THE GREAT RESIGNATION

THE GREAT RESIGNATION

The New Refusal of Work

Francesca Coin

BLOOMSBURY ACADEMIC

LONDON · NEW YORK · OXFORD · NEW DELHI · SYDNEY

BLOOMSBURY ACADEMIC

Bloomsbury Publishing Plc, 50 Bedford Square, London, WC1B 3DP, UK
Bloomsbury Publishing Inc, 1359 Broadway, New York, NY 10018, USA
Bloomsbury Publishing Ireland, 29 Earlsfort Terrace, Dublin 2, D02 AY28, Ireland

BLOOMSBURY, BLOOMSBURY ACADEMIC and the Diana logo are
trademarks of Bloomsbury Publishing Plc

First published in 2023 in Italy as Le Grandi Dimissioni by Einaudi

This edition first published in Great Britain 2025

Bloomsbury Publishing Plc does not have any control over, or responsibility
for, any third-party websites referred to or in this book. All internet addresses
given in this book were correct at the time of going to press. The author and
publisher regret any inconvenience caused if addresses have changed or sites
have ceased to exist, but can accept no responsibility for any such changes.

A catalogue record for this book is available from the British Library.

A catalog record for this book is available from the Library of Congress.

ISBN: HB: 978-1-3505-3435-3
       PB: 978-1-3505-3436-0
       ePDF: 978-1-3505-3438-4
       eBook: 978-1-3505-3437-7

Typeset by Integra Software Services Pvt. Ltd.
Printed and bound in Great Britain

For product safety related questions contact productsafety@bloomsbury.com.

To find out more about our authors and books visit www.bloomsbury.com and
sign up for our newsletters.

CONTENTS

ACKNOWLEDGEMENTS

This text was conceived during a particularly stressful year, when I decided to quit my job in England and move to Lugano, Switzerland. Resituating life and work from one country to another requires a great amount of energy, and there have been moments when the mere thought of finishing this book seemed like a fantasy. If it has been possible, it is also because of all the people who helped me through the storm, reading parts of the manuscript or simply cooking me dinner.

This text would not have seen the light of day without:

Raffaella Baiocchi and Paolo Valoppi, who believed in the project from the start and supported me with great intelligence and professionalism in every single phase, including the most terribly frentic ones, making sure that everything was – against all realistic odds – rolling; my friends and former colleagues at Lancaster University: Giovanni Bettini, Joanne Wood, Bev Skeggs, Joanna Kotska and Ala Sirriyeh, whose closeness and theoretical and political sensitivity I cherish; my beloved DIG family, for their tenacity and for their magnetic and irresistible passion, with which they ensure that, even in August, with forty degrees, there is not a single day of peace; the editorial staff of the Italian magazine *Internazionale*, in particular Giulia Zoli, Giovanni De Mauro and Maysa Moroni for the inspiration that their work provokes, thanks to which the first article on this subject was written; Christian Raimo, Massimo Amato, Giulio Calella, Massimo Alberti, Sarah Jaffe and David Frayne for their intuitions, advice, conversations and suggestions; my dearest family, I have lost count of the reasons why; all the people who agreed to tell me their stories, for their trust and generosity in sharing such valuable journeys.

To them, and to all *quitters*, I dedicate this book.

INTRODUCTION

I have been stuck on the first line of this book for several weeks. I would write a sentence, delete it and try another one. I went on like this, deleting and rewriting, until, just before I threw in the towel, I realized that I was trying to avoid facing a problem: Why quit your job during a recession, when—so they say—having a job is a privilege? Why, in the face of so many problems, tell the stories of those who decide to quit? And again: why talk about those who quit, instead of those who strike, organize mobilizations, and struggle?

I wanted to get there in the end, but let's start here.

Because it is true: the new refusal of work is an ambivalent and contradictory phenomenon. It is not a solution to the deflagration of our working and living conditions; it is a symptom of it. And it is not a symptom like any other: it is the symptom of an epochal rupture. It is the symptom of the end of the era in which hope reigned that work would allow us to realize our dreams of emancipation, social mobility and recognition. When work was thought to be part of a virtuous system that saves the world from hunger and destitution. That era is over. The system we live in is broken and in this context those who quit do not do so because they can afford it. They do it to survive. They do it because they can't take it any more, because they are in burnout, because they need time to care for their loved ones or because they know very well that the real problem today is not the people who can afford not to work, but the people who work all the time and yet cannot scrape together the money to pay for both rent and dinner.

I remember reading the story of a worker at the Fiat Mirafiori automotive factory in Turin who said he wanted to abolish work because he preferred to stay at home and make love. In the 1970s, the refusal of work was also this: the expression of an imaginary of power that set out to radically transform society. Today, those who quit their jobs often do not feel they can change the world, they want to survive. They do not want to abolish work, they are sick of it. The mere thought of it causes nausea, headaches, anxiety and panic attacks. As Anne Helen Petersen puts it in her book *Can't Even. How Millennials Became the Burnout Generation*, 'I can't even … ': everyone may finish the sentence as they wish.

> Because I'm burned out. Why am I burned out? Because I've internalized the idea that I should be working all the time. Why have I internalized that idea? Because everything and everyone in my life has reinforced it – explicitly and implicitly – since I was young.[1]

Petersen is one of the authors who has most readily denounced the way in which the tendency to work all the time often leads us to a kind of paralysis: a state of fatigue so pervasive that it drains our energy from everything else. Petersen continues her article with a list of the things she was having to do while writing it:

> While writing this piece, I was orchestrating a move, planning travel, picking up prescriptions, walking my dog, trying to exercise, making dinner, attempting to participate in work conversations on Slack, posting photos to social media, and reading the news.[2]

The list didn't end there, but reading Petersen made me realize that I too, while writing this introduction, was organizing a move, sorting out paperwork to apply for a visa, closing one life in England, starting a new one in Switzerland, trying to recover from Covid, co-organizing a festival, correcting homework and thesis, getting in and out of zoom calls and trying to ignore the phone because, at some point, I also 'couldn't even'. Our workloads have become so heavy, and the sacrifices they entail so severe, that, at some point, the rope simply snaps. This is not about abolishing work to change the world, it is about evading a system that devours our lives.

There have been many prominent resignations in recent years. Jacinda Ardern, New Zealand's Prime Minister, stepped down in January 2023. 'I of course feel sad', she said, 'but also I do have a sense of relief', she continued, confessing that she had slept well for the first time in a long while after the announcement.[3] Then it was Nicola Sturgeon's turn, the former Scottish prime minister, who declared that 'the time had come' for her to resign. 'I am a human being as well as a politician', she said, before adding that one can only hold the office of Prime Minister by giving absolutely everything of themselves. 'But that can only be done, by anyone, for so long'.[4] Not to mention Susan

Wojcicki, CEO of YouTube, who joins a long list of resignations among women in Silicon Valley: Sheryl Sandberg, former CEO of Meta; Meg Whitman, CEO of Hewlett-Packard; Marissa Mayer, CEO of Yahoo, to name but a few.[5] And then there are the difficult decisions of athletes such as Simone Biles, Naomi Osaka and Michael Phelps, who decided to quit major competitions in order to preserve themselves. Simone Biles withdrew from the Tokyo Olympics, where she was the favourite, due to the enormous pressure she was being subjected to. Biles, who grew up in poverty and was sexually abused by former national team doctor Larry Nassar, revolutionized her discipline and distinguished herself as an exceptional Black gymnast, despite the racist gaze of white America. Her case and that of Naomi Osaka – a tennis star who retired from Wimbledon and refused to speak to the press to protect her mental health – exposed the world of sports and the way it drives athletes to excel, often with such a violence that crushes them. *The Weight of Gold* (2021), the documentary about the multi-decorated swimmer Michael Phelps, is a good illustration of the way in which the sporting system tears athletes apart, whether they win or lose. Sarah Jaffe writes in her book *Work Won't Love You Back* (2021)[6] that athletes are a plastic representation of the concept of 'human capital' as they are forced to think of their bodies in terms of investment from an early age. As Malcolm Harris maintains, 'building muscle is a great way of thinking about human capital because it's so literal: work over time accumulates in the body'. It is when every moment of life is sucked up by the need to create value that people collapse; it is when we are so driven to excel that we cease to function. Anne Helen Petersen writes:[7]

> We were raised to believe that if we worked hard enough, we could win the system – of American capitalism and meritocracy – or at least live comfortably within it. But something happened in the late 2010s. We looked up from our work and realized, there's no winning the system when the system itself is broken.

We may think that these renowned defections are isolated cases. Yet, from the United States to China, from the UK to India, we see very similar processes.

In the United States, 48 million people decided to quit their jobs in 2021. In 2022, the number rose to 50.5 million. It was the *Great Resignation*, the phenomenon that prompted millions of people to quit their jobs at the end of the pandemic. In Italy, voluntary resignations came close to 2 million in 2021 and exceeded this threshold in 2022.

This figure did not take into account those who refused inadequate job offers, consisting of excessively low wages or excessively long hours; those who opted for early retirement, to exit the labour market once and for all; those who decided not to renew a fixed-term contract or those who quit a job in the informal economy or as freelancers all of these experiences do exist but they are not captured by the official resignation data.

In China, the *Tangping* (躺平, 'lying flat') protest movement began as a form of cultural resistance to 996, a system that requires working from 9.00 am to 9.00 pm for six days a week. The protest was followed by another movement, *Let it rot* (*bailan,* 摆烂, 'let it rot'). The *Let it rot* movement maintains that a system that compels entire generations to sit at a desk for years, pushes them to work and compete, and then abandons them to unemployment, does not work. Engaging in such a system, which consumes you and leaves you on the fringes of society, makes no sense, say the *bailan*. It is better to *'lie down and let it rot'.*

In India, the report 'The Great X', published in June 2022 by the recruitment agency Michael Page,[8] warned that 86 per cent of workers in all sectors, of all ages and at all levels, expected to quit their jobs within six months, and that 61 per cent were willing to accept a lower salary in return for a better work-life balance. In both India and China, a counter-culture that questions the work ethic and the obligation to work for wages has been spreading steadily. Self-Help Singh, a fictional character played by comedian Masood Boomgaard, is the embodiment of this trend. Self-Help Singh is a 'professional demotivator' whose aim is to encourage people to do nothing. 'Waking up at five o'clock in the morning? Bad idea. Waking up at eleven o'clock in the morning? A much better idea. Stop doing things you don't want to do. Make excuses, write a book of excuses and always keep an excuse ready. If Nike says *Just do it,* Self-Help Singh says *Do nothing'.*[9] Self-Help Singh is an interesting character as he is the nemesis of our culture. After years of the world praising the virtues of the work ethic, efficiency and competition, suggesting that we should make every moment of our lives productive, Self-Help Singh espouses the spiritual importance of living a purposeless life and freeing time from work, like some strange post-capitalist Guru.

In fact, the pandemic has marked a turning point in our understanding of work. Anthropologist David Graeber showed the prodromes of this trend in his bestseller *Bullshit Jobs,* when he observed that, over the last fifty years, polls, studies and surveys have come to two opposing conclusions about work. The first is that most people hate it.

The Gallup poll, for example, has surveyed a sample of employed people in 140 countries to show that some 80 per cent of the world's employed population hates their jobs, a figure that speaks volumes about the discontent that pervades our age.[10] The second conclusion is that, despite this, most people derive a sense of dignity and self-worth from their work.[11] Drawing on Al Gini and Terry Sullivan, David Graeber called it 'the paradox of contemporary work', that strange contradiction whereby most individuals expect to receive recognition for an activity that they consider demeaning.

> In well over a hundred studies in the last twenty-five years, workers have regularly depicted their jobs as physically exhausting, boring, psychologically diminishing or personally humiliating and unimportant. [But at the same time] they want to work because they are aware at some level that work plays a crucial and perhaps unparalleled psychological role in the formation of human character. Work is not just a course of livelihood; it is also one of the most significant contributing factors to an inner life ... To be denied work is to be denied far more than the things that work can buy; it is to be denied the ability to define and respect oneself.[12]

Graeber reflected on these words in 2018, just before the pandemic brought to the surface the contradictions of work in our society. Two years after this publication, the health emergency became the litmus test of everything that is wrong with the world of work. As the military vehicles left Bergamo, the first European city to be affected by the spread of the pandemic, the healthcare personnel in the hospital ward embodied the sacrifice of essential workers, who toiled day and night to keep the rest of society alive despite the lack of adequate equipment and resources, salaries and recognition. From the factories to the grocery stores, from warehouse drivers to logistics, it was easy in those months to see the distortions of a system of production that operates through the work of the least paid and protected people, especially women and migrants, and only functions thanks to their commitment. The non-essential workers, on their part, in some cases could finally observe the useless drudgery that shapes their lives: the hours in traffic, the eternal shifts and the subordinate role to which work constrains everything important, starting from their loved ones. In those weeks, the pandemic opened a breach in the social imaginary and revealed the contradictions of the world in which we live. Psychologist Anthony Klotz has spoken of *pandemic epiphanies* to describe the moments of truth that, in the darkness of those months, illuminated the need to remove one's existence from an economic framework that, for too many years, has requested sacrifices with the prospect of promises that have almost never been kept. The Great Resignation, in many ways, originated here, as a punctiform and pervasive outcome of the resolutions matured during the lockdown, in a widespread rewriting of the priorities of individual existence, aimed at changing its goals and expectations. From this point of view, the Great Resignation can be considered an anthropological laboratory that springs from within an existential crisis: at the bottom of it there is often the urgency to transform the world of work, its organizational methods and its objectives, as well as the awareness of the obstacles to such an undertaking.

The intention of this text is to restore centrality to the subjective dimension of these experiences, for which the decision to quit is often a total fact, a choice that sees in the inadequacy of the salary the epitome of a productive system that no longer offers an adequate counterpart to the daily sacrifices of the working class. In the following chapters, we will reconstruct the causes of some of these abandonments.

The Italian case is anomalous in the international context, since the difficulty many sectors have in finding personnel coexists with around 5 million unemployed and discouraged people. To understand this paradox, it is necessary to delve into the daily lives of those who work in the sectors where disengagement is most evident. It has occurred to me several times in the last few months that in order to understand the causes of the Great Resignation, all it takes is listening to these stories. It would then be apparent that the increase in voluntary turnover has nothing to do with state subsidies. Rather, it has to do with a toxic work culture consisting of low wages and gruelling shifts, bullying and harassment, insecurity and poor safety at work, victimization and union bashing. In many cases, these elements have been seen as the key to a win-win strategy – enabling lower labour costs and higher profits – only to later become the hallmark of a lose-lose system, in which the flight of workers reveals an unsustainable situation for both workers and companies.

This is not the first time in history that the rate of voluntary turnover has risen relentlessly. A century ago, the growth in absenteeism and work desertion led to the introduction of major transformations. First, a system of direct, indirect and deferred compensation, such as pensions and seniority wages, capable of rewarding staff for their sacrifices. Secondly, it influenced a gradual regulation of working time, taking us from the spinning mills of the late nineteenth century, where shifts averaged sixteen hours a day—to the early twentieth-century introduction of the eight-hour workday, five days a week. Labour regulations are not eternal: they are embedded in history and shaped by the needs of those who struggle in it.

In recent months, there have been important experiments aimed at changing the world of work. Richard Godwin, for instance, explained to *The Guardian* how working less could be 'a solution to all manner of 21st-century ills'[13] and an antidote against staff turnover.[14] The conclusion of the pilot that allowed sixty-one British companies to experiment with the four-day working week without any change in pay was positive in every respect. A four-day working week, explains the report,[15] increases productivity, improves employee well-being, allows for a better work-life balance, improves physical and mental health, helps create a more equal division of domestic and care work, reduces commuting and, along with it, carbon emissions. We 'come back refreshed,' reported one managing director to *The Guardian*. 'It's been great for our wellbeing and we're definitely more productive already';[16] while the environmental charity Platform London noted that a four-day working week would reduce Britain's emissions by over 20 per cent by 2025.[17] In an age gripped by crises, experiments like this should be placed at the top of the political agenda.

'Too many things no longer work', wrote the German magazine *Der Spiegel*, commenting on the words of US investor Ray Dalio. 'Globalisation is crumbling and with it the German model of prosperity. The world is entrenched into hostile blocs. Inflation is causing rich and poor to drift further apart. Almost all climate targets have been missed. And politicians can no longer keep up patching all the new cracks appearing in the system'.[18] For some time, the promises of peace and prosperity that dominated the aftermath of the Second World War have been shattered in the face of poverty, war and the risk of a climate endgame that, according to some scientists, has been dangerously underestimated. The end of the month and the end of the world are the same struggle, say climate justice movements. It is a matter of rethinking the purpose of work in a system of production that cannot merely impoverish human life and the planet: it must regenerate both.

In this context, the determination of those who refuse a job that pays five hundred euros a month is not an expression of privilege: it tells us that we cannot let a toxic system kill us. Those who do not accept a low salary do not act unreasonably: they refuse to lower the bar. 'We are acrobats,' said Luna, as she shared her experience as a freelancer in the publishing industry. 'We have never had certain privileges. The force of our experience has never been fully understood'.

Instead, with the force of their subtraction, *quitters* have managed to turn the spotlight on labour and put a long-delayed discussion on the table.

It is time to listen to them.

Chapter 1

NOBODY WANTS TO WORK ANY MORE

1. A brief history of infidelity

The newspapers keep repeating it: there is an emergency in our society which threatens to bring us to ruin. From restaurants to hotels, from factories to hospitals, nobody wants to work any more. It was January 1860 when the phrase 'Nobody wants to work any more' was first used. On that occasion, a letter to the *Richmond Enquirer*[1] argued that the abolition of slavery would lead nations into bankruptcy. In 1894, a journalist in the *Stockton Review and Rooks County Record* in Kansas[2] used the same words to point out that strikes had deprived coal mines of labour, forcing them to close. According to political scientist Paul Fairie of the University of Calgary,[3] the phrase has been reappearing in the press at regular intervals for two centuries to remind us, with apocalyptic scenarios, what ruin would await humanity if we all stopped working.

For several months, the Italian press has been asking the same question: why, in a country plagued by unemployment, have people become disenchanted with work? Why is there no more staff for our hospitals and restaurants? And how did the moral crisis that threatens to bankrupt the country begin?

Whilst not detracting from these questions, I would like to start with a different matter: how and when did work become the central activity of our lives?

For those who, like me, grew up in the 1980s, it is easy to respond. In those years, it was hard to avoid the question: 'What's your dream when you grow up?' In school, it was common to ask a young girl what her dream job was. Even Hollywood played its part. I vividly remember a film from 1988, entitled *Working Woman*, which held a certain charm for me. The main character was Tess McGill, a Staten Island woman interpreted by Melanie Griffith, who worked as a secretary in a large Wall Street firm. Slowly, thanks to her own initiative, Tess managed to climb the ladder of success which led her to the top of the company. All the ingredients to make an impression in a young girl's imagination were there: the vertigo of New York in the Eighties, well represented by the world of finance, and the emancipation of a young woman moving from the outskirts to the skyscrapers of Manhattan. Between *Wall Street*, the film directed by Oliver Stone in 1987 that portrays work in the world of finance, and *The Secret of My Success* – a film released in the same year, in which Michael J. Fox plays an errand boy who manages to make a career in his uncle's multinational company – work at that time changed its skin and took on a new role in society, aided by the mass media and the film industry. The distance to the 1960s and 1970s was sidereal. Work was no longer a form of slavery, forcing people to toil for a loaf of bread, as it was described then. It was an aspiration, an ambition, the goal of our desires and an instrument of social emancipation capable of bringing self-esteem, prestige and recognition.

The change in work culture is one of the most explicit symptoms of our times. In the 1960s and 1970s, dreams still had a collective dimension. A whole generation wanted to abolish labour and private property, to overthrow inequality and social hierarchies, to abolish colonialism and patriarchy. On the threshold of the 1980s, these grand collective visions had given way to an era of backlash punctuated by talk shows and glitter dresses. For those who found themselves growing up in those years, the impression was that, not much had remained of the desire to change the world. While previous generations wanted to eliminate the division of society into classes, mine could move from one class to another and use the social ladder to buy a car and a refrigerator. In this new historical phase, dreams had become individualized. It was finally possible to abandon the ideological armaments of the last century, said politicians, and celebrate the death of class altogether. 'The class war is over', declared Tony Blair in 1999, 'we are all middle class now', he announced.[4] In this new era of freedom, everyone could become whatever they wanted. 'Everyone can make it' if they just put their talents to use and invest in their dreams and passions. Social justice was no longer guaranteed by the redistributive power of the state, but by the ability to prove one's own personal worth in the market.

Sociology has long dwelt on the factors that drove this transformation, portraying the new era as characterized by globalization, post-Fordism or neo-liberalism. Such were the changes, however, that they overshadowed how the idea of work had irrevocably changed. Work was no longer perceived as a form of violence, as was the case in the 1970s. It was a way of pursuing an individual purpose of freedom. Doing what one loves was *the very purpose of life*. Questions such as 'what do you want to be when you grow up?', and prompts such as 'chase your dreams', 'do what you love' and 'love what you do' were the hallmarks of this grand transformation. And so, in pursuit of its dreams, my generation found itself, over the course of two decades, being hurled from an era marked by the end of History, as Francis Fukuyama put it, the time when humanity reached the peak of its political development thanks to liberal democracy, to another one marked by the climate apocalypse and by dystopian visions of war. In a similarly abrupt manner, we had found ourselves swept from one time in which everyone had the dream of working, to another in which '*nobody wants to work any more*'.

One of the books that help us to set all this in order is *Exit, Voice, and Loyalty* by economist Albert O. Hirschman. Hirschman's text suggests that there are two broad courses of action that a dissatisfied worker can take: he can protest (*voice*) or leave (*exit*). The decision depends on a third concept: *loyalty*. For Hirschman, loyalty to the company leads to constructive protest, prompting employees to express the reasons for their dissatisfaction, using their claims to virtuously shape the organization of work. Low loyalty encourages exit. In essence, workers stay if they can voice their discontent, and quit when they cannot, leaving the burden of solving the problem of turnover and absenteeism to companies. The most useful of the terms used by Hirschman, in this sense, is the one least mentioned: 'loyalty'. Loyalty is a word that my generation doesn't know, inscribed as it is in the expansionary phase of industrial capitalism, when the compromise between capital and labour guaranteed employment security and social protections. To understand how the twentieth century managed to create this bond between workers and companies, we must go back to the origin of this concept and ask ourselves why, at a certain point, the working class became devoted to work.

In the nascent phase of industrial capitalism, in fact, such devotion did not exist. There were, on the contrary, voluntary dismissals, runaways, absenteeism and strikes in the factories. Around 1910, in particular, the number of workers quitting was very high and accounted for over 70 per cent of all terminations on average. In the absence of internal promotion mechanisms, staff had no incentive to stay and often chose to move to some other factory to improve their condition, explains Paul Douglas.[5] To reduce turnover, says Laura Owen, companies were forced to introduce forms of direct, indirect and deferred compensation in an attempt to retain staff.[6] Since voluntary resignations are costly for the company, given the recruitment and training expenses they entail, companies at the beginning of the last century set about changing employment relationships through a series of policies aimed at strengthening the bond between worker and company. These policies were based on offering seniority-based pay, training and internal promotion scales, writes Owen, and had three main purposes. On the one hand, they guaranteed skilled labour in a historical phase in which the increase in technology and the dizzying growth of the industrial sector demanded more skills.[7] On the other hand, they protected technological investments, ensuring that companies were not penalized by an inconstant flow of work. Finally, they prevented unionization because they put workers in a position to earn a decent wage.

The *Five-dollar day* is a good example of this process. In 1914, Henry Ford decided to double wages and reduce working hours to eight hours a day in his automotive factory. We are in the Fordist era, a historical phase accurately described by Antonio Gramsci in a chapter of the *Prison Notebooks*. Ford's choice allowed turnover to fall to 16 per cent as early as 1915. It should be borne in mind that in 1913 turnover had reached 370 per cent – meaning that in that year Ford had had to hire 50,448 people to maintain an average workforce of 13,623: more than 7,300 workers quit the company in March 1913 alone, write Daniel Raff and Larry Summers.[8] Absenteeism was also high in those months:

> In 1913, the company suffered a 10 percent daily absenteeism rate. This meant that on the average day it was necessary to make use of 1300 or 1400 replacement workers each of whom was inexperienced at the specific task they were to perform.[9]

There were multiple reasons for this discontent: Raff and Summers cite the arbitrariness of foremen, unfair wages, inadequate working conditions and monotony of labour, at a time when the introduction of the assembly line had dramatically increased alienation in factories. By doubling wages, it was possible to have a stable workforce capable of running the assembly line. Ford thus managed to increase productivity and profits over a two-year period, turning the salary increase into the best way to reduce turnover, production time and costs.

In general, scholars agree that changes in labour policies and in the terms of remuneration and protection were the reason why voluntary turnover declined substantially during the twentieth century. According to Owen, voluntary turnover declined in the 1920s and then remained more or less constant after the Second World War, providing companies with a long period of relative stability. In the last few decades, however, those forms of direct, indirect and deferred compensation that had made it possible to 'stabilize' the workforce were gradually dismantled, causing the very foundations of the employment stability typical of the last century to be put into jeopardy. In the 1970s and 1980s, the crisis of Fordism undermined the compromise between labour and capital— the idea that workers would respect business prerogatives in exchange for steadily rising wages. This shift paved the way for a service-based economy built on individualised and precarious working relationships, where loyalty became one-sided: employees were expected to show dedication to their jobs, while companies retained the freedom to hire and fire at will, in a disposable dynamic rooted in disloyalty.

As early as 1993, Francis Marion Webster[10] argued that loyalty as a concept belonged to the past. A year later, Hal Lancaster wrote in the *Wall Street Journal* that 'the social contract between employers and employees, in which companies promise to ensure employment and guide careers of loyal troops, is dead, dead, dead'.[11] In fact, the debate on the *end of loyalty* begins in the 1990s – when the employment conditions of Fordism were no longer in place – and suggests that we should consider the growth of turnover as the result of a long-term process marked by the gradual erosion of the forms of protection that characterized it. In fact, the economic downturn at the turn of the century had a direct effect on employment, causing a wave of restructuring and redundancies that profoundly transformed labour relations. The question Webster posed, therefore, was: why should workers be loyal if companies are not?

> Loyalty should be a two-way street. In the terms of expectancy theory, people will be motivated to perform (or be loyal) if they have a reasonable expectation of being able to perform and their performance obtains some valued outcome. When the company demands but does not deliver, why should they be loyal?[12]

The debate of those years is important: it indicates that the growth of voluntary turnover is the epiphenomenon of a long-term process, marked by the gradual dismantlement of the forms of direct, indirect and deferred remuneration that had been introduced during the last century.

Webster continues:

> Until recently it was assumed that if you worked hard and were loyal to the company, you would be rewarded, promoted and, in effect,

taken care of until retirement. It was a reasonable expectation. The employee looked out for the company and the company took care of the employee. But according to many recent articles and surveys, this is no longer true. The 'contract' between employee and employer has apparently changed. As Solomon put it, it now includes caveats such as 'as long as the company remains profitable, and doesn't get acquired, and the economy doesn't get too bad'.

Webster's article ascribes the demise of loyalty to several factors that are still very relevant today. For Webster, the wave of redundancies that, in countries such as the United States, the UK and Italy itself, punctuated the 1990s, triggered a continuous downsizing of the workforce within manufacturing companies. This wave of restructuring was not 'a localized phenomenon' but the symptom of a structural change.

So many companies are reducing staff today that the newspapers keep track, like they do with crime waves and body counts during disasters.

Webster describes the metamorphosis of the industrial structure that was taking place in those years and the way it marked the transition from a manufacturing economy to a service-based economy. This transformation had a strong impact on workers, resulting in a condition of insecurity marked by the constant growth of precariousness. In just two decades, everything had changed: the idea of a 'job for life' no longer existed, and those who lost their jobs could not easily re-enter the labour market. Mergers, restructurings and relocations came with job cuts, an ever-increasing workload and ever-lower wages. It was the beginning of the era of lean production and *just-in-time*, management models that proposed to rethink the organization of work in light of the now universal criterion of *working longer for less*, suggesting to reduce staff, wages, inventory, and wasted time in factories and hospitals, retail and services.[13] In this situation, it was imperative to do 'more with fewer resources', Webster writes, and this increased the sources of stress in the workplace, and described an economy running in the opposite direction to what was hoped for in the 1960s and 1970s. If the slogan back then was 'lavorare meno, lavorare tutti', that means 'work less, work for all', the tendency now was to make a few work to the point of exhaustion, while others remained unemployed and the goal of full employment was gradually abandoned in order to reduce labour costs.[14] Shrinking wages and protections spread a 'pervasive sense of betrayal'[15] among the population – as psychiatrist

David Bruce Robbins calls it – marked by the gradual dismantling of labour rights. Who is less loyal now, Webster asks: companies or workers? 'Loyalty must be earned, not demanded', he concludes.

It is interesting to go back to this debate, because the questions it raised in the 1990s *have yet to be resolved*. It is very clear that when we talk about work today, we are talking about a precarious class that has never had the protections that characterized the twentieth century. Today's work refers, not surprisingly, to an uneven set of conditions and contractual forms for which the very idea of protected employment is an exception. Today, Job insecurity has become the norm. Companies, however, still expect loyalty from workers while offering little to nothing in return. The whole Great Resignation debate, in some ways, stems precisely from the astonishment with which companies realize, thirty years after Webster's writing, that if they do not give workers reasons to stay, they will quit.

It should also be said that 'loyalty' does not mean merely remaining in the workplace. As the American philosopher Josiah Royce[16] wrote in 1908 in *The Philosophy of Loyalty*, loyalty is devotion to a person or a cause. The loyal person does not follow his own impulses but is *submissive* to the cause, which tells them what to do. In this sense, a loyal person must be prepared 'to live or die according to what the cause requires', offering oneself in sacrifice, in the same way that a soldier gives his life to his country and a religious person to God. This, after all, is the form of loyalty required by businesses. Global Ethics Solutions, a company that provides training programmes for companies around the world, explains in its video *The Importance of Loyalty in the Workplace*[17] that loyalty is the ability to put the company's interests ahead of one's own, and to remain loyal to it even if one does not gain any benefit from it in return. 'It is not about what you get, but what you give'. And again: 'Don't let your priorities override those of the company, respect the authority above you'. The comments on the video are also interesting. For example, there are those who admit that they resigned when their boss told them to put their work before their children, and those who question whether companies are loyal to employees when they lay off hundreds of people.

For years, these analyses have been pointing to a one-sided concept of loyalty, in which it is compulsory to be loyal to the company even when it wants to let you go.

Rick Wartzman, in his 2017 book *The End of Loyalty*, argues that expecting loyalty from workers is no longer possible, for the simple reason that the conditions that had enabled the reduction of employee turnover and absenteeism no longer exist. For Wartzman, companies are not loyal to their employees, given the progressive abolition of all of the rights that the workers had obtained. While at the beginning of the last century, it was precisely the demands of technological investments that made high labour retention indispensable, at the beginning of this century we see the emerging tendency to adopt technology as a way of using unskilled-skilled labour in a disposable manner. In this context, the high turnover is structural. It is the expression of a market designed to allow for the hiring and firing of labour according to the company's needs, and for attracting workers when needed and letting them go when they are no longer necessary. For a long time, companies have thought to be the only ones in a position to manage the terms of this process, which allowed them to choose which workers to retain based on the economic conjuncture and on each person's willingness to make sacrifices.

Eventually, the disregard companies showed for their employees became mutual, and people started to quit: if the company does not care about the well-being of the workers, the workers no longer care about the company's business.

2. An unhappy marriage

The interesting aspect of the loyalty debate is how, over the past thirty years, literature on human resources and management has compensated for the loss of salary and the dismantlement of labour rights, with an abundance of references to engagement, a word that has been often used to suggest marriage with work. In this literature, employee engagement is described as a process process of "harnessing people's identity in their productive role, with the hope that it will be fulfilled through work."[18] Introduced by William Kahn, employee engagement became crucial from the 1990s onwards, when the working conditions typical of the Fordist era began to vanish and the question arose as to how to retain employees in the absence of adequate professional and economic recognition. For Kahn, the answer was simple: the employee had to be 'engaged' with his or her business. 'We aren't just looking to get people *"engaged"*, we want them to be *"married."* That is, *fully committed*',[19] wrote Josh Bersin in *Forbes*. From here on, there has been extensive discussion about how companies should become attractive and win the hearts of workers, thus inducing them to *love* their occupation. In an economy increasingly ready to lay people off, the idea was that in order to ask workers to devote themselves to their jobs with dedication, love and loyalty, it was necessary to make them fall in love with the company's values and brand.

Some may remember the video made in 2017 by the employees of the Italian bank Intesa Sanpaolo, in which the manager of the branch introduced her team 'or, rather, our family, or rather, our big family'. In many ways that video exemplifies this tendency. 'We believe in it', the employees say, as they describe their relationship with customers and, after a singing performance, hold up a red heart-shaped cake with the words: 'Intesa Sanpaolo. I'm in'. Swamped by criticism, the video, originally intended for internal use, describes how companies try to motivate employees to work as a team, thereby strengthening their bond with the brand. The heart-shaped cake decorated with the bank's name and the manager's words 'I put my face, my head and my heart into it', indicating the emotional investment in her work, shows the ways in which companies promote brand love in an attempt to bind employees to themselves.

As one of North America's leading business consultants Jim Harris wrote in his book *Getting Employees to Fall in Love with Your Company*, employees must love the company.

> Every day, millions of employees filled with untapped heartpower go to work, where they wait for their organizations to give them a reason to commit themselves, a reason to exert their energies, a reason to excel. Unfortunately, most managers choose to ignore this untapped resource. They prefer to hide behind the bottom line and to manage people on the sole basis of the hard, cold numbers of the business. In doing so, they fail to capitalize on the single greatest motivator of them all. Capture the heart, and you will have captured the employee. For without a vibrant, beating heart, any enterprise is sure to die[20]

Harris' text emphasizes how, at the end of the Fordist era, companies strove to create ways of engaging employees that made up for the lack of job security. For Harris, entrepreneurs must 'capture' the vibrant, beating hearts of their employees, and create bonds 'based on trust, equality and sharing', in order to increase their 'service and productivity'.[21]

In general, over the last thirty years, literature has insisted on the need to transform the relationship with employees into a form of marriage, convincing them to marry the company.

Ah, hearing sweet words of appreciation, surprise gifts that thrill and delight, receiving billet-doux when least expected – we're here to tell you that employee engagement has a lot in common with a marriage![22]

From this perspective, employee engagement is described as a successful marriage, 'one where both parties are striving towards a common aim, growing and flourishing together as their relationship prospers'.[23] This means that the employee must give his or her best and the company must create an atmosphere of trust, showing its appreciation of the employee's contribution and its gratitude.

One of the best bits of marriage advice this author was ever offered was by a Yorkshireman who confided, 'tha's got to gi' a bit', when asked what was his secret to a long and happy marriage. For the non-Yorkshire-speakers amongst you, what he meant was: don't focus on the bad, accentuate the good. No-one wants to feel micro-managed and constantly criticised at work – neither do they want to perceive their hard work is going unnoticed. Just as in a marriage, a note of appreciation can reap rewards far beyond the time and effort it takes to say, 'thanks!'

Creating a climate of trust and expressing gratitude increase individual productivity and, in turn, boosts corporate profit. This is illustrated by Bob Nelson, author of *Keeping Up in a Down Economy* and consultant to major US companies, when he suggests that flattering workers would ensure their commitment, despite inadequate wages. 'Can't pay your employees what you'd like? Praise them instead', headlines an article in CBS News. 'Proper praise can boost a company's bottom line along with its morale'; 'it's probably the most powerful driver of performance known to mankind', says Nelson. 'Whether it's an employee or a spouse, when you praise someone you get more of what you want',[24] he concludes.

As a matter of fact, over the past two decades, managers and consultants have put a lot of effort into writing the rules for a successful corporate marriage.

According to business consultant Grant Herbert[25]

Engagement is the start of any successful marriage. The two becoming one flesh, for better or worse, richer or poorer, in sickness and in health. An engaged employee not only wants to stay, they are excited about the role they play and tell everyone about it with a huge smile on their face. They overlook the little things and concentrate on what truly matters in preparing for the marriage. The size of the ring is not as important to them as is the way they are treated, spoken about, nurtured and respected. They are proud to stand side by side with you, fighting for what you both believe in.

Just like in a big family, an engaged employee is available when it comes to doing something extra, say these insights. When a family member needs help, one immediately steps in to solve the problem, even if such help is neither requested nor compensated. Employees should do the same: be devoted to the company and work for it even when they are not openly asked to do so.

In general, the idea of the company as a family has a long history. Historian Nikki Mandell, for example, traces its origins to the last century, when companies invested in services and non-monetary benefits in order to bind employees to themselves. In her text, *The Corporation as Family*,[26] Mandell suggests that corporate welfare was created precisely in order to reframe modern business by shaping it on the model of the Victorian family. This conception endures to the present day. As business consultant Allison Green[27] noted in *The New York Times*, however, describing a corporation as a family is problematic.

'We're like a family here' tends to be used in ways that really disadvantage workers. It often means that boundaries get violated and people are expected to show inappropriate amounts of commitment and loyalty, even when it's not in their self-interest.

The portrayal of the workplace as a family is often dysfunctional, Green explains.

It means, 'we expect you to be loyal to us even though we won't necessarily return that loyalty when the chips are down'. Or, 'we're going to lean on you to work long hours, accept lower pay and not complain about bad management because, hey, "we're family," and asking for a raise or flex time will mean you're not a team player'.

Over the years, this type of narrative has spread to different sectors of the labour market and has not been exempt from criticism. Rob Goffee and Gareth Jones noted in their text, *The Character of a Corporation*,[28] that in the workplace, the expectation that an employee will do everything possible to solve a problem in an altruistic manner, even before this is requested, has aided 'the imposition of unsustainable rhythms and conditions', 'in many cases through the use of intimidation, threats, blackmail and in some circumstances through psychological violence'. Behind this practice lurks an attempt to extend working hours beyond the agreed limits; the expectation that all barriers between work and private life will fall, that people will be available twenty-four hours a day, and that they will regard work as a passion, a hobby and as an emotional priority equal to the need to spend time with their loved ones.

As Joshua Luna writes in the *Harvard Review of Business*,[29] this work culture has toxic effects.

> When employees work under this mentality, it's only a matter of time until performance and productivity drop due to burnout, leading to conversations with managers or HR about what they did wrong. This creates a perception for employees to believe they're not doing their part. Left unaddressed, employers could foster an environment where burnout is the norm and ultimately impacts the bottom line through employee attrition and lost productivity.

It is interesting to see what has become of the virtuous examples cited by Jim Harris in his book, starting with the airline companies that, according to the author, have been able to make their employees fall in love with them. Southwest Airlines, for example, the low-cost airline that Harris called exemplary, has been in crisis for months. Southwest Airlines has used love for its brand from the very beginning: the in-flight drinks were called 'love potions', the peanuts were called 'love nibbles' and the slogan was '*Feel the Spirit of Luv*'. The problem was that, again, love concealed continuous cost-cutting and exploitative working conditions. In the summer of 2022, Southwest Airlines was shaken by a wave of resignations and strikes, with some one thousand three hundred pilots complaining of being overworked and under-staffed, to the point that, for them, the summer was one of 'delays, rescheduling, cancellations'. The crisis deepened in the winter of 2022, when the airline cancelled thousands of flights and found itself at the mercy of increasing pressure on costs and wage standards. At the same time, Airlines for America (A4A), the organization formed by the eleven major US airlines including Southwest Airlines, did not know how to respond to the shortage of workers.

The group estimates 50,000 employees took early retirement or voluntary separation packages, while 100,000 more accepted unpaid leave of absences. Airlines were surprised to discover the extent to which many workers who had taken leave of voluntary separation did not want to return to work in the airline industry. Workers calling in sick were also an issue that led to operational problems. Between absenteeism issues which "were especially acute on weekends and holidays when travel demand was higher," and extreme weather patterns which began on Fridays, the organization says they were stressed to the max.[30]

In general, the problem with describing a workplace as a family, a marriage, a hobby, a passion or a labour of love is that these definitions violate all the boundaries that regulate the working relationship. It is not just about the airlines. The coexistence of love and precariousness has proven to be explosive in every sphere. From care work to social work, from education to health care, from art to publishing, from communication to retail, entire sectors of production have only been able to provide services thanks to the dedication and commitment of their own workers. In these sectors, the erosion of trade union power, the tendency to cut the workforce and outsource entire phases of the production process, and the continuous recourse to subcontracting have favoured the proliferation of forms of employment that are only partly regulated. Over the years, this has led to an across-the-board deterioration of employment conditions.

In this context, staff have found themselves exposed to continuous 'encroachment' of corporate demands, in a process that has turned unpaid overtime, cut-off breaks, unpaid availability and chronically late hours into a real corporate 'loot'. For freelancers, unpaid labour has translated into a system of downward bids, in which the difference between the remuneration one should receive 'in theory' and what happens 'in practice' is an ever-increasing chasm.

Companies, therefore, have continued to base their services on the workers' willingness to sacrifice. The love of work 'brushes up against the line between what we think should be done for love and what we think should be done for money',[31] wrote Sarah Jaffe, and allows working hours to be extended indefinitely, when necessary. For a long time, this mystification has cemented the bond between an increasingly unprotected labour regime and its prey, turning love into both the trap and the coping mechanism of the precarious class.

To what extent, however, can such dedication to work 'trap' people in their own exploitation, if they receive nothing in return? When, on the other hand, will the epidemic of stress, malaise and burnout that pervades the workplace undermine the happy marriage between the precarious class and work?

3. The Great Repulsion

There is a word in English for the moment when attraction to a person turns into repulsion: '*the ick*'. A friend told me about it while recounting her first attempts to have a new relationship after a difficult divorce. Termed 'sudden repulsion syndrome' by some, *the ick* describes the moment when, all of a sudden, everything that was previously a source of attraction generates rejection. Carrie Bradshaw uses it in the episode *The Ick Factor* of *Sex and the City*, the hit TV series set in New York, when she remembers the words of Alexander, a man she dated, and realizes that they contained so much flattery that it was obvious to Carrie that something was wrong. Alexander flaunted boundless love, as if he could not live without her, even though he had only just met her. His attentions were so intrusive that Carrie went so far as to wonder how long she could stand all that romance before she ran away. After all, as we have seen, flattery doesn't always stem from love. In some cases, flattery conceals a manipulative intention. Here, the '*ick*' factor describes the moment of truth, when repulsion breaks the spell and induces the recipient of so much attention to leave.

Think about what happened after the Second World War, when economic and demographic growth brought back a traditional idea of the family in which a woman's role was to take care of her husband and children. Marriage was presented as an idyll bound to yield a life of joy and fulfilment. The very stability of the Fordist era, a system of production in which men worked in factories and women took care of reproduction, depended on the ability to seduce women to the delights of family life. 'Capitalism depends on domestic work',[32] said the leaders of the *Wages against Housework* campaign, because it was their free labour that guaranteed an influx of stable manpower. As Silvia Federici wrote, what they called love was a manipulation aimed at persuading women to do unpaid work.

In 1971, Jane O'Reilly wrote an article in *New York Magazine* entitled 'The Housewife's Moment of Truth,'[33] in which she listed the small and large moments of truth during which women realized they had been harnessed into a life they did not always want. Each of these little *clicks* shattered the fairytale of marriage, exposing the subordination that structured women's lives at the time.

> In Houston, Texas, a friend of mine stood and watched her husband step over a pile of toys on the stairs, put there to be carried up. 'Why can't you get this stuff put away?' he mumbled. Click! 'You have two hands', she said, turning away.
>
> Last summer I got a letter, from a man who wrote: 'I do not agree with your last article, and I am canceling my wife's subscription'. The next day I got a letter from his wife saying, '*I* am not cancelling *my* subscription'. Click!
>
> In New York last fall, my neighbors – named Jones – had a couple named Smith over for dinner. Mr. Smith kept telling his wife to get up and help Mrs. Jones. Click! Click! Two women radicalized at once.
>
> In suburban Chicago, the party consisted of three couples. The women were a writer, a doctor and a teacher. The men were all lawyers. As the last couple arrived, the host said, jovially, 'With a roomful of lawyers, we ought to have a good evening'. Silence. Click! 'What are we?' asked the teacher. 'Invisible?'

Despite being raised to expect a happy marriage from an early age, reality proved different. The 1970s BBC documentary *Our Time Is Coming Now*,[34] recounting the beginnings of the feminist movement in Britain, shows how there was nothing idyllic about the conditions in which women were expected to live in those years. Their testimonies recounted a life of drudgery and loneliness, of sweeping pavements and washing clothes, which at the end of the day left them exhausted, deprived and alone. This is where second-wave feminism placed on the agenda a critique of the traditional ideas of marriage and the nuclear family, and the provision of all those services necessary for the sharing of care, such as family allowances and childcare, turning each of those little *clicks* into the catalyst of a public discussion on the social division of labour.[35] In that instance, the ability to flee the condition of subalternity in which women were placed had repercussions on society as a whole. Repulsion can be a powerful driver of withdrawal. In those years, it became the fuel for a process of subtraction in which the rejection of the role to which women were assigned became the trigger for a radical process of social transformation.

This also applies to wage labour. We saw it during the pandemic, when millions realised that their workplace was far from a real family. The sacrifice and devotion demanded of them were not adequately compensated. Often, in fact, the workers were used as a sacrificial lamb. In such moments, the pandemic became a revelation of all that was wrong with contemporary work, and revulsion, once again, became the driving force in a disorganized flight from contexts of exploitation.

This was explained by Cornell University professor Kate Bronfenbrenner, who argued that working conditions had been deteriorating over time.

> Workers had been maintaining an astonishing threshold of tolerance for abuses by employers against them. But when this abuse advanced to the point of risking their lives, that threshold was crossed; in the context of Covid-19, employers were asking them to work harder than ever while making huge profits.[36]

The pandemic was 'the last straw':

> The pandemic was the last straw, with people cooped up working from home, or expected to come into work and risk their lives without access to vaccines or personal protective equipment.
>
> Meanwhile, we see the corporate leaders are going to the moon.[37]

We have seen this in hospitals, where staff became aware that their lives 'did not matter'. Recently, a study published by the American Psychological Association,[38] and titled *If I Die, They Do Not Care*, explained how some of the staff felt they were being used as 'cannon fodder', and perceived themselves as victims of an '[institutional] betrayal'.[39]

Consider the stark observation of this nurse:[40]

> If I die, they don't care. It doesn't matter if [they] get like, you know, 600 nurses have died from Covid-19, and you know, with higher exposure being linked to severity and things like that. And it just felt like [they] don't care, they'll just get somebody else in my shoes tomorrow.

Or this:[41]

It felt like we were just the cannon fodder because at the beginning no one knew you know what what's happening. What is Covid? How's it spread? Are we gonna get it? And we weren't wearing masks. [...] And then as research has gone on and they said now you need all this PPE, well we didn't have that and it feels like they knew that we should have had it, but they just weren't gonna say it 'cause they didn't have the equipment and it didn't matter 'cause it was only us going in there.

Or the words of this doctor:[42]

When they ran out of certain things in the hospital like visors and things and they basically were trying to tell us things like chest compressions aren't aerosol generating. [...] Yes, they fucking are. [...] just say we've run out, fine. If somebody is dying, I'm going to go in without anything on and I just accept the risk. But if for instance, my colleague is somebody pregnant or someone at risk then they shouldn't be going in. Just be transparent.

The word 'betrayal', which some of the medical and nursing staff use to describe their experience of working during the pandemic, conveys the depth of the trauma suffered by those who felt used. In many cases, insufficient resources, staff cuts, the abnormal amount of work and the resounding failure of the chain of command made the pandemic an overwhelming experience for them. Management's neglect shattered the illusion of the company as a family. Staff felt betrayed, abandoned in the moment of need, stabbed in the back.

In general, the pandemic has been a harsh reality clash for millions of workers around the world, not only in essential sectors.

'This might sound cold, but regardless of the difficulties you are going through in your personal life, you have a job to do and are expected to continue to perform your job as if nothing is going on outside of work',[43] said the boss of a 58-year-old woman whose mother was diagnosed with lung cancer.

– Hey, my mother died this morning, I can't make it to work today.
– I'm sorry. Are you coming tomorrow?

And again:

Three weeks ago, my sister died, and my boss told me to try to attend an online funeral for her so I wouldn't have to miss work for travel. This entire sub pushed me to quit.[44]

Such stories are tragically frequent, as we shall see.

Despite the love and devotion that companies demand from their employees, what united the experience of millions of essential and non-essential workers during the pandemic was the perception of suffering an injustice for which there is no compensation. In this sense, the word 'betrayal' chronicles the violation of a relationship of trust and it shows that, to quote Sarah Jaffe, irrespective of our devotion, 'work won't love you back'. Love at work, a bit like Alexander's attitude towards Carrie, is often an instrument of manipulation that serves other purposes. It points not to a relationship of reciprocity, but to an uneven relationship in which the sacrifice of one party is functional to the profits of the other. Here is where betrayal, as it happens in pairs, marks the end of the relationship.

From this point of view, it must be recognized that the pandemic has had an extraordinary transformative effect. Repulsion is a force of creative destruction, which drives one to change one's existence at the moment of greatest difficulty. When we talk about the Great Resignation, we are also talking about a powerful mixture of trauma and desire for transformation that takes shape when suffering illuminates the need to change. It is in the darkness of that frightful night that the aversion to all that was wrong became the spark for meaningful change.

This explains a few things about the word '*resignation*'. In recent months, in fact, this term has often been interpreted as 'renunciation'. Resignation, however, is not a form of renunciation. On the contrary, it describes an affirmative process whereby the precarious class claims allegiance to its deepest values. Resignation is *also* an act of renunciation, but not of life.

One day, as we were walking and chatting in Venice, Mark Fisher used the word *sidetracked* to describe the way he felt at work, when he was *derailed* from his priorities. The notion of derailment nicely illustrates the extent to which the quitter perceives the employer's priorities to be distant from his own. In such cases, the choice to leave does not point to renunciation. It rather points to an inevitable divorce, animated by the realization that, in the relationship with work, there is nothing left to save.

Chapter 2

THE GREAT RESIGNATION IN THE WORLD: AN UNDECLARED GENERAL STRIKE

1. Pandemic epiphanies in the United States

When Anthony Klotz, an occupational psychologist at University College London, first coined the term 'Great Resignation'[1] in an interview with Bloomberg in May 2021, he argued that it was the result of several factors: chiefly, stress, exhaustion and burnout, which are prevalent in the working class. Klotz then cited the lack of work-life balance as one of the causes of this phenomenon, as well as the fact that, when faced with death, many people would ask themselves 'existential questions'.

Klotz's analysis can be, at least in part, traced back to the Terror Management Theory (TMT) and to a 1974 text by Ernest Becker, entitled *The Denial of Death*. According to this text, the ability to carry out our daily responsibilities depends on the possibility of removing the thought of death. For Becker, the human is the only living being capable of thinking in abstract terms, and he uses this ability in order to carry on with his small affairs without being disturbed by larger questions about the transience and meaning of life. Influenced by this text, Klotz suggests that during the pandemic, proximity to death forced many people to re-evaluate their lives.

Does it make sense to spend several hours a day in traffic on the way to work?

Does it make sense to spend more time at work than with the children?

Does it make sense, to quote the writing on a wall in East Rome, 'to work to pay for the car to go to work'?

For many workers, the answer is evidently no. These questions became what Klotz described as pandemic epiphanies: moments of truth whereby proximity to death forced people to take a hard look at their lives, even when doing so generated revulsion, discouragement or fear. In an article in the *New York Times*, entitled, 'The Future of Work

Should Mean Working Less', Jonathan Malesic[2] gives some examples of the decisions that emerged from these realizations.

> I am never going back to being the last parent to pick up my
> child from school.
> Sasha, 42
> I am never going back to driving for Uber. It's the definition of
> chaos in myriad ways. It is also the exact opposite of where
> 'employment' should be headed.
> Bruce, 65
> I am never going back to being separated from my children for
> 10 to 11 hours per day as they commute and attend school
> and after-school programs while I work.
> Anna, 48
> I am never going back to sending work-related emails after
> dinner or on weekends.
> Philip, 46
> I resolve to remember my boundaries. 'No' is a complete
> sentence.
> Amanda, 41
> I resolve to try and unionize my fellow employees.
> Richard, 70
> I resolve to put work second. My family and I come first from
> now on.
> Jackie, 30

Since then, the pandemic has been the catalyst for a process of detachment from work, which still has no end in sight.

Overall, in the United States, 48 million Americans quit their jobs in 2021, an increase of 6 million over the previous record. This record was broken again in 2022, when 50.5 million people left their jobs. Compared to initial analyses, which regarded the increase in the number of resignations as a temporary and cyclical process, recent ones speak of *a long-term trend*. This is discussed, for instance, in a study by the BlackRock investment fund entitled *After the Great Resignation: Shifting Expectations for Employers*, published in October 2022.[3] According to the study, the number of employees quitting as a proportion of total employment rose from 28 per cent in 2019 to 32.8 per cent in 2021. In 2009, the quit rate stood at 15 percent, indicating a long-term trend the causes of which can be traced back to structural factors, contrary to what was thought at first. The labour force participation rate is still below pre-pandemic levels. According to the U.S. Chamber of Commerce,[4] 2.9 million workers were missing from the labour force in September 2022: in that month, the participation rate was estimated at 62.2 per cent, 1.1 percentage points lower than the 63.3 per cent recorded in February 2020. The gap, according to the study, is largely caused by adult workers who quit in large numbers during the pandemic. Another problem is childcare services, for which the pandemic has triggered a vicious circle, as staff shortages in childcare services have led to facility closures, reducing the availability of support for families with working parents, especially women.[5] As a result, the participation rate of women is still at one of the lowest levels since the 1970s.

According to data from the Bureau of Labor Statistics, the most affected industries[6] include hospitality and restaurants, which have a quit rate twice as high as the other sectors, followed by retail, professional business services, healthcare and manufacturing.

I still remember a car ride with a friend in the early 2000s in Atlanta, the city in the US Southeast where I was living at the time. We were driving past Ford, the assembly plant of the American car manufacturer. Mike was speaking to me with irritation about the privileges of factory workers. As we drove down a highway with the car in neutral, taking advantage of the slight slope to save fuel, he complained that they enjoyed privileges that he would never have. Ford was one of Atlanta's historic factories. Before closing in 2006, it had about two thousand employees, most of them unionized. Mike worked as a restaurant worker, in a context where the minimum wage under the Fair Labor Standards Act (FLSA) for tipped employees was $2.13 per hour, with no legal requirement for vacation, sick leave, or holiday pay. It was clear that there was no privilege among industrial workers. But, in the early 2000s, precariousness was such in the United States that a traditionally strenuous job in the factory was much more protected than work in the restaurant industry.

The restaurant industry was one of the sectors most affected by closures and layoffs during the pandemic when millions of people like Mike lost their jobs. The report *The Impact of Covid-19 on Restaurant Workers across America*, by the trade union Roc United,[7] shows that 95 per cent of respondents had suffered economic losses due to redundancy, layoffs, reduced hours or loss of employment. Ninety-one per cent stated that they had not received any risk compensation from their employer. One in ten reported working while symptomatic due to financial pressure, lack of paid sick leave or fear of retaliation. Overall,

85 per cent of respondents said they lost income in 2020 due to the pandemic.

The vulnerability of restaurant workers was not limited to the economic sphere. Sixty-eight per cent of the respondents said that the virus had affected them or their colleagues. Fifty-eight per cent said they were worried or very worried about falling ill at work. About one-third of the total respondents said they had been touched by the death from Covid of a family member or friend, a figure that increases to 50 per cent for African American workers.

As a Philadelphia restaurant worker explains in the report:[8]

In my opinion, the lack of care concerning Covid is just a manifestation of the general lack of care ownership has for their employees. At one point we had an employee test positive for Covid-19 and some of us did not feel comfortable coming into work until getting back test results. Several people were fired. If they're not invested in our emotional well-being, of course they are not invested in our physical well-being. In the middle of a pandemic and historic economic crisis, management showed zero care for its staff, who were economically vulnerable and reliant in a way.

According to Sarah Jaffe:[9]

Restaurant workers and essential workers in general have been perhaps the most numerous to die of Covid-19. This is also because many of them were immigrants, did not have papers, did not take much money and lived in overcrowded houses. Then there were the people who decided not to go back to work because their colleagues had died of Covid-19, and they thought their job shouldn't cost them their lives. Many saw it as an opportunity to gain better working conditions.

Unsurprisingly, the restaurant industry in the United States has also been the sector with the highest rate of voluntary resignations.[10]

A study titled *Losing Talent due to Covid-19: The Roles of Anger and Fear on Industry Turnover Intentions*[11] shows that, in order to understand the high resignation rate, one needs to understand anger. For the authors, anger related to the threat of redundancies is the main driver of turnover in the industry.

Consider what was happening in those months. In the first half of March 2020, Columbia University historian Adam Tooze noted on

Twitter the steep rise in unemployment benefit claims. The rise in jobless claims that week was staggering, wrote the *New York Times*.[12] In contrast to an average of about three hundred and fifty thousand requests per week before the start of the pandemic, in the second half of March alone there was a rise of 10 million. The Labour Department's graph was a vertical line merging with the y-axis, indicating how the number of people who had lost their jobs had skyrocketed. In the two months leading from mid-March to mid-May, the total number of new unemployment claims had exceeded 36 million. And eighteen weeks later, the catastrophe was still unfolding. A large chunk of those who had been left at home worked in hospitality and in the restaurant industry. They were, in short, people like Mike.

'We are facing staggering levels of claims', Tooze observed. For Andrew Stettner of the Century Foundation, the trend represented 'the single worst one-day piece of labour market news in America's history'.[13] It was reminiscent of the era of the Great Depression when millions of workers were laid off, in a flash, with traumatic speed. It became clear in those days that no matter how many sacrifices you made at work, the system was ready to spit you out and leave you at home when the crisis hit.

The anger stems from here.

There is a tragic overlap between sectors with high mortality, racial inequality, and pandemic layoffs: these three often coincide, and they are also the sectors most affected by a high rate of voluntary turnover after the pandemic. In many cases, anger at being used as cannon fodder is the main reason why many decided to leave the sector at the end of the sanitary emergency.

We can see this also in retail, where low wages, long hours and unpredictable shifts coupled with high rates of contagion. 'Just wear a mask and don't tell anyone' was how several outlets tried to overcome staff shortages: 'I really need you today'.[14] As we shall see, the situation in retail is similar on both sides of the Atlantic and reveals the existence of widespread malaise exacerbated by staff shortages, pressure from supervisors and low wages.[15] According to a McKinsey[16] report, at least half of all retail workers are considering quitting their jobs. Among the reasons for this trend, the report listed burnout, lack of childcare and economic uncertainty. In retail, moreover, 'flexibility ranks first among the reasons for leaving a job'. This shows how the concept of flexibility is often interpreted asymmetrically: in many cases, companies use it to increase staff presence at peak times, even if this does not meet the needs of employees. In this context, the report continues, pay is too low to meaningfully compensate workers and prevent them from leaving.

In fact, low-wage workers are the main driver of the Great Resignation. In analysing the socio-demographic characteristics of those who resign, the Pew Research Center[17] attributed this choice to three prevailing reasons: low pay, poor career opportunities and the feeling of not being respected at work. As the report explains:

> Across educational attainment, those with a postgraduate degree are the least likely to say they quit a job at some point in 2021: 13 per cent say this, compared with 17 per cent of those with a bachelor's degree, 20 per cent of those with some college and 22 per cent of those with a high school diploma or less education. About a quarter of non-retired Hispanic and Asian adults (24 per cent each) report quitting a job last year; 18 per cent of Black adults and 17 per cent of White adults say the same.[18]

In contrast to the idea that it is only those who can afford it who quit, the Pew Research Center shows that it is first and foremost those with low income and little protections who do so. Up to now we have assumed that having a job is a privilege that must be honoured, in an anachronistic approach that suggests that a job is enough to pay expenses and rent. Evidence shows an opposite pattern. Those who quit their jobs first and foremost are those who are not happy at work. This happens for different reasons, that cannot be limited to the salary. When the salary is low, however, there is no return for the workers' sacrifices.

In January 2023, the U.S. Chamber of Commerce confirmed this trend. In a study entitled *Understanding America's Labor Shortage: The Most Impacted Industries*,[19] it confirmed that the restaurant industry had a quit rate consistently above 5.2 per cent – almost twice the national average of 2.7 per cent. In retail this was around 4 per cent in autumn 2022, closely followed by professional business services and industry. According to the report, voluntary turnover is lowest in areas where employment is more stable and wages are higher, in line with what has been said so far. Labour shortages are also high in other sectors, such as transport, healthcare, social work and schools.

As far as schools are concerned, the National Education Association (NEA), the main teachers' union in the United States, found that 55 per cent of its members are considering leaving education,[20] exhausted as they are by the pandemic, the lack of resources and the high risk of exposure to viruses.

As education lecturer Jo Lambert explains:[21]

> [H]ere is no 'teacher shortage'. There are thousands of qualified experienced teachers who are no longer teaching. There's a shortage of respect and proper compensation for teachers allowing them to actually teach.

In fact, teaching is paid so little that some people cannot afford to do it.

> I am a full-time teacher. And here it is, it's eight o'clock at night and I'm delivering pizza. I am doing this because I cannot survive on my teacher's paycheck. Everyone is talking about all the reasons why teachers want to leave. But what about those who want to stay, but can't afford to?[22]

In fact, the topic of education would deserve a separate discussion. For here, burnout, low salaries and high workload add up to a profound dislocation between teachers' values and institutional values, shaped by a competition-oriented neoliberal paradigm that, in recent years, has changed the organization of work, and the very purpose of teaching. In the entire sector, the health emergency was the final straw, generating an epidemic of Covid among that part of the teaching staff that found itself forced to teach in presence and one of remote-work burnout for those who, instead, worked from home. A recent study on teachers' mental health during the pandemic[23] shows that those who worked remotely were 60 per cent more likely to feel socially isolated and experience symptoms of depression while 18 per cent of teachers showed symptoms of anxiety, had difficulty sleeping or panic attacks.

This problem afflicts the academic world as well. Here, quitting had started well before March 2020. I myself had written about this ten years ago, in light of the growing malaise and burnout in the sector.[24] Recently, a study in the academic journal *Nature*[25] reported that long hours, crushing workloads, meagre salaries and limited career prospects are driving a quarter of mid-career scientists in the United States out of the sector. On the other side of the pond, a study[26] by the University and College Union in the UK reports that about three out of five people want to leave the sector within five years (61 per cent). Three-quarters (74 per cent) of those in research roles consider it 'likely or very likely' that they will leave the sector in the next five years, while four in five (81 per cent) of younger people think they will leave the sector in the next five years due to working conditions.

Data show a desire to escape that cuts across positions and ages, in line with an organizational system in which 78 per cent of respondents say they are unable to do their jobs as they would like due to management demands, and in which a staggering 88 per cent say they are not optimistic about the future of the industry.[27]

In the UK, after all, the pandemic has set in against a difficult situation well captured by a five-year cycle of strikes, during which staff have protested job insecurity, pension cuts and ever-increasing workloads, to no avail. In several universities, the last day of the strike, in 2020, was followed by the first day of lockdown. This allowed the whole country to dismiss the union's demands as untimely. For thousands of people employed in British universities, this meant tackling the pandemic with an extraordinary workload and hardly any support or possibility of interaction with management. I remember that for many months in a row we were teaching online for nearly twelve hours a day, and that I was often only able to carve out a few hours for myself in the morning, before dawn. The inevitable result of this situation has been a loss of staff at the end of the acute phase of the emergency. I also left British academia after the pandemic. The irony is that from the point of view of research and intellectual affinity, that was the best place to be. However, dealing with the convoluted demands of management was simply not sustainable.

The subject of remote working returns among business services, and particularly among professionals in accounting, legal or marketing services. In this case, the U.S. Chamber of Commerce report cited above attributes the causes of voluntary turnover to two factors: the reduction in the possibility of working from home and the absence of childcare services. The issue of remote working is important. For years, research has shown that it often leads to working more, being always *on* and always available, including in the evenings, on holidays and at weekends. According to the *Employee Burnout report*,[28] for example, 67 per cent of remote workers suffered from burnout during the pandemic. Fifty-three per cent worked more hours than they did in the office and almost a third said they worked 'a lot more' than before. Sandra Burchi has written insightful analyses on this, showing the ambivalences of a work regime that brings with it obvious benefits, but also suffering and loneliness.[29] In spite of this, many companies, once the emergency was over, viewed remote work with skepticism and restricted its implementation, precluding employees from the benefits of tele-work: greater flexibility and a better work-life balance. The untimeliness of this choice is surprising, because it shows how the 'empty nest syndrome', the fear of not seeing employees and not being able to control them, takes precedence over flexible policies that benefit both employees and employers.

From this perspective, the refusal of work has been more widespread than commonly assumed. It is not limited to Gen Z, as has been said repeatedly. On the contrary, as a BlackRock report[30] points out, it affects adults more than young people.

> While employees in the 20-30 age bracket have historically comprised a large proportion of voluntary leavers and continue to do so, they have not been the key driver of the great resignation, contrary to expectations. In fact, their resignation rates are actually below their pre-covid levels. [...] Resignation rates have been higher for all other age groups. [...] As of June 2022, resignation rates for employees aged 30-50 in the US were between 6 per cent and 17 per cent above 2019 levels, despite a slowdown in the second quarter from peak levels earlier this year. Resignation rates for older workers are even higher, at 30% or more for employees above age 60, consistent with official data showing larger departures from the labor force for these age groups.

In general, a report by the consultancy firm McKinsey tried to summarize the reasons why people leave.
The first:

> Because they are upset. [...] Employees witnessed how companies furloughed or laid off their colleagues during business slowdowns. Those who remained resented being told to shoulder greater burdens and put in more time (sometimes with suboptimal resources) to help keep operations afloat.

The second:

> Because they are exhausted. Our research shows that poor mental health (burnout and stress), family-care demands, and reflections on purpose because of the Covid-19 pandemic played big roles in why some workers left their companies without another job in hand. Consider the couple who, after two years of stressful, isolating remote work in their respective jobs, realized they could get by on

one income as a trade-off for spending more time with their children. Among those who quit, attrition was most apparent in the consumer and retail, healthcare, and education sectors – industries that have felt some of the greatest social and economic pressures during the pandemic.

There is one last reason, among those reported by McKinsey, that is worth considering:

Because they can. Leaving a job used to be anxiety inducing; it isn't anymore. The cost of switching jobs has gone down significantly. There is much less of a stigma associated with showing a gap in your résumé. Because of the current labor shortage and the greater acceptance of remote work, employees in many industries are confident that they can find work anywhere, whenever they are ready. They have access to more information about the labor market than ever before – through word of mouth and social-media sites, for instance – so they don't need to rely on the usual recruiting resources. They have seen friends and colleagues depart and survive, and they are confident that they can, too.[31]

This last entry is the most interesting. It is complicated, in fact, to prove that quitting a job entails less anxiety than it did a few decades ago. Anxiety is, clearly, difficult to measure. Data also suggest that anxiety disorders are the world's most prevalent mental health problem[32] in contemporary times. It is plausible that the main difference from the past is not the anxiety associated with quitting a job generates, but the anxiety that having a job soothes. Compared to what happened in the past, the very fact of having a job does not settle the anxieties of those in work. Wages are so low and workloads so heavy that some fear they will not be able to pay their rent *despite* working. It is therefore safe to assume that the fear of job loss is proportional to the job's rewards. If a job pays poorly, there's little to lose by leaving it.

2. The antiwork society[33]

In the United States, the declining labour force participation rate has been the subject of several analyses, including one by the investment bank Goldman Sachs, which addressed the problem in November 2021 in a report entitled *Why Isn't the Labour Force Recovering?*[34] At the time, the labour force participation rate was 61.9 per cent. The analysis was largely in line with what we have just read, but offered additional insights. For Goldman Sachs, 3.4 million adults over the age of fifty-five and eight hundred thousand people between the ages of twenty-five and fifty-four had exited the labour force because they did not want a job at that time.

> The first key takeaway is that most labor force exiters are over age 55 (3.4 million) and do not want a job right now, reflecting 1.5 million early retirements, 1mn natural retirements due to population aging, and 900 thousand exits for other reasons.
>
> The second key takeaway is that among the prime-age persons who exited the labor force (1.7 million), more either do not want a job right now (800 thousand) or have not searched in the last year (400 thousand) than want a job and have searched in the last year (500 thousand). The low share of prime-age exiters who want a job and have searched (30 per cent) suggests that most prime-age exits are voluntary.

The report went on to focus on childcare constraints and concluded that the number of people not working because of this had decreased dramatically after schools reopened. The number of workers who did not return to work because of the medical risk and because of the temporary buffer provided by subsidies had also fallen sharply. The Goldman Sachs report included one last point:

> A final long-run risk to labor force participation is that some worker's preferences and lifestyles may have shifted after a year and half out of the labor force. [...] Reddit's antiwork message board – which encourages individuals 'to get the most out of a work-free life' – has surged in popularity this fall and is now even more popular than the Wallstreetbets board that drove a surge in retail trading activity earlier this year. As a result, we see some risk that some workers will elect to remain out of the labor force for longer, provided they can afford to do so.

Reddit's r/antiwork is an anonymous discussion space that claims to be antiwork. 'We are left-wing, anti-capitalist, and want to abolish all work', write the administrators of the page. Over the past two years, r/antiwork has become a popular discussion space where some 3 million users converge to discuss strikes, resignations and unionization. On r/antiwork, users share resignation stories and workplace experiences.

In an article in the *New York Times* in October 2021,[35] John Herrman described the emotion he felt in scrolling through the testimonials on the page, reading about one employee who admonished his boss because his paycheck had arrived late and such a mistake could not be repeated. And of another explaining to his manager the meaning of the word 'loyalty'.

We are witnessing 'what feels like a seismic shift in people's attitudes towards work'[36] said Alison Green. Journalist Farhad Manjoo, for his part, described in the *New York Times* the visceral thrill he felt reading these testimonies and 'seeing people wrest the reins of their lives from the soul-sucking, health-destroying maw of capitalism'.[37]

Overall, r/antiwork marks a radical transformation in the way work is understood and described, highlighting its costs and injustices.

As Kat Cosgrove wrote on Twitter:

«Yeah I worked 90 hours a week, destroyed my marriage, and didn't watch my kids grow up but hey we shipped an important product».
«Ah well at least you're rich now.
«Oh no, no no no, but i have the satisfaction of having made other people rich».[38]

Stories like Kat Cosgrove's capture the heart of r/antiwork forums, which always start from personal experiences to create connections or collective reflections. Like the story of a user who cared for his cancer-stricken wife for five months, spending the savings of twenty years so that she could be cured, even though they both had good jobs and degrees from top American colleges, only to realize in the end that even if you do everything by the book, the system eats you up, spits you out and throws you out on the street.

In fact, r/antiwork is about workers who quit their jobs after being cynically exploited for years. It narrates the damaging impact that unskilled, underpaid, precarious work, plagued by ongoing downsizing, high workload and a toxic culture has on health and relationships. The post explains that wages have only increased by 5 percent over forty years. He also dwells on how many workplaces have become environments of abuse and bullying, where any request from management is treated as legitimate, but workers' requests are routinely dismissed.

As this post points out:[39]

Boss: – Your salary won't be very good starting out. Is that ok?
Employee: – My performance won't be very good until it is, is that ok?

Or this:[40]

Employers asking for references is so stupid and pointless like. Why don't YOU give me 3 references! Go ahead! Let me call three former employees and see if y'all treated them well or like shit, then we'll talk.

In general, stories on r/antiwork recount the disillusionment of those who believed that work was an instrument of emancipation or, at least, a free exchange between equals. Only to realize that in everyday practice, work is often an abusive relationship, marked by a lack of reciprocity. This great disillusion is the cultural subtext to the Great Resignation, transforming personal reckonings into a collective phenomenon aimed at renegotiating the boundaries between what is permissible and what is no longer acceptable.

It is no longer acceptable to work sixty hours a week and fail to pay the rent. It is not acceptable that pay goes down while profits go up. It is not acceptable to work full-time and not be in a position to pay for education or health care. It is not acceptable to consider time off as a form of unpaid availability. It is not acceptable to spend more time at work than with the family, commuting than with their children. It is not acceptable that we have to sacrifice so much for a job that offers so little in return.

We always thought that work was very insecure and that we had to hold on to it because there was no alternative. In the discussion forum, the opposite reasoning reigns: when working conditions deteriorate so inescapably, what do you really lose by quitting a shitty job? Consider someone working in a restaurant earning $2.13 an hour plus tip: The real question is not how one can live without such a job, but how one can live with it

Or again, think of this person who works for Uber Eats:

Decided to try Uber Eats while I'm out of work for a couple weeks.
I drove for four hours. Did 8 deliveries. 3 of 8 people tipped.
After 8 deliveries, I'd made a whopping $30.97.
Filled up my tank to go home. $30.60.
Four hours of my life for 37 cents. And accounting for my car's depreciation, it cost me money to drive for Uber Eats.
Fuck this gig economy bullshit.[41]

Recently, the Edelman Trust Barometer 2020[42] found that many people no longer believe that working hard will give them a better life.

But if work does not help to improve our living conditions, what is it good for?

These questions cross workplaces from one side of the world to the other, but find no answers.

In fact, the stories shared on r/antiwork represent a fundamental shift in how work is viewed. Compared to the 1970s, when it was possible to work a certain number of hours and buy a house, today you have to work a certain number of jobs to be able to pay the rent. The problem is not just that wages have declined while the cost of living has soared and continues to do so; the problem is the way in which the toxic culture of work has deteriorated the well-being of millions of people. In this context, people's disposition to sacrifice has changed. There was a time when sacrifice was rewarded by economic, professional and social recognition. Today, it is not uncommon to find oneself without the bare minimum to live on despite work. Today, in too many cases, sacrificing oneself serves no purpose.

According to Noreen Malone, this does not only affect people on low incomes:

> At Citi, according to New York magazine, an analyst typed 'I hate this job, I hate this bank, I want to jump out the window' in a chat, prompting human resources to check on his mental health. 'This is a consensus opinion,' he explained to H.R. 'This is how everyone feels.'[43]

And at Goldman Sachs.

> Junior bankers in San Francisco felt alienated over their long hours, what they considered low pay and lack of Seamless stipends while working from home. They made a formal presentation to their office's top executives, relying on survey data they gathered that showed, for instance, that three-quarters of them felt they had been victims of workplace abuse. It was something a little like collective action by America's future elite.[44]

Perhaps this is why the decision to quit is often met with relief and even excitement.

> Sex is great, but have you ever quit a job that was ruining your mental health?[45]

And again:

I hope this email doesn't find you. I hope you've escaped, that you're free.[46]

Or lastly:

I am currently out of the office and don't plan on returning[47]

For Noreen Malone[48] the Great Resignation marks the beginning of an era of 'anti-ambition', the phase that causes people to relate to work 'As just a job, a paycheck to take care of the bills! Not the sum total of us, not an identity', she writes. The term 'quiet quitting' has been used to describe this phenomenon: the decision to do the bare minimum, without identifying one's entire life with work. This is a controversial definition: rightly, there are those who think that it is wrong to consider as a form of *quitting* the decision to limit oneself to doing what is stipulated in the contract, because it implies that exceeding one's contractual duties without compensation is expected. It remains true, however, that in a work culture punctuated by expectations of devotion, 'relating to work as just a job' is already considered an affront, a form of insubordination, a stance often interpreted as lacking deference or gratitude. In short, it is easy to perceive it as a scandal, and in many instances this is enough to become the object of retaliation and reprisals.

The former US Secretary of Labour, Robert Reich,[49] explained better than anyone else how the Great Resignation should be interpreted.

Corporate America wants to frame this as a 'labor shortage'. Wrong. What's really going on is more accurately described as a living-wage shortage, a hazard pay shortage, a childcare shortage, a paid sick leave shortage, and a healthcare shortage.

For Reich, it is wrong to speak about the shortage of workers. There is a shortage of adequate wages and protections.

Unless these shortages are rectified, many Americans won't return to work anytime soon. I say it's about time.

3. Don't just quit, unionize!

On 13 October 2021, the former US Secretary of Labour, Robert Reich, wrote an article in *The Guardian* in which he asked whether the high number of resignations amounted to an unofficial general strike.

'*Is America experiencing an unofficial general strike?*', the economist asked, as he summarized what was happening.

> You might say workers have declared a national general strike until they get better pay and improved working conditions. No one calls it a general strike. But in its own disorganized way it's related to the organized strikes breaking out across the land – Hollywood TV and film crews, John Deere workers, Alabama coal miners, Nabisco workers, Kellogg workers, nurses in California, healthcare workers in Buffalo. Disorganized or organized, American workers now have bargaining leverage to do better. After a year and a half of the pandemic, consumers have pent-up demand for all sorts of goods and services.

Reich drew a connection between the strikes and the growing wave of resignations. Whether organised or not, in both cases they stemmed from the need to rebel against existing working conditions. After a year and a half of pandemic, 'consumers have a suppressed demand for all kinds of goods and services', Reich wrote. Labour demand surged, while labour supply lagged behind. The labour force participation rate was stuck at 61.6 per cent, and there were a large number of vacancies on the market for which no workers could be found.

Reich was clear about the causes:

> Years ago, when I was secretary of labor, I kept meeting working people all over the country who had full-time work but complained that their jobs paid too little and had few benefits, or were unsafe, or required lengthy or unpredictable hours. Many said their employers treated them badly, harassed them, and did not respect them. Since then, these complaints have only grown louder, according to polls. For many, the pandemic was the last straw. Workers are fed up, wiped out, done-in, and run down. In the wake of so much hardship, illness and death during the past year, they're not going to take it anymore.

The issue has not escaped mainstream economists. In February 2022, Alex Domash and Larry Summers of Harvard noted that the pandemic had changed the world of work. On the supply side, there had been 'some movement away from the labour market', while on the demand side there was an increasing difficulty in finding workers. In December 2021, there were almost 11 million job vacancies. At the same time, there were 6.3 million unemployed workers.[50]

In practice, there were about two vacancies for every immediately employable person, a ratio that remained almost stable for much of 2022. Declining labour force participation risked driving wages higher. In light of these considerations, the authors predicted that there would be significant inflationary pressure in the United States for some time.[51]

Another reason led them to this conclusion: the labour market was shaken not only by resignations but also by strikes October 2021 was called *Striketober*,[52] the month in which more than one hundred thousand people decided to go on strike. There were many sectors involved. They ranged from the ten thousand employees of John Deere[53] – who went on strike for seven weeks in a row to obtain, among other things, a 20 per cent wage increase – to the staff of Kellogg's,[54] via the miners of Alabama[55] – who were still on strike in January 2023, after twenty-one months – up to the nurses[56] in California, the students and precarious workers at universities like Columbia and Harvard, not to mention the difficult unionization drive of Amazon workers in Staten Island.

And then there were the small businesses, from which workers decided to resign en masse, in a kind of spontaneous strike that occasionally took on the appearance of a case of collective resignation.

This is what happened at a Hot Top chain shop in Rochester,[57] Minnesota, where all employees decided to leave by posting this note at the entrance:

> Almost all our staff walked out due to the inability of the Hot Topic Company to support and give a living wage.
>
> We cannot support ourselves and our families. We have worked so hard and cannot do this any longer.
>
> You cannot pay your workers in passion. Sorry for the inconvenience

It also happened at a Burger King in Lincoln,[58] Nebraska, where workers decided to leave en masse, putting up a sign outside the restaurant that read: 'We all quit. We apologise for the inconvenience'.

The same happened at several McDonald's and Taco Bell restaurants, where workers simultaneously walked out and did not return, wishing their boss good luck in finding people willing to be underpaid. Labour journalist Mike Elk, in October 2021, counted more than 1670 worker walkout[59] since the beginning of the pandemic, on top of these cases.

Then come the union-organizing efforts. For instance, workers managed to establish a union at Starbucks in 2021. 'During the pandemic we realised they didn't care about us', a former Rochester employee told

Recode. 'They'll call me a partner all they want, but corporate will allow me to die on the floor if it made them money',[60] said Brandi Alduk, a 21-year-old employee at a Queens shop. By the following year, more than 260 additional Starbucks shops had voted to unionize, creating a domino effect in shops across the chain.[61]

In general, 2021 was a year of mobilization, in which mass resignations added to strikes. In 2022, both increased. The Workers Institute[62] of the School of Industrial and Labour Relations (ILR) at Cornell University, which monitors strikes in the world of work, showed an increase of almost 50 per cent in 2022. Working conditions worsened during the pandemic, said director Cathy Creighton[63] in an interview. Subsequently, labour shortages aggravated the situation because they forced few people to do more. In this context, strikes and resignations reinforced one another and pushed employers to sit at the negotiating table with the unions. 'If there's nobody in line to take your job because there are just not enough people, that gives you incredible strength in striking',[64] Creighton stated.

Such is the case with nurses, who managed to negotiate a 19 per cent wage increase after three days of strike action, in what has been called a historic victory.[65] The sector, after all, has been on a state of unrest for months: think about the fifteen thousand nurses' strike in Minnesota, described as the largest in the private sector in US history.

Then there is Big Tech. Apple is the first of the big tech companies to agree to sit down at the negotiating table with the union, after receiving a complaint from the National Labor Relations Board for banning the posting of union leaflets in a New York Apple Store break room.[66]

Amazon, on the other hand, has so far refused to acknowledge the union. The multinational corporation is the second largest private employer in the United States, with a workforce of around 1.5 million, which has more than doubled during the pandemic.[67] Amazon also has a long history of anti-union practices: practices of coercion, intimidation and retaliation against union-supporting workers in order to undermine their organizing efforts have been documented for years, in full violation of labour law, as well as strategies to launch reputational initiatives in the press and 'neutralize' critics.[68] For years, these strategies mirrored the high turnover rate in the company, entirely focused on the replaceability of employees, creating an environment in which high turnover and low unionization rates reinforced one another. 'Successful companies either hire well or fire well', writes Nick Dimitrov:[69]

As the adage goes, successful companies either 'hire well' (e.g. Google, Microsoft) or 'fire well' (e.g. Facebook, Netflix,

Amazon.) This is true: Amazon is exceptional at removing its underperformers quickly. What enables Amazon to 'fire well' is its strong culture, which obsesses over results. Nothing else matters, but output. In an environment that sheds an incredible and constant amount of light on accountability, it's impossible for underperformers to hide.

'Amazon seeks out underperformers and jettisons them from its organism like foreign bodies', Dimitrov writes. For a long time, high turnover was part of the company's strategy. 'Bezos really wanted turnover. He was afraid of a stagnant workforce – what he would call a "march to mediocrity".'[70] For Jodi Kantor, coauthor of a major *New York Times* investigation into the way Amazon treats its employees, 'some of this turnover is actually by design. [...] The turnover is almost built into the system. If you look at how they pay, you can see that they don't expect to keep people for very long'.[71] In this sense, dismissals without just cause and the high rate of voluntary resignations, for Amazon, have not been a problem: on the contrary, they have always been part of a production model in which high turnover has an essentially anti-union function. Certain levels of growth, after all, are only achievable that way: by creating a culture of efficiency that discourages the retention of all those workers who do not always perform at their best.[72]

The problem is that, in a context of full employment, a high turnover rate can be counterproductive. This was disclosed in a confidential report published by 'Recode', according to which the American multinational could run out of staff in its US warehouses by 2024.[73] The report was confirmed by a later document,[74] which highlights the company's difficulties in retaining employees.

As journalist George Anderson summarized:

The internal documents reviewed and reported on by *Engadget* support a similar *Recode* report from June on a leaked 2021 Amazon memo speculating that turnover rates at its warehouses would far outstrip its abilities to hire and train new workers by 2024 unless the company responded quickly with higher wages and increased automation. These changes were positioned as triage actions designed to give the company more time.[75]

The topic has been discussed extensively in the press over the past year: after eight months of investigative work, journalists from the *New York Times* seemed to sense concern at the top of management about the unsustainability of its production model.[76] In fact, the confidential document, published by Engadget, made it clear that workers choose to leave the company in numbers twice as big as those of the workers who were laid off and that 'only one in three new hires in 2021'[77] stays with the company for at least ninety days – a very high quit rate.

To get out of this bottleneck, Amazon started 2022 by buying 'the largest number of robots in a single quarter'.[78] According to some analysts, the company is betting on automation to cope with staff shortages. Robots, after all, don't call in sick, don't quit, and don't demand raises and don't go on holidays. Full automation would therefore allow the company to confirm its production model, irrespective of economic cycles and cultural transformations.[79]

Transformations made even more powerful by the union. In 2021, an extraordinary organizing effort succeeded in establishing the first Amazon Labor Union in Staten Island, thanks to the positive outcome of the successful vote on the introduction of the union. The union's historic victory was the result of previous efforts lasting several months, during which workers organized strikes and demonstrations, stationing tents outside the plant to meet the rest of the workers. In the spring of 2022, the Amazon Labor Union won the right to represent some eight thousand workers at the huge New York warehouse.

Amazon, however, has not yet sat down at the table with the union.

On 9 January 2023, a federal official ruled that the multinational must recognize its first unionized warehouse, and desist from further retaliation against the union.[80] Analysts wondered if Amazon could afford to continue ignoring their demands.

The corporate decision to ignore the union was a show of strength, whereby the company wanted to reaffirm its operating model without making concessions. In some ways, the decision to lay off eighteen thousand workers – which doesn't include warehousemen and transporters – as announced, should be placed within this context, marked by the need to downsize the workforce following the extraordinary growth in recruitment during the pandemic, when the company had recruited half a million people. The Amazon example shows the antagonism that exists between a Big Tech trying to assert the legitimacy of its production system through dismissals, anti-union practices and the race for automation. While quitters and trade unionists, on their part, embody two different forms of revolt of the precarious class.

We see a similar contrast in the macroeconomic scenario.

In 2022, the pressure on companies increased. In several sectors, the combination of walkouts and strikes forced companies to make concessions and led, in some cases, to slight wage increases, especially in low-income professions such as hospitality and restaurants. Sarah Jaffe recounts:

> I spoke to a young woman who had participated in the establishment of a fast-food workers' union in North Carolina: she worked for a chain, Freddy's, and was hired by McDonald's because they were understaffed and offered her sixteen dollars an hour. But while wages were rising at an unprecedented rate, the Federal Reserve decided that the inflation crisis was caused by spiralling wages – which was not true – and they raised interest rates to crush the bargaining power of workers.[81]

For companies, high voluntary turnover resulted in rising recruitment and training costs on top of rising labour costs. In the public discussion, such an increase was presented as a wage-price spiral that attributed inflation to rising wages. Against this scenario, the Federal Reserve rushed to raise interest rates. This was suggested by Harvard economist Larry Summers, for whom the only way to reduce inflation was to increase unemployment: 'we need five years of unemployment above 5% to contain inflation – in other words, we need two years of 7.5% unemployment or five years of 6% unemployment or one year of 10% unemployment'. The starting assumption of Summers' considerations was that the extraordinary rise in inflation in recent months depended on the upward wage pressure generated by the post-pandemic wave of strikes and resignations.[82] Given this premise, Summers argued that the only way to reduce inflation was to raise interest rates.

The problem is that as high as wages have risen, they have not kept pace with inflation. In June 2022, consumer prices rose by 9.1 per cent in the United States. In the same months, wages increased by a few percentage points at most. Real wages have fallen, both in the United States and in the rest of the world, as documented by the International Labour Organisation (ILO).[83] Former Secretary of Labour Robert Reich made it clear: the rise in inflation is not caused by wages.[84]

> Using high unemployment to attack inflation is like reducing someone's fever by putting them in a freezer. It may work, but at a horrendous cost. American workers are not responsible for today's inflation. Their wage gains have trailed inflation.

After all, Reich said this for months: it is not wage inflation, but profit inflation. This is demonstrated by a study by Amherst University economists Isabella W. Weber and Evan Wasner,[85] which gained international attention at the end of March 2023. According to the researchers, US corporate profit margins in 2022 reached their highest level since the post-war period. The same was true in Europe, where companies took advantage of inflation to boost profits. We are 'in the grip of a profit epidemic', a trade unionist told the *Financial Times*.

Summers' suggestion, in this sense, aimed at reducing the negotiating leverage of labour, rather than inflation. As Federal Reserve Chairman Jerome Powell noted in the summer of 2022, the availability of two job vacancies for every person seeking employment 'has led to a real imbalance in wage negotiations'.[86] The existence of more open positions means, in fact, that those in employment can say no and choose. 'Fighting inflation will require a decrease in vacancies and an increase in unemployment. There is no magic tool', wrote Larry Summers, Oliver Blanchard and Alex Domash in a policy brief from the Peterson Institute for International Economics in July 2022.[87] Only in doing so is it possible to force everyone to accept the jobs that are available, without complaints, even if this means undermining the very drivers that have enabled a modest improvement in working conditions. 'It's profits, not wages, that need to be controlled', Reich warned.[88]

Behind the decision to raise interest rates, once again, lies a political decision to counter the bargaining power of labour. Full employment has always been a threat. This was clarified by the economist Michael Kalecki[89] in his *Political Aspects of Full Employment* (1943), when he observed that in a regime of full employment:

> Under a regime of permanent full employment, the 'sack' would cease to play its role as a disciplinary measure. The social position of the boss would be undermined, and the self-assurance and class-consciousness of the working class would grow. Strikes for wage increases and improvements in conditions of work would create political tension.

Clara Mattei discussed this in her book *Operation Austerity. How Economists Paved the Way for Fascism*, in which she observes how the decision to increase the cost of money has historically been one of the paths chosen to discipline labour. Monetary austerity, as Mattei defines it, is a political measure aimed at crushing the resistance of labour, that is, at reducing voluntary turnover, absenteeism or strikes. The *Financial Times*[90] named Mattei's books one of the most influential books of 2022. The book narrates how the proprietary order has turned to austerity to regulate labour since the 1920s in order to suppress the struggles of workers and peasants who fought for shorter working hours, higher real wages and, more generally, to support a democratization process in the country. Unfortunately, there are more analogies between our era and those years than we like to reckon. The Federal Reserve's decision to raise interest rates can be traced back to this paradigm.

Mattei sees Jerome Powell's interest rate hikes as a form of 'economic warfare.'

> Powell described the process of resetting the economy – through the introduction of increased unemployment and possible recession – as a necessary form of 'economic pain.'[91]

As the economist wrote in *The Guardian*,[92] this has been the aim of austerity for more than a century: inflict pain to preserve existing power relations. The introduction of restrictive monetary policies is no exception.

> For capitalism to work in delivering economic growth, the social relation of capital – people selling their labor power for a wage – must be uniform across a society. If prices or salaries rise, the system fails, and economic disaster follows abruptly.

The Great Resignation did both. On the one hand, it put pressure on wages. On the other, it challenged the belief that life holds no alternative to selling one's labour for a wage. This is why, at first, the great resignation was considered a *temporary anomaly*, caused by the intemperance of the younger generation. With time it became clear that what was happening could not be reduced to either one of these things.

The decision to impose monetary austerity, therefore, was seemingly designed to protect the labour relations and discourage people from quitting. Such is the aim of the central banks' tightening policies, the consequences of which add to a situation of uncertainty caused by the war and rising energy prices.

> That's exactly the function austerity serves: it preserves the basic class relations at the core of our economy, especially in times of social changes.[93]

Economist Bryce Covert stated the same in an article published in the *New York Times* on 31 March 2023: 'The Federal Reserve's war on inflation is a class war'.[94] The problem is not to lower inflation, but to reduce the negotiating power of labour, even at the cost of generating unemployment and putting the banking system at risk, as happened with the collapse of Silicon Valley Bank. From this point of view, the Great Resignation seems the embodiment of a cultural and anthropological change, intended to reshape lifestyles and question one of the pillars of the world in which we live: the labour relation. To this end, the post-pandemic debate in the United States has focused on the need to 'slow down' the economy. At first, it looked like a paradox: during the pandemic, the focus was solely on achieving a rapid rebound. A few months later, the economy had to slow down. For only by cooling down the economy could workers be stripped of all those vacancies that allowed them to choose and, *scandalously*, to reject the least advantageous job offers.

In this context, austerity entailed an undeclared class war, aimed at crushing an unorganized general strike. It is interesting how both things unfold blatantly before our eyes, without having been announced: Perhaps our fragile democracy cannot bear to acknowledge the resurgence of a long-standing class war. Such unraveling of political and social order often prompts reactionary responses. There is always someone who seeks to restore the social order with reactionary measures, while others desert and break ranks.

4. Let it rot: The case of China

Refusal of work has also become a significant issue in China, where the protest movement *Tangping* (from 躺平, 'to lie down') began as a form of resistance to 996, a system that requires working from 9.00 am to 9.00 pm for six days a week.

In a 2021 article in the *New York Times*,[95] Vivian Wang sought to shed light on this system. According to Wang, the term started to be used around 2015, when Chinese Big Tech firms—including 58.com, Alibaba, Huawei, and ByteDance (owner of TikTok) resorted to longer working hours to compete with Silicon Valley. At that time, several companies introduced 996 and imposed longer shifts on employees.

Although '996' suggests a 9 am–9 pm schedule, in reality 996 is merely indicative. In fact, work often ends at midnight or in the early morning hours.

In the Chinese public debate, several entrepreneurs have defended these schedules. Jack Ma, founder of Alibaba, declared that working long hours is a blessing and that people who are unwilling to do it should stay away from his company. For Richard Liu, founder of JD.com, work-life balance is for slackers. Richard Liu also argued that no one is obliged to work hard. According to critics, however, his company classifies staff based on overtime hours worked and punishes those who work less. Jia Guolong, managing director of Xibei Canyin, said that 996 is not enough: we should stick to the 715 model and work fifteen hours a day, seven days a week. Chinese law limits working hours to eight per day and forty-four per week, with at least one day off. In 2021, furthermore, the 996 system was ruled illegal by the Supreme Court.[96] However, weak enforcement in China allows companies to impose much longer actual working hours and, in several cases, to work more than one weekend per month.

In 2019, the founders of the online forum 996.ICU,[97] which collects anonymous complaints from Big Tech workers, warned: 'If you continue to tolerate the 996 schedule, you will put your health at risk and end up in the intensive care unit of a hospital'. Among the testimonies in the forum, there were people who complained of leaving their homes to go to work between two and three o'clock in the morning, and those who admitted they were only leaving work at that hour.

> Boss: Keep it up, try to stay in the office until 3AM.
> Employee I already stay until 3AM every day. Can I take on sick leaves without penalty?
> Boss That is not possible.[98]

In 2021, the death of two workers at Pinduoduo, an e-commerce giant, prompted a major debate over the 996 system. The first, Fei, was in her early twenties when she collapsed on the 29th of December after leaving work at 1.30 am. She died in the emergency room for unknown causes, wrote the *Washington Post*;[99] she had worked at least three hundred hours in a month – twelve a day plus overtime. Two weeks later, Tan, twenty-three, died by suicide in his hometown of Changsha, falling from the 27th floor. Tan had completed his internship at Pinduoduo and left without giving an explanation. Following his death, Wang, an employee of the same company, posted a video in which he described the 'constant exploitation' of the staff, forced to work up to 380 hours a month, including Sundays, with no bathroom breaks, and called Tan 'another martyr'.[100] Wang was fired for publishing the video. Meanwhile, Pinduoduo founder Colin Huang had become the second richest person in China in the same months.[101]

Death due to overwork is not new. In Japan it is called *karoshi* and has been killing ten thousand people a year for the past thirty years. In South Korea, it is called *gwarosa*,[102] while in China, *guolaosi*[103] causes roughly 600,000 deaths annually.

In 2022, the death of a 25-year-old man, an employee of the Bilibili platform, who was forced to work until four in the morning, made headlines.[104] The same happened to a young woman who lost consciousness after working for five days straight until dawn at a company in Hangzhou.[105] Recently, the International Labour Organisation estimated that, globally, about 745,000 people die from heart attacks and heart disease every year due to working excessively long days.[106] Generally speaking, in Chinese Big Tech, it is difficult to escape similar working hours, due to the psychological pressure from a hierarchical system that uses digital surveillance to monitor productivity.

Tangping originates here.

In April 2021, a post by Luo Huazhong went viral, igniting the cultural movement known as *tangping* or *lying flat*. Luo Huazhong was a factory worker who toiled for several years, before he quit his job and cycled from Sichuan Province to Tibet, covering about 1300 kilometres while he sustained himself through odd jobs. 'After working for so long, I just felt numb, like a machine. And so I resigned', he said.[107]

> I have not been working for two years, just having fun and don't see anything wrong in it. Pressure mainly comes from people around you who position and compete with you, it also comes from the values of the older generation. All sorts of pressures keep popping up before you all the time. Every time you search for a popular news, it is all about romances and pregnancies etc. of celebrities in 'procreative surrounding' (生育周边), as if some 'invisible creatures' (看不见的生物) are creating a kind of thinking and pressure on you. But we don't have to be like this. I can lie in the sun in a wooden tub like Diogenes, or I can live in a cave like Heraclitus and think about 'logos', since this land has never had a school of thought that exalts human subjectivity, I can develop one of my own. Lying flat is my wise movement. Only through lying flat, can humans measure up to things.[108]

According to Ivan Franceschini, a researcher at the Australian National University and an expert on China, the expression *tangping* describes 'a kind of passive resistance to the unbridled pace of working life in China, experienced mainly by young workers in technology or new economy companies'.[109] Behind this form of protest is the criticism of a business model based on overwork, which puts people in the impossible position of having to choose between ruining their health in order to work or quitting work and not having enough money to live on. For years, this culture of competition in China has been justified by the promises of an emerging market that was meant to enable everyone to improve their living conditions. In 2010, China's Gross Domestic Product was growing by about ten percentage points. In the following years, growth slowed to 6.8 per cent in 2016 and 2.3 per cent in 2020, the year of the pandemic. For a long time, economic growth drove employment by creating jobs for almost 800 million people. Such a high growth rate also drove higher education, which has increased almost tenfold since the 1990s, in a process that has been called 'the great expansion'.[110] In 1997, there were about 1 million new enrolments per year in universities. In 2020, these were over 10 million. In 2021, the total number of students enrolled in a higher tertiary education institution was 44.3 million and about 15 per cent of Chinese had a university degree.

After the pandemic, the economic downturn in China jammed the mechanism.

'It has never been so difficult to find a job', a young worker who had accepted a 30 per cent pay cut in order to keep his job told the *Financial Times*.[111] By July 2022, the unemployment rate for 18–24-year-olds had reached almost 20 per cent, a record for the country. In this context, education no longer secured employment, but generated high rates of stress and burnout among students. At the same time, house prices were unaffordable. In China, the ratio between house price and income, which shows how many years it would take to pay for a house if all income was spent on it, is among the highest in the world and shows that housing is unaffordable for most.[112]

When the socio-economic framework changed, many of the promises underpinning people's lives disappeared, highlighting the irrationality of a system of production that, on the one hand, forces people to work hard to succeed, and, on the other hand, condemns those who excel to failure. In this context, Tangping proponents argue that working oneself to exhaustion is pointless, because this system no longer offers a reward for people's sacrifices. For *tangping* it is pointless to strive, because with or without effort you are doomed to fail. Similarly, with or without work you are bound to be poor. So you might as well stop trying: at least, by doing so, there will be no more suffering and no more injustice. In the words used by Zhang Xinmin, a musician from Wuhan, in a piece of music censored in China: 'Lying down is the way to go / If you lie flat, you can no longer fall down'.[113]

In recent months, the mainstream media have painted a stereotyped image of *tangping*, describing the tendency to lie down as an exotic and, in some ways, childish choice. Reality, however, is more complex. It is worth recalling what happened at Foxconn, the world's largest iPhone factory, where some three hundred thousand workers produce half a million phones every day, working as subcontractors for large multinationals such as Apple, Sony or Nokia.

It was 2010 when the company hit the headlines with a wave of suicides. For a while, young employees jumped out of the factory windows into the void, up to twenty suicide attempts in one month. To prevent this, Foxconn installed nets under employee dormitories, so as to intercept their bodies when they threw themselves down, like fishermen use nets to catch fish. The inhumanity was explicit in every detail. A recent reportage by Viola Zhou[114] recounts asphyxiating work rhythms, in places that stink of chlorine, where everyone has to keep their heads down without communicating, lest they be punished. It is like 'being under constant threat of whipping', one employee told her. 'iPhones are made in hell',[115] said Hunter, a man who worked intermittently for ten years at Foxconn, speaking of a windowless space where it is not possible to distinguish day from night and in which the passing of the hours is punctuated only by the number of parts to be produced each minute and by the shouting of a supervisor. 'I was having mental breakdowns all the time', says Hunter as he recalls colleagues bursting into tears in the middle of their shifts from stress. Hunter describes Foxconn as a place where money is more valuable than life. During the pandemic, thousands of people fled the company as management asked both people sick with Covid and healthy people to work side by side. 'Working at Foxconn means surrendering one's dignity', he concludes.

Tangping emerged in response to these situations, which shaped the imagination of an entire generation. *Tangping* choose to stop working to escape a production system based on exploitation and humiliation. From this point of view, the improvised image that the press has sometimes given of them does not reflect their political philosophy, which stems from an era of suffering and trauma, in which, as mentioned, sacrifices no longer come with a payback. Unsurprisingly, an anonymous manifesto named '*Tangpingist Manifesto*' (躺平主义者宣言) claims a closeness to the principles that led to the founding of the Paris Commune:

> Tangpingists try to find inspiration and enlightenment from their attempts. We are grateful to the following pioneers: the anarchists and Marxists who founded the Paris Commune, the workers who took over the factories in the Spanish Civil War, the escaped slaves who formed marron communities in the Great Dismal Swamp in the United States, the homeless, artists, students and queer people who occupied houses in Berlin, Germany, the autonomous Zapata aborigines of Chiapas, Mexico, and the women who fought patriarchy and organized cooperatives in the Kurdistan region of Syria.[116]

The manifesto resolves to 'contact all those who refuse coercion and obedience, men and women, workers and the unemployed, citizens, farmers and nomads, hooligans, students and intellectuals, heterosexuals, homosexuals and other queer people, vagrants and pensioners'.[117]

In some cases, the *tangping* movement has been compared to *quiet quitting*, the trend in the United States that recommends not to quit work but to do the bare minimum. *Tangping*, however, do not exclusively profess the desire to do the bare minimum, but to stop participating in its economic system, opting out of social practices designed to turn each individual into a consumer or producer that can be exploited.[118]

Young people have abandoned 'the rat race, with all its pain and distress', wrote journalist and author Jianan Qian in an article in the *New York Times*.[119] For Jianan Qian, Chinese history has long been soaked in pain: from the Japanese occupation in the 1930s and 1940s to the Chinese civil war to severe exploitation, malnutrition and extreme workloads. For decades, the population endured this pain in the hope that it would lead to a better future. The author gives the example of how her parents prevented her from using painkillers as a teenager, to get her used to bearing the agony. People suffered for years, convinced that if there is no pain, there is no gain. Today, however, this pain no longer yields anything. It is a 'pointless hamster wheel' that no longer leads to emancipation. Rather, it leads to *involution*.

Anthropologist Xiang Biao has described this involution as an inward retreat, trapping participants in an 'endless cycle of self-flagellation'.

If involution is said to originally have referred to a structural pattern in agricultural society which is repetitive, lacks competition, and prevents progress, then involution today is an endless cycle of self-flagellation, feeling as if you're running in place and constantly having to motivate yourself day in, day out. So, it's a highly dynamic trap which consumes a lot of energy. Living in a smallholder society was physically tiring, but this kind of mental torture didn't exist.[120]

For Xiang Biao, competition has come to a standstill. It has developed into a practice that forces you to work all the time, but prevents you from having any social mobility. Involution is therefore 'the experience of being locked in a competition that one ultimately knows is meaningless', he said in a long interview with the *New Yorker*. 'It is acceleration without a destination, progress without a purpose,[121] Sisyphus spinning the wheels of a perpetual-motion Peleton'[122] for all eternity.

For the *tangping*, competition no longer makes sense: it no longer yeals a good job or social stability. It seizes life and holds it captive in an involutional process.

After the pandemic, *tangping* was followed by another movement, Let it *rot* (*bailan,* 'let it rot'). Several observers have suggested that the *bailan* movement was more cynical than *tangping* because it did not just advise to flee the system, but to let it rot, as suits a hopelessly compromised machinery that cannot be reformed. 'Let it rot' is the movement's slogan, because any other course of action will be futile.

In both cases, these movements have been strongly stigmatized by the Government. China's hope lies in young people, said President Xi Jinping in a speech on 6 May 2022. The refusal of work undermines the 'Chinese dream' and cracks open the work ethic that has enabled its extraordinary economic growth. In recent months, *Tangping* and *Bailan* have often been called slackers and the refusal of work has been described as a danger to China's future.

At a historical stage of faltering growth, these movements embody the need to change the idea of development that dominates the present. Despite their contradictions, they are a grain of sand in an increasingly unsustainable economic system. A nest of uncertainty and hope overshadowed by the imperial ambitions of rival geopolitical blocs.

Chapter 3

THE ITALIAN ANOMALY

1. Blame it on the Citizenship Income

One evening in June 2022, I received a phone call from Luigi Ambrosio, a journalist from Radio Popolare, who asked me to participate in the live broadcast of *What's Going On*,[1] the programme he was hosting at the time. The subject of the programme was a survey carried out on behalf of the national television network La7, according to which, in the event of a referendum, 54 per cent of Italians would vote to abolish the Citizenship Income,[2] the support measure that, according to the INPS Annual Report, in the first three months of 2022 provided an average monthly amount of EUR 548 to 1.5 million households, about 3.3 million individuals.[3] The 'Citizenship Income' (Reddito di Cittadinanza, RdC) has been introduced on 1 April 2019. Although the name suggests a universal basic income, the RdC is instead a means-tested benefit aimed at poor and socially excluded households, conditional on participation in job-search activities. In Italy, this measure allowed one million people to make it through the pandemic,[4] when the healthcare emergency required thousands of activities and businesses to close. Nevertheless, it was hotly contested. Progressives argued that a real citizenship income should be unconditional rather than tied to an obligation to work, while conservatives argued that it disincentivized work and created a nation of slackers.

On that day, the discussion was heated, but at the core of the programme was a phone call from the owner of a small business in Milan, who said she was 'experiencing firsthand' that people 'don't want to commit' and continue to refuse a part-time job in her business because they simply 'don't want to work anymore'. For the owner, it had to be blamed on the Citizenship Incomes if, all of a sudden, young people had so little incentive to work. The call dropped before I could respond, but I was captivated by the woman's words. In a place like Milan, a 'part-time' job is often a cause for concern: the cost of living is so high and part-time jobs pay so little that it is plausible that such a position would not be attractive to people living in the city. In this sense, it is not uncommon for those seeking full-time employment to choose not to accept a part-time job if it does not allow them to meet their expenses. When it comes to work, however, the point of view of the workers is never taken into account. The basic idea, in fact, is that work should be accepted with enthusiasm and gratitude, regardless of its conditions. The fact that work is poorly paid, that it is only partially regular, or that it does not allow any real economic independence is irrelevant, because the prevailing political narrative is that there is, on the one hand, an entrepreneur who has 'broken his back' with sacrifice – and, on the other hand, loafers who have no desire to do anything despite the good heart of those who offer them an opportunity. In the words of Flavio Briatore: 'I have never seen a poor person create jobs, but instead of thanking you they also give you shit'.[5]

We have known for a while how the situation in the Italian debate has gotten out of hand. Suffice it to recall the way in which, in 2015, Expo Spa and the confederal trade unions made an agreement to 'hire' eighteen thousand five hundred volunteers to work for free, suggesting that this would give them a chance to 'make new friends', 'listen to fifty languages', 'be tagged in hundreds of photographs' and 'get lots of likes'.[6]

The underlying idea was that work is always a blessing, even when it is unpaid. For years, the creation of a business model based on precariousness and the dismantlement of labour rights has appealed to political leaders more than it has alarmed them. For many years, the demolition of the protections painstakingly conquered during the 1960s and 1970s has been presented as an opportunity to create employment and reduce the rigidity of the labour market, even though these reforms have amounted to a real assault.[7]

In general, from the 1980s onwards, in Italy, it was not a priority to tackle low wages, gruelling shifts or high rates of undeclared work, but rather to create a more flexible world of work, allowing companies to attract new staff and to let it go when it was no longer needed. In those years, work was not presented as a right or as a duty: it was a gift, a favour that companies granted to those who worked, and an opportunity to make new friends and acquaintances.

From this point of view, that thousands of unemployed people would be reluctant to accept a job is perceived as an *unfathomable mystery*. 'Nobody wants to work any more', in essence, was an attempt to address this mystery. People 'don't want to put themselves out there', they have no gratitude for the opportunities that their bosses offer them, and all too often decide to leave companies in the lurch for no apparent reason. It is no coincidence that the Italian debate on the Great Resignation has for a long time revolved around the emotional tones of disbelief. 'Companies do not understand why people quit', commented an article on Forbes Italia on 7 February 2022.[8]

In this context, the interpretations of this phenomenon were the most varied. Federico Fubini, for example, dedicated a long article to investigate the causes of the current labour shortage in the province of Modena. 'I passed the selections for *X Factor*', confessed a young 22-year-old girl to a placement agent, upon turning down a job.

> It is not just because of the (admittedly correct) literature on the exploitation of young workers or because regular, protected work is nowhere to be found, that being a placement agent has become hard. But because workers are nowhere to be found [...]. Especially, but not only, young workers. They don't want to let salt on their tails, they don't want to feel married to a typical family business in the Centre North, one of those companies that have been the backbone of Italy for three generations and that are now seeking new workers to train for the next thirty years.[9]

The *X Factor* and the lack of interest in marriage were not the only the reason that was used to justify the labour shortage. 'Blame it on the millennials', it was said, a generation that is notoriously lazy, choosy and unwilling to sacrifice. Nothing to do with the virtuous examples of *happy* workers who earn more than managers in doing menial jobs. Like the food delivery driver who:

> rides about a hundred kilometres a day on a bicycle, carrying a large delivery bag on his back and delivers pizzas and lunches and groceries. He earns two thousand euros a month and, on certain months, even four thousand. That's a manager's salary. And he is happy.[10]

Not to mention the woman who leaves Naples every morning to go to Milan, where she works as a school cleaner, making a 1,600 km round trip each day to save on rent. Every morning she takes the train, and in the evening she is 'happy to return home to my family with my parents, my grandmother and my little dogs'.[11]

These widely discussed and often debunked stories[12] praise individual sacrifice, the readiness to accept the harshness of life, the humility of those who give their all at work, despite exploitation and low pay, thus obscuring the reality of an increasingly unequal country, in which desertification of production makes it difficult to get out of unemployment even for those who want to.

In fact, behind these guilt-inducing narratives, there are areas of the country where work cannot be found, not so much due to voluntary unemployment, but rather to the decades-long absence of an industrial strategy and of R&D investment, which has turned entire areas of Italy into a manufacturing desert.

In order to understand what is happening, therefore, it is necessary to leave this framework and take into account the contradictions of the Italian anomaly: the bizarre case of a country in which over 5 million unemployed coexist with a widespread labour shortage.

2. Life in a cage

In Italy, the rise in the number of voluntary resignations is an anomaly.

When the Great Resignation first came to the fore, such an outcome seemed unlikely. On the one hand, it could not have been clearer why so many people quit their jobs. Work engagement has been in free fall for years. According to the *Global Workplace Report*[13] of 2022, the survey that 'measures' the satisfaction of working men and women, it is low on all five continents. In Europe, only 14 per cent of the workers are satisfied at work. In Italy, the situation is even worse. According to the Gallup Poll, 4 per cent of people are satisfied with their jobs: the lowest percentage in the world. At the same time, Italy is last in terms of perceived opportunities: the people surveyed think it is not a good time to find a job. A high discontent rate, therefore, in a context lacking in opportunities: these two conditions, as we shall see, well describe employment in Italy. This is why, when the international media started discussing the rise of voluntary resignations in the United States, it did not seem plausible to me that something similar might happen in the country: the absence of opportunities makes it difficult to quit, even when dissatisfaction is high.

Christian Marazzi explained this clearly in one of his texts, *E il denaro va. Esodo e rivoluzione dei mercati finanziari:*[14] 'The flight from work is made possible by the availability of free land', he wrote. Echoing the words of Edward Gibbon Wakefield, he added: 'Where land is very cheap and all men are free, and anyone who wants it can easily get a piece of land, labour is very expensive'. Edward Gibbon Wakefield was an English politician and a leading advocate of the colonization of South Australia. Karl Marx dedicates a chapter to him in the first book of *The Capital*, where he thanks him for revealing the secret of a 'steady' and 'regular' labour supply. Forcing people to sell their ability to work means depriving them of the means of subsistence, he observes. Wage labour is not a natural condition. It is a social relationship that is contingent on access to the material conditions of reproduction. As soon as the land is cheap and people are free, workers stop selling their capacity to work, except at a very high cost.

This is why, according to some commentators, the availability of wage labour depends on the threat of hunger. As the political scientist George Kent provocatively puts it:

> For those of us at the high end of the social ladder, ending hunger globally would be a disaster. If there were no hunger in the world, who would plow the fields? Who would harvest our vegetables? Who would work in the rendering plants? Who would clean our toilets? We would have to produce our own food and clean our own toilets. No wonder people at the high end are not rushing to solve the hunger problem. For many of us, hunger is not a problem, but an asset.[15]

For these reasons, as I have mentioned, when the Great Resignation debate unfolded, a potential rise in job quits in Italy seemed unlikely: the conditions to refuse wage labour do not exist in the country. In the United States, unemployment was at an all-time low; in Italy, in the third quarter of 2022, the unemployment rate was at 7.9 per cent, rising to 23.7 per cent among young people. At the same time, the vacancy rate, that is, the ratio between the number of vacancies and the total number of jobs, was around 2 per cent,[16] which corresponds to approximately five hundred thousand jobs.[17] In the same months there were about 2.3 million unemployed and 2.5 million discouraged, for a total of almost 5 million people out of the labour market. This scenario is very different from the one we have seen in the United States: in Italy, in fact, there was one job available for every four, almost five, unemployed people, without even taking into account the discouraged. Those who quit their jobs, therefore, run the risk of not finding another one. Despite this, voluntary resignations have risen.

In 2021, there were almost 2 million voluntary resignations and 2.2 million in 2022.[18] In the third quarter of 2022, the quit rate was at 3.2 per cent, the highest in fifteen years.[19] The 2022 Annual Report by the Ministry of Labour and Social Policies offered an overview of the geography of voluntary resignations in Italy. According to the report, the year-on-year increase in 2021 was 30.6 per cent. In 2021, the phenomenon mainly involved the North, in particular in the Italian regions of Lombardy and Veneto, where voluntary departures increased by +37.7 and +34.9 per cent, respectively, compared to 2019. In the South, such increases were lower but nonetheless high: Molise (+21.8), Lazio (+23.9), Puglia (+17.3) and Sicily (+18.9).

In recent months, several reports have tried to explain what was happening. A useful analysis of the situation was offered by the *5th Censis-Eudaimon Report on Corporate Welfare*, which described the working condition in the months immediately following the pandemic. According to Censis,[20] workers in Italy are deeply dissatisfied: 82.3 per cent of them are dissatisfied and believe they deserve more, a figure that increases to 86 per cent among young people and 88.8 among blue-collar workers. Despite this impatience, 56.2 per cent of the employed are not inclined to quit their jobs.

According to Censis:

There is a latent, hidden, but intense dissatisfaction with work. The prevailing idea among employees is that they deserve more and that work does not provide them with the recognition they need to develop a sense of identity and belonging.

However, the report continues:

The majority of workers are dissatisfied with their jobs, but do not quit [...] People do not run away from their jobs, but instead survive in them as if it were an inescapable necessity, and minimise their impact in their lives. In the coming years, this psychological tendency may become even more pronounced, as a powerful lust for life arises that will presumably seek valorisation outside and beyond the workplace.

The picture offered by Censis is both interesting and tragic, though not surprising. According to the research institute, 'the majority of workers are dissatisfied with their jobs, but do not quit'.[21] What is surprising, on the other hand, is how much dissatisfaction there is among both those who quit and stay.

The Censis report paints a very similar scenario to that of the Gallup Poll, consisting of workers with a high dissatisfaction rate, in a world devoid of opportunities. The causes of dissatisfaction are manifold. Censis speaks of low wages: average gross annual wages have fallen by 3.6 per cent in real terms in twenty years compared to a 17.9 per cent increase in Germany. The poor salary levels go hand in hand with the lack of rewards, in an increasingly precarious context, punctuated by fixed-term contracts and de-skilled work. In such a market, the absence of universal welfare and the scarce alternatives make the majority of individuals feel caged in, forced to keep their jobs *obtorto collo* despite the high level of intolerance.

It is certainly not a reassuring picture, indicating a work normality marked by insecurity and dissatisfaction, in which the desire to change is discouraged solely by the fear of not finding a different occupation.

The Censis report of 2023 supplemented this reading with an even more disturbing analysis. According to the report, about one in two people would change jobs if they could.

> 57.7 per cent of people with at most a secondary school diploma, 45.7 per cent of high school graduates and 37.9 per cent of university graduates. A widespread restlessness and intolerance towards one's job that, with varying intensity, involves the many different players in today's labor market.

According to the research institute, moreover, the *subjective* relationship of people with work has changed. This transformation is best epitomized by this phrase, which indicates a radical change from the working culture of a few decades ago: 'work only serves me to get money I need'. According to the report, 64.4 per cent of those in employment think so, and this *instrumental* approach to work as a way of getting the money they need and then devote themselves to something else rises to 76.6 per cent among people with at most a secondary school diploma. The Censis warns, in this sense, that retaining such workers will pose a challenge, as

> disengagement, estrangement from work in the workplace and, even, the propensity to leave and move on to other companies is

very strong among them, and their mass departure or widespread disengagement could have tremendous effects on the companies involved.[22]

In February 2022, the resignation report by the Fondazione Consulenti del Lavoro offered a useful and, in some ways, complementary analysis. Starting with data from the Ministry of Labour, in fact, the report focused on those who quit their jobs in the first three quarters of 2021. In that period, there were 1.3 million voluntary terminations, an increase of 6.3 per cent compared to the same period in 2019. One million eighty-one thousand workers had been affected, a figure 13.8 per cent higher than that of the same period in 2019, predominantly consisting of men (41.3 per cent women). According to the report, 52.9 per cent quit a permanent job, in the remaining cases it was a temporary job while the share of part-timers was 37.9 per cent. The interesting fact is that one out of two (44.7 per cent), *had no alternative* at the time of leaving and is still unemployed three months later, indicating, as we shall see, a prolonged state of aggravation that often leads to quitting even without an alternative in hand.[23]

At sectoral level, most resignations are concentrated in services (69.4 per cent), particularly in retail (13.4) on top of accommodation and restaurants (12.6). The healthcare sector is also affected with 7.1 per cent of the total number of resignations.

In general, the Foundation traces the decision to quit back to two main patterns. First, those who quit their jobs to improve their conditions, for example, the highly specialized and technical professions at the top of the professional pyramid, which together contributed 17.9 per cent of the resignations in this time. Then there are those who choose to resign out of disappointment and dissatisfaction, as is the case for those employed in the retail and hospitality sector; for the over-55s, for whom the number of resignations grew by 21.5 per cent between 2019 and 2021. Lastly, there are women, for whom resignations frequently entail a withdrawal from professional life, writes the report.

The 2022 INPS Annual Report allows us to complete this picture and look at relocation rates by sector. The study, which has a different baseline than the data from the Ministry of Labour, shows the relocation movements of those who resigned within three months of the date of termination, excluding workers over sixty years of age. According to the report, those who resigned from transport, construction and engineering have the highest relocation rates (over 70 per cent). Construction and transport are also the sectors that attracted the largest number of relocations from other industries in 2021, confirming the dynamic nature of this segment in those months. The sectors with negative balances are accommodation and restaurants, professional services, retail and steelworking industry.

Fifty-seven per cent of people found employment in the restaurant sector, a figure rising to 64.5 per cent in retail and around 60 per cent in the textile industry where, similarly, the balance between arrivals and departures in the sector is negative.

> The lowest level of *stayers* can be found among employees in the accommodation and restaurant sector (77 per cent). If we consider those who remained in the same sector as in 2019, the accommodation and restaurant sector has once again the lowest level of stayers (59 per cent). Here, the proportion of those who left employment is also substantial (23 per cent), as is that of those who moved to other tertiary sectors (14 per cent), while the proportion of those who moved to manufacturing is smaller (4 per cent).[24]

The Randstad[25] analysis on the mismatch between job vacancies and unemployment, from this point of view, leaves no doubt: there are sectors in Italy where labour dissatisfaction is acute and alarming.

According to the analysis, after the crisis of 2007–8, the Italian labour market has been characterized by a series of bottlenecks: patterns of mismatch between supply and demand, which have different determinants depending on the sector. In this context, the absence of opportunities, a condition that scares those who would like to quit their jobs, coexists with the inability of companies to recruit staff. This is a real Italian anomaly, a context of divorce in which supply and demand no longer meet.

Based on Randstad's analysis, the highest labour shortage is in IT, where there is very little unemployment. In fact, IT specialists are highly skilled and sought-after professionals. In the sector, demand exceeds supply. Universities, on their part, often do not have the necessary programmes to train students, so difficulties in recruitment coexist with the need to attract professionals from abroad. In contrast, labour shortage in the hospitality sector is associated with high rates of unemployment, indicating that the increase in vacancies coexists with a widespread decision to leave the sector.

For the purposes of our analysis, dissatisfaction in the sector is important: when a high number of vacancies coexist with a high unemployment rate, it is necessary to understand what creates this bottleneck. The Beveridge curve, after all, assumes that the exit from unemployment has a direct impact on vacancies, which are reabsorbed as each unemployed person finds a job, hence the inverse relationship between unemployment and vacancies. In our case, for one hundred fewer unemployed, vacancies increase by twenty-four, which means that for every one hundred people who find work, twenty-four new jobs open up.

If this is confusing, that's OK: the magazine *Bloomberg* described the Beveridge curve as 'the thing that keeps economists awake at night'.[26] In this sense, it is common to read that vacancies are increasing because the market is dynamic and there is a lot of demand.

This is true, for example, of the construction industry, which experienced a surge in activity at the end of the pandemic. In other cases, it is the shortage of existing skills that creates a bottleneck. In other cases, the increase in vacancies indicates areas of disaffection where it is particularly difficult to convince staff to stay, such as in the restaurant and hospitality sector or in retail. In the case of hospitality and restaurants, the report notes 'a marked disaffection' of staff. In this sector, 'both in Italy and in the United States, many unemployed people who previously worked in the industry do not seem inclined to return to this market'.[27] In these cases, one often speaks of the so-called supply-side rigidity, the phenomenon whereby companies are unable to find staff despite high numbers of unemployed, discouraged and inactive people.

The question is: why do some people refuse a job, even though they need it, and why do others quit, even though they have no other alternative at hand? To answer this question, we need to interrogate the workers in some of the hardest-hit sectors, mainly healthcare, restaurants and retail. We will do so by listening to their stories.

3. A short methodological note

In 2022, while working on this book, quitting was emerging as a global phenomenon. During those months, the main challenge was identifying the sectors these workers came from and reaching out to those involved. Contacting quitters and interviewing them was not straightforward and required different methodological approaches. First, I asked two Italian magazines I collaborated with to include my email address at the end of an article I had written on the topic, along with a request for quitters to reach out, share a brief testimony, and provide their contact information if they were open to an interview. This method allowed me to connect with around a hundred people from various professional backgrounds. However, the sample overrepresented certain worker demographics in terms of sector, geographic area, gender and age while underrepresenting others.

To address this, I simultaneously searched for online forums where discussions about specific labour sectors took place. This proved challenging as Italy's labour market is highly fragmented and often lacks real representation. Where does the political debate on work happen today? Where do workers in logistics, retail or hospitality discuss labour issues? In which physical or digital spaces? And with whom – if anyone – do they engage in these discussions?

Anonymous online forums, particularly those used by retail workers, proved especially valuable. In addition, I reached out to trade unionists from different organizations, many of whom provided data, testimonies or interview contacts. Workers' associations, such as Occca (the Association of Waiters and à la Carte Cooks), were also helpful, having conducted extensive research on sector-specific issues in the years before and after the pandemic. In some cases, snowball sampling was particularly effective – especially for interviewing healthcare workers leaving the profession. In industries like hospitality, where work is highly individualized, reconstructing networks was especially difficult due to the sector's structural fragmentation. Conducting research in such a context presents the same challenges and barriers that characterize fragmented communities, where engagement and outreach are all the more complex. It goes without saying that all interviews have been anonymised unless the interviewees have explicitly requested otherwise, in which case this choice is indicated and explained in the text.

Chapter 4

THE TIME TO BREATHE: THE GREAT RESIGNATION IN HEALTHCARE

1. Like a teapot on the fire

They drained us. They harassed us. They humiliated us. And, when we tried to say that the law did not allow us to do the things they were asking us to do, they granted us an injunction like we were soldiers during wartime, threatening us in a rather overt fashion with repercussions.

This is Silvio, an anaesthesiologist and a critical care specialist who decided to move with his wife and daughter to France after the first two waves of the pandemic. Francesca Nava, the journalist who has followed the course of the pandemic in Bergamo and unveiled the political responsibilities behind it, suggested that I talk to him. Her book, *Il focolaio (The Outbreak)*, is a wake-up call on the disastrous ways in which the emergency in Lombardy was handled and a heartfelt acknowledgement of the work of those nurses and doctors who, in spite of everything, tried their best every day to save lives. Francesca interviewed Silvio for an investigative TV programme called *Presa Diretta* in February 2020.[1] When I met him, Silvio did not look like the same person. In the video from two years earlier he was about twenty pounds thinner and had a hollow, sunken face. His voice sounded as though he was trying hard not to stumble into dismay. The dismay of someone who has realized that everything he has dedicated his life to had become a mere function of profit.

I had a video call with Silvio in June 2022. He was uncontainable. There was no hesitation in his words: no fatigue, no turmoil, no frustration. If anything, there was anger. Silvio had decided to leave his job in January 2021. Before ending up in France, he considered taking a job in Norway, 'where it rains all the time'. He and his family lived a good life in Milan; they had their own routines, friends and relationships, he tells me. Over time, however, work had started to eat him up. Silvio worked gruelling shifts, often being on call three weekends out of four, and a situation that kept getting worse due to the number of staff decimated by retirements and the hiring freeze. This is also why, when he received a job offer from France, he decided to accept it, even though he had not spoken the language for a quarter of a century. He asked his wife and eight-and-a-half-year-old daughter to follow him and left. 'This gives you the measure of how strong my need was to escape in order to make a living. In order to *survive*: perhaps that is the most appropriate word'.

During the pandemic, Silvio was in the front line. His hospital was in one of the areas that had been most severely affected by the virus, and as a critical care specialist, he was particularly exposed to the enormous increase in workload in the operating theatre and intensive care unit. In this sense, Silvio worked for months at the heart of the emergency.

> The first and second waves were terrifying. We didn't know what to do, we had no treatment, we had no instructions, we had no hospital beds. We had no doctors and nurses, most of the nurses working in the emergency room got sick, we had no face masks, we had no proper face masks—just one FFP2 for a twelve-hour shift.

I ask him what kinds of shifts they worked. He says he does not remember. 'We were always in the hospital'. Then he tells me about fourteen, fifteen-hour shifts, without a break, without even a chance to eat or use the bathroom. It was a constant flow of work without interruption. In those days, it was not uncommon for Italian hospitals to work gruelling shifts, even up to twenty-four consecutive hours. In fact, European Directive 2003/88/EC – which brought together in a single text the existing provisions in terms of rest, breaks, holidays and working time – establishes a working week for physicians of a maximum of forty-eight hours, including overtime, and a minimum period of rest of eleven consecutive hours per day.[2] In Italy, this directive is systematically disregarded due to staff shortages, which means that doctors and nurses often have to work very long shifts. These conditions are particularly noticeable in emergency rooms and emergency medicine, such as ICU, anaesthesiology and reanimation, where Silvio worked, areas where, not surprisingly, the incidence of burnout is very high.

Christina Maslach, author of *Burnout: The Cost of Caring*, observes that such intense working conditions often lead to a situation of emotional exhaustion, what we call burnout. Christina Maslach quotes

Carol B., a social worker who uses the metaphor of a teapot to explain this syndrome.

> When I try to describe my experience to someone else, I use the analogy of a teapot. Just like a teapot, I was on the fire, with water boiling – working hard to handle problems and do good. But after several years, the water had boiled away, and yet I was still on the fire – a burned-out teapot in danger of cracking.[3]

Like a teapot that sits on the burner for too long and needs water, so energy and dedication in a healthcare worker slowly give way to emotional drying up, punctuated by cynicism and frustration, when denied time to recover and rest. Therefore, Christina Maslach does not describe burnout as an individual issue, but as an institutional problem. Burnout does not result from people per se, but from the environment in which they work, she argues:[4] from the corporate decision not to provide adequate staffing, adequate wages, adequate rest shifts, for budgetary reasons. In this context, the mismatch between the organizational priorities of the healthcare company and the needs of the staff turns the workplace into a potentially dangerous environment, for both workers and patients. Silvio continues:

> I have seen 65-year-old physicians cry with helplessness. People went mad.
>
> I lived for a month and a half away from home, for fear of infecting my wife and daughter. The hospital, in association with the municipality, gave me a one-room apartment. I lived in this one-room apartment by myself: I would go to work, come home, drink some wine, smoke a cigarette, eat, throw myself on the bed and faint. Then I'd wake up the next day and start again. It was like that for forty days. Forty days in which I lived alone in a one-room apartment of fifteen square metres. During that period some of my colleagues would shower until they almost peeled their skin off before going home, and they would make it the hottest they could, because they were terrified of infecting their loved ones.

In an article in *The Atlantic*, the founder and director of the Trauma Stewardship Institute, Laura Van Dernoot Lipsky, noted that during the various phases of the pandemic, the emotional state of healthcare workers changed. 'As hard as the initial trauma is', she added, 'it is the aftermath that destroy people'.[5]

In general, those who find themselves working during a crisis, be it a pandemic or a natural disaster, experience a kind of emotional freeze to keep working with their heads down. To explain this phenomenon, psychologist Paul Slovic of the University of Oregon spoke of *psychic numbness*. According to Slovic, this numbness is vital, because it allows one to continue functioning, despite the turmoil, and to continue doing everything possible to face the emergency. For Laura Van Dernoot Lipsky, who in the course of her career has dealt with subjects who had been traumatized by mass shootings or by natural disasters, it is precisely at the end of the emergency, when the adrenalin wanes and normalcy returns, that all the torment that had been buried and shelved finally breaks loose.

In Silvio's case, this was not an issue. When the pandemic was over, in fact, the medical staff were not given time to rest: they were ordered to keep on running, because they needed to dispose of the long waiting lists arisen during the pandemic.

But how? I needed to rest, to pause for a moment. Why did I still have to keep running? In my ward, seven people quit over three years, so we had to do the same things that we did a year and a half earlier with twice as many staff. Obviously, at a certain point you can't take it anymore. During that period I couldn't sleep, I had high blood pressure and nausea, a feeling of sickness and vomit, and I couldn't concentrate. You realise all these things and say, but hey, we've been pulling the cart all this way and we didn't say anything, even though there were organisational flaws that were complete disasters.

In those days Silvio was *nauseous*.

I would arrive at the hospital, and I would feel nauseous, almost vomit at the entrance. Covid kept us all in a state of emergency. After the pandemic, it was like finishing a university exam: the stress fades and you begin to see things clearly. You had to start running again without asking yourself too many questions. One had to work, work, work. Holidays? Holidays are not needed, time off is not needed, we're paying you, aren't we? What are you complaining about?

He lists his symptoms:

Cardiovascular diseases, increased tobacco consumption. Difficulties in normal sociability, because by then we had all become like machines. So we had all more or less fallen into depression. In my company, the doctor in charge confirmed that many had problems of this type, related to burnout. In fact we never stopped. The problem is that today, at the hospital where I used to work, they're working even more. The nurses are running away because they are working round the clock: operating theatres by day, emergency shifts by night. But you have to be healthy to treat others! You cannot get sick to do your job. But they don't understand that, because, I repeat, the manager doesn't care how you are. You just have to work.

One morning, after yet another night in the hospital, Silvio asks to schedule his annual leave. After two waves of Covid, he wanted to take three weeks off to stay with his wife and daughter. This hadn't happened for a long time, and he needed to rest. The chief physician replies that he cannot authorize them. 'So you are making me quarrel with my wife', said Silvio, who has had to put himself and his family on the sidelines for more than a year. The chief physician patted him on the shoulder: 'Silvio, we all quarrel with our wives'. There may seem to be a disproportion between this exchange and the decision to switch jobs, cities and countries in order to leave. However, if we consider the context of this sentence, Silvio's reaction becomes not only understandable but almost inevitable.

Silvio had requested annual leave after a prolonged period of self-sacrifice, during which he had been constantly exposed to death and trauma. For once, he asked that his own needs and health be considered—alongside, not beneath, the hospital's budget. The chief physician's refusal to authorise the leave not only denied him the exercise of a basic right, but also revealed the institution's disregard for the physical and mental wellbeing of its staff. Let us bear in mind that, according to trade union data, in Italy, on average, each doctor arrives at retirement with as many as three hundred days of outstanding vacation while nurses arrive at retirement with approximately one hundred and ten.[6] According to Silvio, the amount of unpaid overtime and unused vacation days in the Italian health service is so extreme that it is, in his words, akin to 'practically kidnapping people'.

In all these cases, the employer, who insists that we continue to work in emergency mode even when the emergency is over, knows no reasons. Neither contractual limits nor union organisers are able to challenge the continuous and unilateral imposition of ever-increasing workloads. Silvio himself tried for a long time to change things as a union representative for the anaesthesiology and critical care staff. Yet, he says, 'you would write to management, and they wouldn't even reply'. A line has been crossed. There is clearly no incentive to stay if the company that asked you for flexibility and devotion is deaf to your requests. It is only legitimate, at this point, that those very people who for a long time have carried on doing an untenable job because they thought it was the right thing to do, who have accepted extreme levels of sacrifice and have tried in every way to change things, decide to leave.

> At some point, the world around me clearly began to crumble. [...] I couldn't go on like this, I couldn't get sick. And we were getting sick, I was getting sick. My body was giving me signals I couldn't ignore. It was telling me to stop, to change, to try something else or I would have a heart attack. It was as if my body had metabolised at an unconscious level that the situation was not adequate and therefore it was starting to give me these signals. I would arrive at the hospital door, punch in, and feel like vomiting. So I decided to change my life. I decided to quit on 1 January 2021, and by 15 January 2022, I had moved to France.

It didn't take Silvio long to find a job abroad. Had it not been so, however, he would still have left: 'I couldn't take it any more: I had to leave'. There is a fundamental point to make here. For it has been said that the Great Resignation was an attempt to rethink life after the trauma of the pandemic. For Silvio, the problem was not to rethink his own life, it was simply to survive. 'I had to leave' means that work had devoured his life so much that, had he stayed, there would be nothing left of him. With no social movement pushing to defend and reinvest in public healthcare, there were no alternatives.

2. The soul at war

Flavio decided to quit his job in October 2021. He was an anaesthesiologist in the operating theatres and intensive care units of one of the largest hospitals in Lombardy, at the epicentre of the pandemic. It was a state-of-the-art facility, boasting one of the highest ratios of intensive care beds to inpatient beds in Italy. In the first days of March 2020, the hospital was overwhelmed by the emergency. The decision not to close the Seriana Valley, one of the most important manufacturing areas in the country, allowed the virus to circulate undisturbed for weeks, until it was too late. In those days, says Flavio, you could only wait for the lockdown to take effect. And it did act fifteen days later, as we all learned. But those fifteen days, the second half of March, were the worst.

Flavio recounts that on 1 April 2020, there were almost a hundred people intubated – about two times the capacity for which the hospital was designed. The incoming flow was overwhelming. In those days, some doctors explained what it was like to work at the heart of the pandemic during the most critical weeks of March. In a letter to the *New England Journal of Medicine*,[7] they wrote that:

Three hundred beds out of nine hundred are occupied by Covid-19 patients. Fully 70 per cent of ICU beds in our hospital are reserved for critically ill Covid-19 patients with a reasonable chance to survive. The situation here is dismal as we operate well below our normal standard of care. Wait times for an intensive care bed are hours long. Older patients are not being resuscitated and die alone without appropriate palliative care, while the family is notified over the phone, often by a well-intentioned, exhausted, and emotionally depleted physician with no prior contact. But the situation in the surrounding area is even worse. Most hospitals are overcrowded, nearing collapse while medications, mechanical ventilators, oxygen, and personal protective equipment are not available. Patients lay on floor mattresses. The health care system struggles to deliver regular services – even pregnancy care and child delivery – while cemeteries are overwhelmed, which will create another public health problem. In hospitals, health care workers and ancillary staff are alone, trying to keep the system operational. Outside the hospitals, communities are neglected, vaccination programs are on standby, and the situation in prisons is becoming explosive with no social distancing. We have been in quarantine since March 10. Unfortunately, the outside world seems unaware that in Bergamo, this outbreak is out of control.

In those days, Flavio's role was to answer calls from wards where there were doctors in distress to help the most serious patients.

They would say, 'Come and see this patient. He needs to be intubated'.
But we had no places.
So what could we do?

In the same days, the Italian Society of Anaesthesiology, Analgesia, Reanimation and Intensive Care (Siaarti) published the report *Recommendations of Clinical Ethics for Admission to and Suspension of Intensive Care in Exceptional Conditions of Imbalance between Need and Available Resources*,[8] aimed at supporting doctors who were forced to decide who had a chance of survival and who did not. In a context of scarce resources, where not all patients could be treated, Siaarti sought to provide 'concrete guidance for doctors and nurses engaged in difficult choices'. In general, the healthcare paradigm aims to ensure equitable access to care; that is, everyone should be able to be treated regardless of age or survival chances. In that situation, it was difficult to ensure equity. The scarcity of resources caused by years of cuts in funding, hospital beds and personnel had created, in the words of Marco Revelli, a 'mortal dilemma'.[9] As Flavio explains, within the medical community physicians at times decide that some treatments are medically futile. The notion of futility indicates that, under certain circumstances, treatments fail to produce the desired result.

> For instance, if we have had a person in hospital for a long time, months for example, there comes a time when we must ask ourselves what to do. In such cases, protocols require discussions with families and collective decision-making. In those months, we had to make a decision three, four times a day.
> It was unbearable.

For Flavio, not being able to ensure equal access to care created an emotionally overpowering situation.

> For me, the most painful part was being unable to guarantee equity. We knew that we couldn't make miracles, but even basic equity was difficult to achieve, because access and possibilities varied continuously, every day, like a roll of the dice.

In 2020, doctors and nurses did everything they could to provide the best possible treatment for the population. The very letter to the *New England Journal of Medicine* was a *j'accuse* that insisted on the need to change and strengthen community-based healthcare in Italy, to prevent what was happening in Lombardy from occurring elsewhere. To this end, the letter emphasized the importance of a *community-centred* approach to care, that is, one that would place the community, rather than the individual, at the centre. But these proposals remained unheeded. Medical personnel were asked to respond to an unmanageable emergency without sufficient resources, without sufficient decision-making power, without a chain of command up to the situation, without a territorial healthcare service capable of cushioning the blast and without sufficient protective devices: in short, without anything.

> In those days I would take drugs to sleep and cry in the car. I would cry at night over trivial things, like small moments of tenderness. My wife said I looked like an old woman. But the worst thing, by far, was that I no longer felt like talking to my young daughters. I felt polluted, corrupt, ugly, inhuman. I didn't want to be around them. Even on the phone, I felt like when you catch a glimpse of yourself in the mirror on a particularly bad day, and you don't really want to see yourself and avoid your own image. I realized that this was not good, and I sought help.

Flavio's words describe the impact of the pandemic on the mental health of healthcare professionals and the distress that many of them experienced. During that time, Flavio and many others resorted to the psychological support service provided by the hospital. They felt guilty for being unable to prevent the traumatic events they themselves had suffered.

> This phase lasted three weeks: it felt as though we had never seen anything different, as if we could never see anything different, just like my grandfather's war stories. I remember feeling very close to him, in fact I wished he was alive to talk to him and ask him how he managed.

It's no coincidence that Flavio draws a parallel to war.

An article by Kari Lydersen[10] reports an encounter that occurred in a Minnesota emergency room during the early days of the pandemic between a nurse and a Vietnam veteran. After asking how the nurses were doing, the man said: 'This is your war'. The nurse there and then did not understand and gave a puzzled smile. 'We dealt with this in Vietnam. You don't know it yet but none of you will ever be the same again'.

Some time later, the meaning of that phrase had become clear. The veteran foresaw the guilt, anger, and betrayal that they would feel during the pandemic when they found themselves in an overwhelming situation, where it was impossible to provide the quality of care they wanted to provide.

In recent months there has been considerable mention of 'moral injury' to indicate this condition. *The Diagnostic and Statistical Manual of Mental Disorders* defines 'moral injury' as the act of 'perpetrating, failing to prevent, bearing witness to, or learning about acts that transgress deeply held moral beliefs and expectations. This may entail participating in or witnessing inhumane or cruel actions, failing to prevent the immoral acts of others, as well as engaging in subtle acts or experiencing reactions that, upon reflection, transgress a moral code.'[11] Often, the notion of moral injury describes an individual in agony who blames himself or herself for the traumatic event he or she has been subjected to, even though the guilt often stems from a distorted view of what happened. Originally, the concept was developed to describe the suffering of veterans, for whom burnout or post-traumatic stress disorder was often not enough. As a soldier returning from Iraq[12] explains:

> I accepted the diagnosis from the VA [Veteran Affairs] and from everyone else, and I'm sure that my condition was in part that, but inwardly I knew that the greatest pain I felt was not linked to those moments when violence was being directed at me but when I was involved in inflicting it on others. Post-traumatic stress didn't seem to fit. What else could I call this pain? It felt a lot like guilt, so that's what I started calling it, but in the *Diagnostic and Statistical Manual of Mental Disorders* (DSM) under PTSD there is no mention of guilt, except for "survivor's guilt" … The term "moral injury" has recently come afloat, and it applies to exactly the kind of guilt I'm talking about.

When I was a PhD student in the United States, I happened to work with war veterans.[13] In some cases, moral injury described the stories of those who had joined the army to escape poverty, only to return home condemned to a life of torment and remorse. In certain cases, the memory of war could be so lacerating that veterans were unable to sleep or stay awake, medicated their agony with alcohol and drugs, and sometimes imploded into a terminal phenomenon called *pancaking*, referring to the moment when a former soldier's life unravels in a spiral of despair that ends with the loss of a job, home, suicide or imprisonment. The veteran Janci, for example, admits:

> I went into such a dark depression that I couldn't handle it. I couldn't relate to my children. I couldn't spend time with them. I couldn't take care of them the way they needed.[14]

As Rita Nakashima Brock,[15] one of the foremost experts on moral injury in the United States, writes:

> In the spring of 2015, In spring 2015, Janci spoke at a Soul Repair Centre conference in Fort Worth, Texas, about her struggle to return home. After two years of alcoholism and battling everything, she called a friend and asked him to pick up her children from school and take care of them. When he tried to convince her not to kill herself, she hung up, locked the doors and windows, grabbed a bottle of pills and drank an entire bottle of wine. He got into his van and rushed to her house, kicked down the front door and forced her to walk all night to avoid dying.

The torment faced by veterans who, upon returning from war, struggle to come to terms with their actions is excruciating.[16] In such cases, enduring agony involves a trip to hell and back. War, writes psychiatrist Jonathan Shay in *Achilles in Vietnam: Combat Trauma and the Undoing of Character*, rewards the ability to kill, even though deep down everyone knows that what armies are asked to do in wartime is troublesome. This inconsistency haunts veterans, when the moral code they've built their identity on collapses under the weight of nightmares and remorse. Often, behind that remorse is a conscience struggling to regain control of its own life.

But that effort doesn't always succeed. I have seen veterans crushed by remorse forty years after the end of the Vietnam war unable to communicate with family members to the point of losing them, unable to keep their jobs, unable to avoid crying as they recalled the facts, even though such facts had occurred decades ago. As Arundhati Roy writes in *God of Small Things*, social norms carry with them laws of love that decide 'who is to be loved. And how. And how much'.[17] And those who think they have broken them may not necessarily feel worthy of understanding or, even less, forgiveness, from others or from themselves.

In recent months, literature has repeatedly dwelt on the analogies between the suffering of healthcare workers and that of veterans.

As Dr Francesco Bulli writes:

> Moral injury entails damage to one's conscience when a person commits, witnesses or fails to prevent acts that transgress one's moral convictions, values or ethical codes of conduct. Or it can involve a

deep sense of betrayal when one feels inadequately supported by others in a position of power who have an obligation to do so.[18]

While there are many similarities, however, there are also differences. The medical personnel build their professional lives on the basis of a code of ethics that is radically different from the military one, and which often defines the very core of the person. *First do no harm*, together with respect for the patient's autonomy and preferences, is the cornerstone of that code. In this case, the injury does not depend on the questionability of the values of one's moral code, as is the case of war veterans, but on the impossibility of adhering to them for reasons beyond one's control. It may be, for instance, that the priority of the healthcare workers is to guarantee equality and quality of care, but that this is impossible due to inadequate leadership and the chain of command of the hospital itself.

In this situation, people find themselves in an untenable position, in which the contradiction between their own moral priorities and those of the system in which they operate becomes lacerating. Michele DeMarco[19] is right when he writes that moral wounding 'is neither a problem nor a pathology': it is the way in which conscience begs to regain control over one's actions and over the context in which they occur. It is not uncommon that, in order to reconquer the right to act in alignment with one's own values, some people decide to quit, because the institution for which they work is no longer trustworthy, because they have felt betrayed or because they have fallen out of love with it. This happens more often than we think. We see it in the emergency rooms, where doctors and nurses operate under gruelling circumstances, often unable to perform as they would wish.[20] Simon G. Talbot and Wendy Dean, respectively, a Harvard Medical School lecturer and a psychiatrist, write:

> Most physicians enter medicine following a calling rather than a career path. They go into the field with a desire to help people. Many approach it with almost religious zeal, enduring lost sleep, lost years of young adulthood, huge opportunity costs, family strain, financial instability, disregard for personal health, and a multitude of other challenges. Each hurdle offers a lesson in endurance in the service of one's goal which, starting in the third year of medical school, is sharply focused on ensuring the best care for one's patients. Failing to consistently meet patients' needs has a profound impact on physician wellbeing – this is the crux of consequent moral injury.[21]

'It's as if part of my soul had been shredded with a knife, the part that connects me to my Hippocratic oath and personal values. I don't know who I am any more … just a monster in scrubs',[22] says a doctor, and unfortunately the consequences of this helplessness fall entirely on the individual, even when the causes are rooted in much wider areas. It must be said that the mental health impact of emergency situations like this has long been underestimated. Christina Maslach listed the dislocation between personal and company values as one of the possible causes of burnout, a condition that, even without external conflict, can lead to excruciating inner turmoil.

We see this in other sectors as well. As the *Harvard Business Review*[23] has observed, companies that produce or distribute polluting materials, those that profit from poverty, debt or people's illness can create a moral laceration in those who work for - work for them. Some manage to compromise with their conscience for a while, for instance in return for higher pay. Researchers such as Florian H. Schneider, Fanny Brun and Roberto A. Weber,[24] have shown how companies that engage in potentially harmful practices – sell toxic financial products, encourage tax evasion, create significant strains on public finances or even contribute to serious public health crises, use differentiated compensation to incentivize unethical practices. Jobs that people may find morally objectionable because they entail the risk of physical harm to public welfare, in short, ultimately reward participation in unethical conduct. In less extreme cases, workers find other ways to soothe their sense of powerlessness or inner conflict, perhaps through solidarity with colleagues or involvement in union activity. In other cases, however, people opt to quit.

When I ask Flavio why he resigned, he hesitates for a moment. Then he tells me about the distance to his place of work: his children are growing up and doing so many kilometres every day had become burdensome. He adds: 'I fell out of love with the hospital'.

The crisis has revealed, like a magnifying glass, the true nature of people. Something inside me cracked. I stopped seeing the hospital as a nice place to work and to spend most of my time.

I fell out of love with my hospital.

I was raised with a sense of duty, to a sense of community. I work in a healthcare service, working together is very important to me. The style, the way of working, the organisation of work, all matter. When I started to doubt that the processes were ethical, I couldn't ignore it. It was the last in a series of turning points that led me to resign. Personal aspects, relationships with colleagues, the question of distance – commuting fifty kilometres every day while my daughters are growing up – these became the most relevant aspects.

I ask him how he felt when he resigned.

The moment I resigned, I received a hollow expression of courtesy. A little forced, a little belated. Which served as a confirmation of my decision. I thought, someone like me — with twelve years of experience and mid-career — just isn't as valuable as an active young man who doesn't ask questions. We are pawns, cannon fodder.

3. Whatever it takes

Silvio and Flavio were not the only ones to quit. A survey by Anaao Assomed – authored by Chiara Rivetti, Carlo Palermo, Pierino Di Siverio and Costantino Troise[25] – shows that among medical specialists there are around three thousand cases of voluntary resignation per year, to which we must add retirements. Summing up the two figures, it emerges that around eight thousand medical specialists leave the National Health System (NHS) every year, in what has been described as 'a haemorrhage'.[26] According to Anaao Assomed, between retirements and voluntary departures there will be around forty thousand fewer doctors by 2024.

Resignation rates among doctors are high across all regions. According to data from Anaao Assomed, 2.9 per cent of doctors left the NHS in 2021, but in regions of Southern Italy such as Calabria and Sicily the average rises to 3.8 and 5.18 per cent, respectively, while it triples in Liguria and stands at 3.29 per cent in the Southern region of Puglia. Again for Rivetti, Palermo, Di Siverio and Troise, this represents 'an unprecedented exodus from regions with entirely different histories, systems, and healthcare structures. And if this were not problematic enough, a survey by Anaao Assomed showed that only 54 per cent of doctors still see themselves in a public hospital in two years' time, which would make the picture even more critical.[27] The situation is just as dramatic if we look at nursing staff. According to the Nursing Up union, in 2021 there were more than two thousand resignations in six months among nurses and care technicians.[28]

According to the doctors' union Anaao Assomed, around seven doctors and eleven nurses resign from the national healthcare system every day.[29] In both cases, staff shortages both cause and result from resignations.

Recently, the national agency for regional health services, Agenas,[30] tried to take stock of the situation of the healthcare workforce, and found that, in Italy, in 2020, the number of people employed by the national healthcare system was approximately six hundred and seventeen thousand (68 per cent of whom were women), of whom 72 per cent were healthcare workers while the remaining 27 were technical and administrative staff. According to the report, the number of doctors appears adequate: there are about four doctors per thousand inhabitants, compared to 3.17 in France and 3.03 in the UK. In Italy, however, doctors are getting older: one in three will retire in the five-year period 2022 and 2027, and there is still no adequate planning to replace them. In Italy, 56 per cent of doctors are over the age of fifty-five, which means that in the next few years the country will be at risk of falling in the ranking of active doctors per thousand inhabitants.[31] In this sense, the sector's attractiveness is being overestimated. According to Palermo and Liuzzi, of the approximately sixty-five thousand neo-specialists who will be trained in the coming years, only one in two will accept to work for the NHS, which gives us a picture of the organizational difficulties ahead.

For its part, the nursing staff is hardly in better shape. According to the National Federation of Nursing Professions (FNOPI), there is a shortage of around seventy thousand nurses in the country, both in hospitals and on the territory. The severity of this shortage is set to worsen due to retirements – an estimated outflow of around twenty-one thousand between 2022 and 2027 – and the termination of temporary staff – hired in increasing proportions in recent years due to the hiring freeze.

According to the Eighteenth Health Report drawn up by the Centre for Applied Economic Research in Healthcare (CREA),[32] thirty to forty thousand new nurses per year would be needed to compensate for this situation, an unlikely scenario given the low propensity to enter the profession in a country like Italy, where salaries are 40 per cent below the European average. As a result, fewer students are enrolling in nursing programs than there are available spots.[33] The shortage of personnel in this situation is bound to worsen.

The picture would not be complete if we did not consider the profound discontent of the nursing staff, who have been hit hard by the pandemic. In Italy, three hundred and fifty thousand nurses have been infected by the virus, according to INAIL data, 82 per cent of all healthcare personnel. According to a study promoted by FNOPI,[34] moreover, about one third of nurses have been victims of an episode of physical or verbal violence. Increased working hours and worsening employment conditions, finally, have exacerbated symptoms of stress and burnout. Data collected in a survey conducted on a sample of 2195 staff members of the University Hospital by the University of Verona, and coordinated by Antonio Lasalvia,[35] show that 86 per cent of staff members have high levels of work-related stress and 63 have experienced highly stressful or traumatic experiences. More than half reported symptoms of post-traumatic stress disorder, 50 per cent showed significant generalized anxiety symptoms, while signs of moderate depression were found in 27 per cent of cases. Similarly, a study co-ordinated by Valentina Simonetti, a researcher at the Department of Biomedical Sciences and Human Oncology at the University of Bari Aldo Moro, revealed the condition of great suffering developed by nurses, the operators who are closest to the patients, and among whom prolonged stress has led to the development of post-traumatic stress syndromes and, in extreme cases, to suicide. Thus, 71.4 per cent of nurses still complain of having sleep disorders, 33.2 have anxiety problems and about half have difficulty coping with stress, which, according to Simonetti, is an important indicator of mental health.[36] It is not surprising that the number of dropout rates are rising, or that the profession is no longer attractive to the younger generation. The study by Nurse forecasting in Europe,[37] for example, shows that 36 per cent of nurses in Italy intend to leave the workplace within twelve months, while 33 intend to leave the profession, a figure in line with what happens in the rest of the world.

In fact, when we speak of resignations in public health, we are talking about a sector plagued by inadequate pay, irregular shifts, staff shortages, and insufficient rest — factors that render working conditions intolerable and jeopardize the sustainability of the National Health Service.

a. The history of the National Healthcare Service

In 1978, Italy established the National Health Service under Law 833/78. Chiara Giorgi and Francesco Taroni,[38] two of the scholars who have most carefully chronicled this story, describe the law as an expression of the democratic fervour of the time. The universal, public and decentralized structure of Law 833/78 was based on four cardinal principles: globality of services, universality of recipients, equality of treatment and respect for the dignity and freedom of the individual. In the 1970s, the achievements of the labour and trade union movement, the feminist movement and radical psychiatry had nurtured a demand for free healthcare services capable of enabling the expansion of social services and the universal right to prevention and treatment.[39] At the same time, Taroni[40] recalls, the deficits of the mutualist bodies had created the window of opportunity needed for the establishment of a national health service with those characteristics, in a country deeply marked by social and geographical inequalities.

It is useful to read Francesco Taroni's reconstruction of those years, because it allows us to give due importance to the aspects of innovation that characterized the reform, but also to the opposition that underpins it.

As Taroni explains,[41] the establishment of the National Health Service was anything but linear. It took place with little public attention, at the end of the expansionary phase of industrial capitalism. In those years, the election of Margaret Thatcher in the UK and Ronald Reagan in the United States had prompted a new political pressure to reduce public spending. In this context, the introduction of the NSH in Italy was an anomaly, which made use of the deficits of the mutualist system to make a reform that seemed impossible at first and then turned out to be impossible to avoid', as Giovanni Berlinguer put it. Thus, in 1978, Law 833/78 gave Italy a pioneering National Health Service capable of combining universalism and equality, prevention and diagnostic-therapeutic objectives, and of integrating healthcare and social intervention, thus overcoming the profound inequalities and fragmentation of the system that had preceded it. Finally, this set-up made it possible to implement Article 32 of the Constitution, which envisages protecting health 'as a fundamental right of the individual and as a collective interest', and 'ensure free medical care to the indigent'.

More than we have ever liked to admit, the idea of an egalitarian and universal healthcare system has never appealed to everyone. For many, taking healthcare away from the private market has always been a problematic political choice, like the very idea that there may exist a universal right to healthcare. It is from this perspective that one must start to explain the evolution of the NHS in the years following its introduction, in order to understand why, only fifteen years after such introduction, Law 883/78 was already followed by the 1992 Amato-De Lorenzo 'reform of the reform'.[42] The latter, Giorgi and Taroni explain, regionalized, corporatized and privatized the health service, transforming the Local Healthcare Units (USL) into Hospital Boards (Aziende ospedaliere – ASL), thus exacerbating the imbalances and inequalities in the national territory.

This is not the place to examine the legislative vicissitudes that have made it possible, since the 1990s, to subtly dismantle the NHS. It is useful, however, to recall how the tendency to cut public spending eventually hollowed out its original structure, bringing to the foreground the policies of containment that had already been prevailing in the international context. After all, the flight of doctors, nurses and care technicians originated here: in a process of disinvestment that began well before the pandemic.

b. *The perfect storm*

During the pandemic it became apparent how this slow and often imperceptible transformation had undermined the national healthcare system.

As the Gimbe Foundation[43] shows, Italy's national healthcare system has suffered cuts amounting to some 37 billion in only ten years, funds that were saved by introducing a hiring freeze and cutting staff costs, thus preventing the replacement of retiring doctors and hampering the alignment of the salaries of Italian doctors to European standards. The consequences are right in front of us.

Between 2010 and 2020, in Italy:[44]

> eleven healthcare agencies, one hundred hospitals, one hundred and thirteen emergency rooms (including ten pediatric ones) have shut down, and eighty-five mobile critical care units have been decommissioned. These closures have entailed the loss of almost thirty-seven thousand beds, twenty-eight thousand of which are ordinary beds and almost ten thousand day-hospital beds: but while beds in public facilities have been drastically cut (-38,684), those in private facilities have increased (+1,747).

According to the report, over the same ten years, the NHS lost around thirty thousand professionals. On-call medical services suffered a cut of seven hundred doctors, resulting in approximately one thousand five hundred fewer on-call doctors for every one hundred thousand inhabitants. In general, the reduction in territorial assistance has resulted in 'a less equitable, less public, less sustainable health care system'.

Over time, this has begun to directly affect life expectancy and mortality rates, increasing deaths from cancer, as well as those from diabetes mellitus, blood diseases and immunological disorders, diseases of the nervous system, pneumonia and influenza, and – the report continues – of the circulatory system.[45]

During the pandemic, the result of these policies became manifest. As Carlo Palermo and Chiara Rivetti write in their survey *Less beds more deaths*, the insufficient number of beds, the suspension of check-ups for chronic diseases, the overcrowding of wards and emergency rooms, and the postponement of ordinary check-ups and non-urgent operations caused a tragic increase in mortality. In Europe,[46] the overall mortality rate has increased by 2 per cent for every 1,000 fewer beds per thousand inhabitants. In Italy, by 17 per cent.

In the face of the tragic increase in mortality, healthcare workers have done everything possible to protect public health, often at the expense of their own. Resignations declined during the first two pandemic waves, indicating the willingness of many doctors to stand by their colleagues during the emergency. However, they started to increase again soon afterwards, due to the disheartenment resulting from the realization that nothing would change.

In the first pandemic wave, writes Chiara Rivetti:

Unless the relocation had been planned for some time, doctors slowed down their resignations in order not to abandon their colleagues during the worst health crisis of the last century, which they all faced with an admirable sense of responsibility, that earned them the appellation of 'heroes'. Unfortunately, the heroes were soon forgotten. In the following waves, the doctors faced the same organisational approximation as in the spring of 2020.[47]

At the end of the pandemic, the prolonged state of emergency, and the rise in violence and physical and verbal aggression against healthcare personnel have generated a new surge in the number of resignations, exacerbating the difficulties of an organization already severely afflicted by staff shortages, writes Rivetti.

At the 25th National Conference held in Naples on 26 June 2022, Anaao Assomed spoke of a 'perfect storm, an unprecedented crisis in the National Health Service that the Covid pandemic has amplified and blown up', made up of 'extremely high levels of psychological and physical stress due to the numerous night and weekend shifts', both in emergency rooms and in all hospital and non-hospital departments.

'A "Dantesque circle" with unlimited shifts and hours, rarefied career progressions, asphyxiating bureaucracy, debasement of the professional role, an increase in legal complaints as well as in physical and verbal aggression, and a total lack of economic recognition':[48] structural problems that undermine the sustainability of the healthcare system.

4. *The qualities of care*

Michela is an anaesthesiologist and reanimation specialist who took early retirement in 2022. She had been working in the public health service since 1987 when the working conditions were very different.

> There have always been many problems, but very good cooperation. When hospitals became businesses, the problem was to make money at the detriment of others. I'm fine with you being a business manager, if you make it work better. But you cannot exclusively expect to make money at the expenses of staff and nurses.

Michela is used to working intensively and in emergency situations. She is used to making quick decisions and to prioritize the well-being of others. Like all the people we have been meeting so far, she decided to quit after the second wave of the pandemic. In her case, the problem was her health situation, in particular her back pain, leg pain, hernia. She had asked to be relieved of the night shifts. After all, the contract allows doctors over 62 to be exempt from night shifts. The fact that this right is envisaged, however, does not mean that it is conceded. In order to claim this right, Michela made a visit with the competent doctor.

> When I applied for an exemption, the answer was that I had to see the company doctor first. When he visited me, the answer was: 'Do some stretching, maybe you won't be able to run the New York marathon, but you can run the half marathon'. I left the room crying in anger.

Michela took early retirement. She would have liked to stay longer, but the conditions were not there. She was told that if she did not work nights, the burden of her absence would fall on her colleagues, so she had to continue to do it, regardless of her health. It frequently happens that management uses similar arguments to respond negatively to employees' requests, both in health care and in other sectors. Often, it is the same management that decides to cut the workforce to the bone that accuses employees who fall ill of being a burden on their colleagues. Yet, it was not Michela who decided to introduce the hiring freeze in the NHS, nor to cut public funding for healthcare. Michela simply wore herself out to make up for the staff shortage.

> The meeting with the doctor was a decisive moment for me. For a long time I had been getting up, taking a painkiller and going to work. I said to myself: look, you're crossing the line. What you are doing is not good. You are taking care of people's bodies but you are not taking care of your own. Why? Do you think you are a superhero? You think you're going to live forever? You think you're a woman of steel? It's very hard now because my condition has worsened. It was a mistake not to respect myself. After all, if I treat you, why can't I treat myself?

Michela speaks with great passion about her work. She tells me about a patient in the ICU who – it was clear to her from the start – was not going to make it. She recounts how she learned to comfort family members only through the tone of her voice, when the pandemic forbade visits. As I listen to her I remember all the times that, after an operation, I waited for the doctor to tell me how it went. I am reminded of the hurried meetings in the corridors, the surgeon standing there talking in an undecipherable language, spouting incomprehensible words and then walking away, leaving me more confused than before.

> I didn't deny them the seriousness of the illness, but I didn't lay it all on them straight away. Gradually we made a journey together. It was not long, because it lasted three or four days, but it was intense. The day this gentleman died, we could no longer find his wedding ring in the hospital. We looked for it everywhere. When we managed to find it, it felt like we had found a treasure. Sometime later, when I had already retired, I received a message from the chief physician, who forwarded me an e-mail from them. They thanked me for how I had gently taken them by the hand and helped them to cope with death. I cried, I had just retired, and I was still distraught. I responded by thanking them, because they had done so much good for me. They managed to make me shed all the tension I had been withholding

for those months. And they responded by comforting me (laughs). We left that I had to comfort them but in the end they comforted me (laughs again).

The care Michela puts into her work is palpable. Sociologist Lisa Huebner speaks of professional intimacy, to describe the set of psychological, medical and spiritual skills that are part of the therapeutic journey.[49] Yet, care does not always receive the appreciation it deserves.

> Sometimes people tell me that my work is a mission. A mission! Are you kidding me?
> I love my job and I do it to the best of my ability, but I am not a missionary. I would go elsewhere to be a missionary.

Michela is highlighting a dangerous semantic slippage: care work is a job, not a mission, and there's no vocation to martyrdom required to undertake it. Despite this, the work of doctors, nurses and social workers is sometimes described as a mission of those who are naturally inclined to abnegation. This tendency is particularly frequent with regard to women, who are often considered to be intrinsically predisposed to caring for others. The image of care work as an altruistic sacrifice or a mission, however, prevents one from acknowledging all that is really needed for healthcare to work, inside and outside hospitals.

In many ways, Italian healthcare has managed to get through the pandemic despite the lack of resources and funding, banking precisely on the idea that care work is a vocation or a sacrifice that can withstand a situation of chronic underfunding, thanks to the sense of responsibility of the staff.

> We are trapped by a culture of martyrdom: 'I suffer, but I suffer for something important'. But sometimes we also have to make sure that we are well. Being well should be the norm, at work. On the contrary, we often have a completely distorted view of the conditions under which one can work.

For years, the request for sacrifices from healthcare workers has made it possible to conceal the effects of cuts by appealing to the staff's values of altruism, generosity and compassion in order to demand a willingness to work longer shifts, give up time off and holidays for the sake of service. There is an aftertaste of blackmail in the tendency to exploit the dedication of staff in order to manage constant emergencies — a pattern that threatens serious consequences on both patients and staff.

> In my opinion, people have yet to realise how much this jeopardises the quality of care and their own health. I am saying something terrifying, I know. There are very big staff shortages. With no time off, with holidays that are not authorised, not to mention that nobody cares about their health. So the staff shortage has been masterfully resolved by introducing piecework staff. In the hospital where I used to work, there are currently 70 per cent pieceworkers. There are only a few of us left [as permanent staff], so there is no sense of cooperation. And if we want to go and see, they cost more than the permanent staff. If you reduce the staff you have already lost the war.

Pieceworkers are doctors or nurses who work on piece-rate pay in the national health service. One of the first investigations into this trend was published by the 'Corriere della Sera', on the occasion of the death of a woman who had given birth to her third child in a hospital in the province of Brescia, assisted by a doctor who had been on duty for thirty-six hours.[50] Freelancers are paid by the hour to compensate for staff shortages, and recruited by cooperatives to cover uncovered shifts. This system is extremely costly for the public sector: health care companies can offer up to one thousand two hundred euros per shift per doctor — which is, in effect, more than half of what a specialist earns in an entire month, Ravizza and Viafora write in *Corriere*.

Michela recounts her experience with pieceworkers.

> I have met many of them and they have introduced me to a reality that I ignored, and I did not think could exist in the public. As in any industry, there are good pieceworkers, but that is not the point. The point is that with pieceworkers you cannot create a team. Their shift ends at 8 p.m., and they leave immediately. In addition, they earn a lot, they get one hundred and twenty euros per hour gross. While it's true they have many expenses, the system still incentivizes those facing financial difficulties to leave the public sector. There is an incredible pressure to make doctors and nurses migrate to the private sector. It's a vicious circle, a process that has already started and that is working very well, even if it implies a general deterioration of the very health care system.

Michela is emphasizing how the dismantlement of public healthcare is an advanced process, that uses different tools, including economic incentives, to induce hospital staff to leave a protected position in the public sector and start working as freelancers.

> There is a ready and voracious private sector. Take for example the new private hospitals that are being built: in Milan they are building a ninety-four-metre-high hospital that will have thirty-two operating theatres. Who will operate it? That's how the private sector recruits doctors today: like a vacuum, pulling doctors away from public hospitals.

Michela is raising a central issue. A study by Anaao Giovani analysed the flow of medical personnel in healthcare and found that the number of doctors working in public facilities fell by 9.5 per cent between 2010 and 2017, while the number of doctors working in the private sector increased by 15 per cent. In a situation of staff shortage, the public sector empties as private facilities fill up, and vice versa, in a symbiotic process in which the constitutional right to healthcare is being eroded day by day.[51] In recent years, this process has taken place with increasing speed.

As the national secretary of Anaao-Assomed Pierino Di Silverio explained in an interview with Vvox,[52] by law the Italian healthcare system is subject to spending caps for personnel, which means that the hospital company cannot decide to hire based on treatment needs, but must do so according to precise spending constraints. An understaffed hospital outsources the work to the pieceworker in order to work around budget constraint. Pieceworkers' costs are accounted for under a separate budget category from standard personnel expenses. In this way, to plug one problem, they generate another one.

First, a transformation of hospital staff, who resign from a permanent contract to become freelancers. Paying freelancers more than staff incentivizes precarious work arrangements, eventually stripping them of protections they would otherwise be entitled to. This undermines the quality of care, not to mention that it removes the main barrier to the complete dismantling of public healthcare: its personnel.

It is not surprising that, in a context in which work within the NHS is continually mistreated, the use of freelancers is tragically on the rise.

The investigation conducted by Simona Ravizza and Giovanni Viafora shows how recruitment takes place via Telegram, bringing freelancers into hospitals all over Italy. The main destination is emergency rooms.

Every day, thousands of professionals reach 'Italian hospitals, hired by external cooperatives on behalf of health companies, to cover the growing number of staff shortages', the authors write. Asked about the matter, Pierino Di Silverio explains that the problem is not freelancing *itself*.

> The problem is the attractiveness of medical work in Italy today within the healthcare system. Today a doctor within the national healthcare system is subjected to constant violence. Verbal, when all goes well, physical, when it doesn't. It is the only profession in the world to be simultaneously subjected to three courts. A hospital's internal review board, a professional licensing board, and civil or criminal court. In addition, it is poorly paid, because salaries have been at a standstill for ten years with inflation at 8 per cent, with an already expired union contract yet to be discussed, and with no possibility of making a professional career, or having the gratification that each of us would like to have. Moreover, the quality of work, given the endemic shortage of personnel, is very poor, just think that an emergency room doctor today finds himself having to manage eighty, ninety, one hundred emergency patients at the same time. This is then corroborated by hospital conditions that are undeniably dire, to the point that a doctor who should be doing thirty-eight hours of work a week, including four hours of refresher courses, is forced, according to our latest survey, to do sixty, seventy hours a week, and is thus deprived of time, because behind the doctor there is a human being, and this is not considered.

The companies explicitly request shifts of twenty-four or even forty-eight consecutive hours, and the cooperatives, meanwhile, make money. 'Anthesys itself has almost doubled revenues in 2021: fourteen million euro against eight million eight hundred thousand in 2020', write Ravizza and Viafora. And all this is a catastrophe for the healthcare system.

Di Silverio continues:

> The unregulated use of cooperatives and outsourcing has catastrophic consequences for the quality of care, because when the company asks the cooperative to cover a shift in the ER, the cooperative will not put a specialist in emergency medicine in there, also because there are few such specialists in Italy, but it will put a specialist in a branch that is defined as 'equivalent', that is, a doctor who has not studied to

be an ER doctor. The same applies to other departments, and thus the quality of care is objectively and potentially at risk. But just as the quality of care is at risk, so is the legal and professional safety of those who work in the ER. A doctor working on a piecework basis does not have the same protection as an operating doctor employed by the company, from a legal point of view. Before the pandemic, we had succeeded in banning outsourced work in hospitals. Covid has reintroduced an unbridled precarisation of work and we should return to making it illegal.

5. Encouraged to leave

Luca has been an anaesthesia nurse for many years. In the summer of 2022 he resigned and now he does the same job as a freelancer. In some ways, Luca is one of those nurses who have been *incentivized* to leave. As we speak, he has been off work for a month, but his voice is strained, as if he has yet to realize that he can finally rest.

Luca is tired but clear-headed. I ask him to tell me about his work and he casts his mind back to the months of the Covid emergency.

We were disarmed. I went into the first wave in a desperate condition, with a pair of pierced gloves and a snowboard face mask to assist intubated patients in a ward that had no protective gear.

Luca recounts how, in the early days, everywhere he turned there were people wearing the so-called 'helmet', the one made for patients with severe respiratory failure, in every corner, as if it were a film. He remembers the face of a nineteen-year-old boy wearing a helmet inside the red room of the emergency room. 'I met his gaze, he was distraught. He seemed to be looking for help, it was as if he was asking me with his eyes: am I going to die?' At that moment it became clear to me that what was about to happen was more serious than we had been told.

At the hospital we had crazy shifts and on-call time. I worked from 7.30 a.m. to 3.30 p.m. in the operating theatre, where the level of attention is highest and you can't afford to be tired. Then I was on call during the night, and the next day I covered the afternoon shift until two in the morning; the day after that I was again working in the morning and on call during the weekend. So the quality of life was non-existent, the salary was out of proportion compared to the actual hours worked and everything costs so much that just making the journey between home and work became unbearable.

I ask him how long his shifts were.

I remember one day I came into the hospital in the morning at 7.30am and did a 24-hour shift at least. I spent the morning in the operating theatre, then found myself intubating people in the wards and setting up intensive care. I then transported patients to other hospitals and organised ambulance transports. I remember that by then things just kept going and I didn't even think about my physical needs anymore. I remember that I came to realise after twenty-four hours that I had not eaten and I had not even thought about it.

I ask if it was adrenaline that kept them going.

Let's say that what you were seeing led you to this. Maybe that's what happens in burnout, when the priority of looking after the other is such that you try to do everything you can. For me the real difficulty wasn't the lack of rest, the real struggle was trying to sleep, because an inner voice kept saying that I should stay at work. I felt guilty when I went home to sleep instead of staying at the hospital.

Luca also benefited from the psychological support service provided by the hospital. The public debate has never adequately addressed the traumatic impact the pandemic has had on healthcare staff. Words such as burnout or exhaustion have not found the space they deserved in the press, perhaps because hospitals are companies that must protect their reputation, and they have no incentive to admit that staff are unwell.

According to Luca, however, burnout became a constant state. In this sense, its causes were not in individual behaviour, but in the organization of the workplace itself, in particular in staff reductions, excessively long shifts and in the absence of adequate breaks. This must be why the phenomenon of large-scale resignations is easily understood by psychologists, psychiatrists and psychotherapists, and hardly by entrepreneurs and economists, who are often lacking in tools when it comes to grasping the subjective aspects of the world of work.

In cases such as this, it is clear that burnout and prolonged exposure to fatigue and death produce traumatizing effects. Conversely, the economic uncertainties arising from the decision to quit take a back seat when compared to the urgency of getting back on one's feet.

Luca explains what it means to quit while having a mortgage to pay. He tells me that in his first month as a freelancer he billed four thousand euros gross with one hundred and twenty hours of work, while as a public employee, his salary was around one thousand eight hundred net. Luca now earns significantly more as a freelancer. Of course, now he has no labour protections: he has no fixed salary every month, no pension, no paid holidays or sick leave. But what nostalgia could he have for sick leave when he had to work even though he was sick to compensate for staff shortages? And why would he miss holidays, if the possibility of taking them was tied to an authorization that could never arrive, due to service requirements?

What I have witnessed over the past twelve years has been a continuous dismantlement of the conditions that allowed us to do our work. When I worked in a small county hospital, I saw entire services being hived off and gradually given to private contractors. First it was the management of the mortuary. Then it was the turn of the laboratory, which decentralised to another department of the same company; finally it was the turn of the centre for blood transfusion, with all that this entails - for example, that if you need a bag of blood products during surgery you have to send an ambulance.

The pandemic could be an opportunity to make society understand what happens when the territorial health services are no longer there.

All sorts of things arrived in the ER: the lady with Covid and the child with a cold, all the people who, instead of accessing appropriate care through local services, had to go to the hospital. That's how emergency rooms started to overflow and could no longer cope with demand.

The problem is that this led to nothing. On the contrary, people began to feel neglected and to lash out at health personnel.

I was attacked by a guy who had taken cocaine and arrived drunk in the emergency room. First he punched my colleague and left him on the ground, consider that my colleague is two metres tall and has two shoulders like that, and then it was my turn. And I could tell you about other people, such as the man who smashed a monitor in the emergency room because he had been assigned a green code, and became angry when others with more urgent needs were treated first.

Unfortunately, the number of assaults in hospitals is only increasing. According to the National Federation of Nursing Professions Associations, 33 per cent of nurses are victims of some form of physical and/or verbal violence every year, particularly in the emergency sectors. That means a total of approximately one hundred and thirty thousand assaults per year, 75 per cent of which involve women.

People felt they were not being helped. And at a certain point they started to forget that we were forced to work in those conditions and that we were doing anything we could to save them. They started to forget the deaths in Bergamo, the nonexistent intensive care beds. They grew tired of the bulletins and began to resent us. When you abandon people, it happens that, instead of revolting, they start to react the way you do in situations where there is no hope of survival. They begin to think that dog eats dog, and so it was.

It is at this point that many co-workers have chosen freelancing, he says. 'It is too heavy a burden to carry'.

In recent months, the media have given space to stories like Luca's: *la Repubblica* reported on Sara Risi, who at the time of the interview had decided to give up a permanent contract. Thirty-one-year-old Francesca[53] specialized in emergency medicine in 2020. The cooperative pays nine hundred and sixty euro gross for a twelve-hour shift, which means that her monthly remuneration with four night shifts per month would be three thousand euros net. 'With eight days of work per month I earn one thousand euro more' than she used to she says. 'And I have time for me, for my family'.

It is hard not to see such enormous economic disproportion as an incentive to leave public healthcare, and in some cases it is hard not to understand the heavy heart of those who do. Among the stories in the press, for instance, is that of Ilaria Giubbilo, who resigned after twelve years working as a nurse. In her letter, her discouragement at the lack of professional and economic recognition shone through. Her resignation letter is a scathing critique of how public healthcare is managed.

I presented my resignation not because I expected anyone to mourn my decision. But simply because at 42 years of age I feel I still have the desire, the drive and the need to change, to learn, to grow. Someone else will take my place, that is OK. Maybe someone better. Maybe someone randomly recruited by a staffing agency, simply because a pawn is missing. I never wanted to have to say this: the healthcare system is collapsing. It is losing professionalism without batting and without demonstrating that it can or even wants to do anything about it. So things get worse. Because they impose endless symptomatic fixes that never solve the problem. It only patches the problem, wasting resources in the process. This is the choice. I adapt. I still wonder if I did enough, that I have not sufficiently demonstrated my love for public service. [...] I have simply decided that I am no longer in. I no longer agree with a system that has abdicated solidarity, charity and the universality of care for corporatism. A system that does not reward but flattens human resources. [...] I leave with my head held high. I know I have done my best always.[54]

It hurts to read letters such as Ilaria's, because they recount the suffering of those who leave, unwillingly and reluctantly, simply because they want to do their job well. Unfortunately, in contexts of creeping privatization such as the healthcare system in Italy, it is often the most capable people who quit first, because they can't abide by values that they do not share or because they see the limits of a dysfunctional management.

For Luca, incentivizing people to leave is dangerous.

The problem is that if you are dealing with people who may be on a permanent contract and you don't know how to get rid of them, then you completely discourage them from keeping their job. This is what we went through and it is horrifying. You want a healthcare system that works? Do you have a professional who can benefit the company? Why not put him in a position to work? Why not incentivise people to stay?

Indeed, there is no satisfactory answer to this question. The impression is that a decision has been made to undermine the very foundations of the public health system, or what is left of it.

6. *Essential struggles*

In Italy, there are nearly 2 million people without a family doctor,[55] a number that is rapidly growing. A report on healthcare needs in inland areas[56] speaks of real *deserts*, marked by the absence or rarefaction of services in various parts of the country. Under these conditions, an increasing number of citizens are forced to turn to emergency rooms to access diagnosis and treatment.

In fact, every ninety seconds there is an emergency in the country's ERs. 'Every minute and a half, a heart attack, stroke, polytrauma, sepsis, septic shock, or acute respiratory failure arrives', explains the president of the Italian Society of Emergency Medicine (Simeu), Fabio de Iaco.[57]

The situation is exacerbated by the growth in the number of departures within ERs and by the decline in applications for the specialization in emergency and urgent medicine. Simeu estimates that around one hundred doctors per month have left their jobs in 2022, a number that is roughly equivalent to closing five emergency rooms each month.[58] For Simeu President Fabio De Iaco, this is an inevitable consequence of a profession that is becoming less and less attractive.

> Why should medical graduates choose to go to a place where they have no career progress, no financial benefit, have to spend 75 per cent of their holidays on call, and have to do six to eight on-call night shifts each month? It is understandable that young people are not attracted to our work, I would never wish them to lead the life we do.[59]

It is also to stem this haemorrhage that Italian hospitals use pieceworkers. According to a survey carried out by *Simeu*, there are fifteen thousand freelance doctors who provide 18 million treatments a year. In Veneto, a region in the North-East of Italy, they account for 70 per cent, in Liguria, which is a region in the North-West, for 60 per cent, in Piemonte, a region that is also in the North-West of Italy, for 50 per cent of the workforce. Far from being a solution, piecework has become part of the problem: the epitome of a process of privatization, which foreshadows a chronic state of emergency.

Behind this is a kind of existential crisis, in which two different visions of healthcare clash: in the first one, healthcare is a political priority, because it contributes to public health. In the second one, it is a cost and an opportunity for private profit.

For Pino Visone, one of the emergency doctors at the Cardarelli hospital in Naples, the emergency room safeguards not only the constitutional right to health, but also 'the right to life'.

> A healthcare system stands or falls on its emergency system. If I go to the emergency room and do not find anyone to assist me my right to health care is suspended, and at that moment my life is only worthwhile if the system that receives me is organised, otherwise it is worth nothing. [...] The ER has been marginalised by a health care system corrupted by a poisonous seed that has now grown into a monster. Rights and profit are fundamentally incompatible. So, once profit was allowed into the system, it has increasingly ostracised the ER because that can't be monetized. So hospitals themselves have turned the emergency room into a ghetto. When it finally became that the demand for doctors is greater than the supply, everyone who could leave, has left. If you ask doctors in the emergency rooms if they want to leave, 90 per cent will answer yes.[60]

To defend this right, on 4 May 2022, in Naples, twenty-five doctors of the Cardarelli emergency department gave a collective notice of resignation, because under the given conditions they were no longer able to do their job and provide adequate and dignified care to patients.[61] Cardarelli is the largest hospital in Southern Italy. During the pandemic, it was repeatedly overwhelmed by the influx of patients, forcing emergency doctors to manage daily admissions of around two hundred people. After the dismantlement of community care services, the Cardarelli became a point of reference for patients in the area. Recounts speak of dozens of mobile beds stacked next to each other and filling every inch of the triage area in a highly uncomfortable situation with few bathrooms and no privacy.

For Visone, the threat of resignation did not signal a desire to leave. Theirs was a 'cry for help'.[62]

It's hard to fully capture what's happening in this sector. Italy has long abdicated the primary goals of the 1978 reform to reduce territorial inequalities and has become a country divided into twenty-one different healthcare systems, each of which even has a different life expectancy. The situation promises to get worse in the years to come. In the meantime, the ratio of healthcare expenditure to GDP continues to be lower than it is in other European countries (11 per cent in Germany and 10.3 in France), and it is bound to be reduced to 6 per cent in 2025.

In this context, the slide towards the insurance system seems increasingly inevitable, given the continuous lengthening of waiting lists and the growing recourse to private healthcare. In 2021, the ISTAT report on Fair and Sustainable Welfare (Bes) noted how the percentage of people who had to forego care due to financial problems almost doubled in two years, rising from 6.3 per cent in 2019, up to 11 per cent in 2021.[63] Unfortunately, in view of the contraction of public spending, 90 per cent of private healthcare expenditure is covered by household savings[64] and often those who cannot pay out of their own pocket simply give up treatment.

From this point of view, the growth in the number of voluntary resignations is a symptom of a crisis affecting the entire sector. The drain of personnel, however, does not only stem from the issues we have seen. Two years ago, the tragedy of Sara Pedri brought to light the climate of harassment that dominates some hospital departments. Pedri was a young doctor in the gynaecology department at Trento hospital. She resigned in March 2021 and disappeared the next day, never to be found. The Trento Public Prosecutor's Office confirmed that the chief physician mistreated the doctors, showing how threats, sanctions, mistreatment and devaluation were the order of the day in her department. 'That constant mistreatment broke her',[65] her sister said.

In general, mobbing – from the English root *to mob*, which means 'to attack' – indicates a persecutory process against a designated victim, where the latter is marginalized and harassed to the point of laceration. It is not uncommon that this process targets women such as Sara Pedri, underlining an extreme form of domination, flavoured with patriarchal contempt. In other cases, it plays a key role within corporate restructuring, aiming to bend the resistance of staff with abuse.

A very experienced doctor recounted to me that he had resigned after being insulted, sworn at and humiliated in front of patients and colleagues by superiors. He reported of colleagues who were humiliated to such an extent that they had to take ten drops of valium before their shift. Of a frequency of insults, demotions and criticism that made practicing the profession feel '*incompatible with life*'. These episodes often go unnoticed. It is clear, however, that in many circumstances, resignations hint at the existence of toxic situations, which make it hard to continue working.

In this context, resignations are the symptom of a situation of crisis that often progresses in silence and, just as often, feeds on itself, because for every person who quits, there is an even heavier workload left for those who remain, indicating a vicious circle from which it will be difficult to re-emerge, unless there is a sudden turnaround, which is not in sight.

A study published in *The Lancet*[66] estimated that there is a worldwide shortage of 43 million health workers: doctors, nurses and care technicians, on top of dental and pharmaceutical personnel. The global perspective is crucial because, in this context of shortage, high-income countries contribute to reducing the already small number of health workers in low-income countries by draining them northwards.

There is an urgent need to ensure effective planning, encourage students to undertake such studies, refinance the sector and increase salaries. In recent months, doctors, nurses and medical personnel have mobilized in different corners of the world[67], from India to Pakistan, from Venezuela to Mexico, from Chile to Argentina and from South Korea to Morocco. Health care, however, should not only be a concern for healthcare staff. It is an essential struggle for the whole of society.

Chapter 5

WANTED: RESTAURANT OWNER WHO PAYS PROPERLY, IN GOOD STANDING

1. The labour contract: a stranger still

During the pandemic, when the restaurant industry shut down, all of us working without a contract were suddenly let go. I ended up working on the streets during those days. I was collecting things to sell at charity markets. We couldn't even afford bread.

Gaia is thirty-eight years old. If we exclude her five years of living in Barcelona, she has always worked in her region, Puglia, in the South of Italy. Gaia is a precarious worker, one of many forced to juggle a job that pays a fistful of euros and a rent that costs more every month. Gaia started working in the restaurant industry when she was sixteen. Back then, she toiled fourteen-hour shifts for €21.50 a day, about one euro and fifty cents an hour.

The most I could get in those years was twenty-five euro a day for twelve or thirteen hours of work, because that's how it works in the restaurant business: if you're the last to arrive and you're the youngest, you're also the one who will get the least of all. If you are also female, that's even worse.

During the pandemic she found herself at home overnight. The business where she was working dropped its shutters, and Gaia invented a makeshift job in the street markets. Undeclared work is like that: no one warns you if you are going to end up on the street. No one pays into your pension, no sick leave, no unemployment support. Nobody asks you how you are. You must figure out a way to survive on your own.

Gaia has been trying to get out of the quicksand of undeclared work for a long time. In her last job she was promised a contract. The owner did not know how to run the place. His father had given it to him as a gift to stop him from feeling like a complete failure, says Gaia. She ran that place: she worked as a waitress, cashier, counter assistant, and cleaner, while the owner, in the kitchen, prepared burgers and fries. When he got sick, Gaia would open the restaurant in the morning and close it in the evening. She would also substitute for him in the kitchen. She had to keep it open, or she'd lose a day's pay. After all, if you work off the books and the owner stays closed, you don't earn anything.

During those months Gaia often asked about her contract. In the end, promises are a clever way to extract free labour. As Marco Bascetta[1] has written, in the age of precariousness, promises are a lure that extracts unpaid labour from those desperate to believe that, by doing so, they will access future earnings, higher pay or, as is the case here, a labour contract. Gaia agrees to work off the books, once again, hoping the owner would finally hire her. But again, he didn't.

> I was getting fifty euros a day, two hundred and fifty a week, and I was the only one working with him, the only staff member working there. When August comes, in the middle of the summer season, he tells me: 'you cost me too much'. Consider that I never received my thirteenth month salary, holidays or sick pay. So when he told me 'you cost me too much', for the one thousand euros a month he was giving me off the books, I remained silent. I just thought, well, if you think I cost you too much you'll see how much I cost you. I went to a union, and they told me that between the national contract, thirteenth month, fourteenth month, severance pay, etc. they ought to give me around five thousand euros. In the past I shrugged my shoulders, left and looked for something else. This time I went to the labour inspectorate and filed a complaint.

Gaia quit her job. Her resignation will never appear in official statistics, because her contract never existed. The press, in recent years, has been repeating that there is one problem in the restaurant industry: no one wants to work anymore. Instead, one of the main problems is the black economy, that sinkhole of undeclared work through which employers try to beat the competition by offloading their costs onto staff.

The Oxfam report *Disuguitalia: Giving value, power and dignity back to work* (2022)[2] examined the use of undeclared work in different sectors of the Italian economy. In the hospitality and catering sectors, there is widespread use of part-time contracts, in which a few formally contracted hours are flanked by large portions of 'out-of-pocket' pay; long probation periods paid little or nothing; not to mention the spread of short-term contracts, punctuated by very high turnover rates. Increasingly, the catering and hospitality industry is a jungle of undeclared work, pirate contracts and wage dumping, the attempt to circumvent collective bargaining agreements through parallel dealings with minor trade unions compliant with companies.

Recently, a survey by the Italian Federation of Public Establishments (FIPE) studied contract dumping in public exercises.[3] The report is invaluable in mapping the pressures to which workers are subjected in public services, at the mercy of an environment rife with irregularities, where it's rare for all hours to be properly and regularly paid. Lazzeroni[4] spoke of a 'paroxysmal market of collective agreements', referring to the proliferation of downward contracts. The aim is simple: to reduce labour costs and existing protections. This can be done in several ways: offering less than the minimum wage; paying overtime, night and holiday work less than it should be; increasing the length of the probationary period from the stipulated thirty days up to even one hundred and forty days; creating advantageous conditions for companies in the treatment of holidays, sickness and maternity leave. As Andrea Garnero and Claudio Lucifora[5] have shown, the number of national collective labour agreements filed with the National Economic and Labour Council has increased by 80 per cent over a decade and reached 992 at the end of 2021. This is an increasingly widespread practice that progressively erodes the collective bargaining system and worsens the quality of work, forcing people to juggle between different but equally problematic offers.

Gaia, in fact, was in this situation. For years, she had only been offered two alternatives: working illegally or with involuntary part-time work, working conditions that have repercussions on everything: first of all on pay and on housing.

Today in Puglia, a 50-square-metre flat costs. They also ask you for bank guarantees, for a series of guarantees for which you are shut out. Even if I wanted to, the only contract they give me is a part-time of twenty hours and the economic proposal that corresponds to that contract is seven or eight hundred euro. And this means that when you then go to ask for unemployment you end up with next to nothing because the unemployment you receive is 75 per cent gross of a pay slip on which there were half the hours you did. In these conditions, you can only turn to the black market to get a house.

I was lucky in the past, but now it's not enough. A contract's not enough anymore—you have to show pay slips too, because now they ask for many more guarantees. I'm going to have to leave home soon because I've been evicted, and I don't know how to get another house. I live in limbo, just taking it day by day. There's no other option now.

In Gaia's case, living means being caught between a precarious job that pays too little and a house that costs too much. Not ending up on the street is a matter of luck.

Nobody thinks about housing. Everyone talks about the Citizenship income, which allows small traders to pay you very little. A €500 Citizenship Income won't solve unemployment. It is one tool to address the poverty that exists in this country. Unemployment is a different story; a Citizenship income is not going to make jobs pop up. Even a child can see it: Citizenship Income doesn't solve unemployment. Adults, on the other hand, have a hard time understanding this.

When Gaia says that Citizenship income is for small traders, she has a point.

According to the 21st INPS Annual Report, 20 per cent of Citizenship income recipients had a job in 2021. This is three hundred and ninety-three thousand people who received the Citizenship income on a stable basis and had, at the same time, an active working position.[6] Most of these, writes the report, worked as employees in the private sector and 22 per cent worked in the restaurant industry.

According to the INPS report, the restaurant industry is the predominant sector of activity among Citizenship income recipients. These are people who receive such a low income that they cannot get out of poverty even by working. Catering, from this point of view, is perhaps the clearest example of poor work in Italy. Often, those who work in this sector need an integration of income in order to survive.

Tragically, this situation is reminiscent of nineteenth-century England, when the Speenhamland system allowed people, whose wages were below the poverty line, to supplement low wages with a subsidy of varying amounts depending on the price of bread and the number of family members. Work was very poor in those years and had to be integrated with subsidies. Subsidies, on the other hand, were so low that they had to be supplemented with work to enable subsistence. For a long time, this situation locked the working class into a kind of vicious circle of poor work and poor subsidies.

Sociologist Karl Polanyi best described the violence of this strange combination of paternalism and impoverishment when he wrote that while the Speenhamland system was in force, the poor 'almost lost their human form'.[7] It is tragic to recognise, in a period of history when neither trade unions nor universal suffrage yet existed, such a striking parallel with the present. As Karl Polanyi clearly explained, in nineteenth-century England, low wages and public subsidies helped pave the way for the free market, which was seen at the time as the only escape from poverty. Today, the persistence of meagre subsidies and depressed wages signals not progress, but the systematic dismantling of rights—fitting for an age of crisis that seems to be moving in reverse.

Today in Italy, precarious labour wears the same inhuman face as it did in the 1800s. So inhuman it's become unspeakable: What happened to the people suddenly left jobless by the pandemic? How did they survive? How much anger did they accumulate towards their employer? And after the pandemic, how many decided to go and work in a call centre, a department store or in a factory in order to escape precarity? Gaia's case speaks of undeclared work, but her experience is not unrepresentative of what happens in the restaurant industry. The irregularity rate of over 83 per cent found by the labour inspectorate in 2022 confirms that cases such as Gaia's are all too frequent, and reminds us of the urge to increase inspections and act on undeclared work.

By virtue also of this, it is fair to say that citizenship income helps small traders, as Gaia explained. The national collective agreement envisages, in her case, around one thousand five hundred euros of salary per month. Gaia has none of this: she barely makes a thousand euros off the books, and she has no social security coverage, nor the protections provided by law. In this context, if Gaia, in addition to her monthly salary, were to receive the Citizenship income, she would receive an income supplement, which would allow her to integrate her monthly earnings for a small part. In this sense, the Citizenship income allows small traders to pay their employees off the books and less than they should, leaving it to the state to compensate for poor wages with a monthly subsidy. As Sarah Gainsforth wrote in her book, 'seen in this way, it looks less like an incentive for slackers and more like a state subsidy for private entrepreneurs who do not pay their workers enough'.[8]

Gaia recounts further:

My frustration lies precisely in the relationship between life and work, because I don't believe that work dignifies anything. The moment someone asks me 'what is your dream job?', I answer that

I do not work in my dreams. In my dreams I do not work. But I realise that in order to work as little as possible you have to earn as much as possible and that also causes me frustration, because in this situation you have no future prospects. Many times when I am tired and have to go to work I wonder how much longer will I resist, because mine is a physical job. I stand, I walk back and forth, and my back hurts, my knees hurt, and if it ever happens for any reason that I can't go to work, I will be without income. They say that the new generations don't want to work, lucky them! Had it taken all this trouble of ours to make any young girl understand that she should expect things to be different, it would have been worth it. I know many waiters in their seventies who have no personal life and now live for the restaurant. For if you work a schedule that goes from morning to midnight, what kind of life do you have? Why do you work? Only to find yourself in a shared flat, the only thing *I can afford*, doing the laundry on your day off. I tell you, I don't do six days a week anymore, I do five, and for me that extra day off is a godsend, because it means seeing my friends, staying with my dogs an extra hour, putting a mask on my face, taking care of myself and allowing me to realise that I don't want that from life. I hope you have a lot of time in your life, that is the best we can wish for. I wish you have lots of time.

Gaia's story allows us to understand what is happening in the restaurant industry. The increase in voluntary resignations and the shortage of new applicants suggest, in fact, that we are facing a crisis in the sector.

Over the last twenty years, the growth of the sector has gone hand in hand with the gradual disinvestment in other areas of production, primarily in manufacturing and trade. The process has been particularly intense in the South, where the industrialization rate has always been lower than the national average, and where tourism has compensated for a decade-long lack of investment. Here, catering and hospitality have represented, and continue to represent, one of the few possibilities to escape unemployment. The growth of the sector, however, rather than a quality employment opportunity, has become synonymous with poor work, as it has been linked mainly to part-time and fixed-term contracts.[9]

According to INPS, 64.5 per cent of restaurant workers are poor.[10] Businesses operating in the sector, in turn, are not in good shape.

As the FIPE[11] annual report 2021 shows, some twenty-two thousand businesses have lowered their shutters in 2020, a number that rose to forty-five thousand in 2021. After the pandemic, the situation did not improve due to the rising prices of raw materials, which put 30 per cent of the companies at risk. It is therefore not surprising that the sector lost around two hundred and forty-three thousand people in the first year of the pandemic alone, including those who decided to quit, those who have been made redundant, those whose contracts expired and those who chose not to renew them. In many ways, the pandemic was a watershed. First, it exacerbated uncertainty for both companies and workers, many of whom found themselves, or feared to find themselves, out of work from one day to the next. Secondly, because many began to question whether working in the restaurant industry was really worth it. Why stay in an industry that offers low pay, gruelling hours and such high level of insecurity?

The FIPE report observes that 28 per cent of the enterprises claim to have lost some of their staff because they have 'chosen to leave voluntarily to work elsewhere', and 21.5 per cent of these claim to have lost 'experienced' staff who have been trained for some time. In addition, during 2021, 32.6 per cent of public establishments conducted searches for new staff, and 64 per cent found it difficult to recruit them because of inadequate skills (40.3 per cent). In general, the FIPE estimates that in 2021 the number of employees was one hundred and ninety-four thousand lower than in 2019. This contraction hit restaurants and bars hardest, with the steepest decline among migrant workers (who were 22.9 per cent fewer in 2021 than they were in 2019).

Based on these numbers, we can assume that the shortage is due to a flight of personnel rather than a lack of skills: the skills are there, but those who left do not want to return to work in the sector. what are the causes of such a dispersion of know-how between 2020 and 2022?

In an article of 19 July 2022 entitled 'What the restaurant owner doesn't want to understand',[12] Marco Natali summarizes the stories of some of his colleagues and acquaintances who have decided to abandon the restaurant industry. The first comes from Francesco, a chef.

> After all the negative experiences one can imagine, Francesco had ended up as a temporary worker in a hotel. Unfortunately, in Lombardy, the region that was more severely hit by Covid. He thus found himself without a job. In the summer of 2020, he tried to get

back into the game but ended up in the golden cliche of the restaurant business, where he received a proposal of 1,200 euros per month because 'you know there is a crisis'. Francesco thought 'as if there was no crisis for me'. At that point, fed up with being treated like a peasant, he resumed studying graphics and is currently a freelance graphic designer.

The second story is that of Daniel who worked in the lounge.

He worked there for 26 years. The problem was that he knew when he started but didn't know when he finished. Now he works in a factory, he knows when he begins, he knows when he ends. He earns the same money as before, but works two days less. 1700 euros, Monday to Friday, 8 hours a day, paid overtime. He is keen to point out that at 40 it is possible to change.

The third story is that of Giulia from Alba.

She firmly believes that she is good at her job, which she has been doing since she was 17. From the lounge to the bar, passing also through the kitchen, she has juggled wherever and whenever she could. She is now a shelf-stacker in a supermarket but she has decided to quit due to the following reasons:

- Brigades created with improvised staff
- Unreasonable wages (€ 2.50/hour) and people who accept it
- Colleagues who don't make a team and don't give a damn about the work
- Restaurants that expect you to work for 1 hour at lunch, 2 hours at dinner, 4 days a week and do no other work
- Getting called at 11.15 to be at work at 12.
- Late paychecks
- working without contracts
- Very long working hours without a break (plus they charge you for lunch)
- Pay from € 4.5/hour to do 4 jobs (cook, waitress, barmaid, cashier)
- 2 employees to manage 300 people per night (for months, not exceptional events)
- Regular contracts of 14 hours per week, doing 55
- Working without proper tools (shaker, strainer, squeezer, proper glasses, etc.)

Then it is the turn of Lorenzo, who used to be a sommelier but after the pandemic decided to work in a factory for a company that makes furniture.

> Now that he has a permanent contract he can finally think about taking out a mortgage to buy a house, after which – 'The first thing I'll do as soon as I've bought a house will be to change jobs, but for sure, FOR SURE', he emphasises – 'not in the restaurant business'.

A graphic designer, a factory worker, a retail worker and another factory worker: because you earn more, because there is less uncertainty, because you don't work seven days a week, because there are working hours that allow you to have a life, because a factory pays better than a restaurant.

The XXI INPS annual report confirms these relocations and shows that, three months after the termination date, slightly more than half of the people who had a permanent contract have relocated: the relocation rate in 2021, in fact, was 57 per cent. If we look at the balance between incoming and outgoing relocations, moreover, we will see that, again in 2021, the accommodation and catering sector is the one that, more than the others, has a negative balance, which means more people are leaving the sector than entering it. Finally, the accommodation and catering sector has the lowest level of stayers, people remaining within the same sector between 2019 and 2021 (59 per cent). Meanwhile, a significant share of those who left who moved to other sectors in the service sector (14 per cent) or in industry (4 per cent) is substantial. The conclusion of the INPS report, in relation to these data, is that the loss of employees for the sector is 'entirely due to the prevalence of mobility to other sectors. [...] It does not therefore appear to have counted so much the difficulty in recruiting as the difficulty in retaining'.

But why does the restaurant industry struggle to retain workers? Marco Natali sums it up as follows:

> To sum up
> – The problem is that you cannot find staff.
> – You can't find staff because you don't pay them properly.
> – You underpay them because a proper contract costs 2.2 times their take-home pay.

Not only that, but he wonders if it is not the restaurant owners who are the problem.

Isn't it that maybe if there were more qualified entrepreneurs in our sector, then we would have more people looking for work, rather than so many who, after one lousy job too many, decide to change careers? Scratch that—that's not a question. It's just the truth.

Natali's provocation allows us to go a step further, in analysing the Great Resignation: because, more than the Citizenship income, the problem is the organization of work in the restaurant industry and in all the sectors particularly affected by the Great Resignation. Natali, not surprisingly, ironically suggests giving restaurant owners a 'restaurant income' (this is what he calls it) and allowing employees to take over the boss's business: 'after all, why should employees lose their jobs because the owner's incompetent?'

The fact is that when businesses are poorly organized, problems cascade. Instead of paying regularly one does it in black. Instead of hiring two people, they make one person do the job of two. Instead of hiring an experienced professional (which costs a lot), they enlist students in internships, which cost little or nothing. The picture is complete: gruelling shifts, no days off and unpaid overtime. As if that were not enough, once they have created a workplace full of injustice, they need harassment to force people to obey. If this seems like an exaggeration, just read some of the testimonials collected by 'Fatto Quotidiano' during the *No to Underpaid Work* campaign. The long title of an article by Charlotte Matteini[13] is already emblematic: 'Underpaid Work – 'Broken' Shifts, No Rest, 17 Hours behind the Counter for 800 Euro a Month: For Workers, the Restaurant Industry is a Jungle. Harassment and Threats are the Norm'. Here are some stories that appeared in the piece, starting with Carlo's:

I only had one day off per week, but if there were bookings on that day, I was called on duty for 25 euros. Could I refuse? If I did, there was retaliation. Some colleagues were even denied time off on the following days. Plenty of us bolted, but the real problem is that in the Syracuse area, almost all restaurant owners offer the same exploitative conditions: take it or leave it. What frustrates me most is the lack of enforcement. Sure, the municipal police drop by occasionally to check that the restaurant owner has paid for the public land at his disposal, but I have never seen any other checks. And everyone does what they think, with total impunity. We are not protected by anyone.

Giuseppe worked as a chef on a part-time contract for four hours a day:

I pointed out that I was receiving Citizenship income, and I wanted to be put on full-time status. They said no because they would have to pay too much tax: it was either part-time or nothing. I had to accept because I had been idle for more than two years and my family and I lacked even bread on our table by then. I was working 10 to 12 hours a day for 250 euro a week. The waiters, on the other hand, young guys, were paid 25 to 30 euro a day for 13 hours of work.

This is Gabriele:

I have never had a labour contract in Italy. I was always working off the books, underpaid. The attitude was: 'I am giving you the job, you should thank me for it'. When it comes to small restaurants, disrespect and insults from the owners are practically daily. Forget sick leave or holidays — you show up bleeding if you have to. You work with headache, fever, a burning back — doesn't matter. You show up.

Carlotta worked in a bar in Rome:

A two-month part-time contract. In April I was entitled to take one day off a week and spent 17 hours a day behind a counter making coffee. The pay was 800 euro per month. During the entire month of May I had three days off. Even on May Day — a public holiday — the café stayed open, and I worked the usual 17-hour shift. Even then I was paid 800 euros a month.

These are just a few examples, but they help to understand why people leave the restaurant business: because they are sick of it. This is the one reason that is often forgotten when it comes to the causes of staff shortages.

2. Burnout: An organizational problem

First, go into your kitchen. Put a giant pot of boiling water on the stove and stand in front of it for eight hours. Occasionally stab yourself in the hand with a sharp knife. Find a right-wing radio show, the more rabid the better, and turn it up to ear-splitting volume. Pretend that when they are yelling at the president they are actually yelling at you. Imagine that each insult is very personally directed at your stupid face. Try not to cry. When the eight hours are up, imagine that this is every day of your life and ask yourself if you still want to be a chef. Yes? Then congratulations! You are exactly the kind of masochist who is ready to cook in a professional kitchen!

– Amanda Cohen, chef and owner of *Dirt Candy* in New York, 2012[14]

a. Racism in the kitchen

American chef Harold Villarosa, who was born in the Philippines and grew up in the Bronx, traced the shortcomings of the restaurant industry back to its militaristic organizational structure. Villarosa recalls how it was chef Georges Auguste Escoffier who introduced the brigade system into the kitchen. Escoffier had served in the French army and drew on the military order to devise the system that still governs the hierarchical structure of the kitchen today. Escoffier demanded an absolute commitment from his staff and considered the willingness to work to the point of exhaustion as a demonstration of dedication. From then on, psychological pressure became the norm in the kitchen. According to him, today's shouting, punishing shifts, and abuse all trace back to that system.

> The hierarchy quickly slid into abuse. Abuse from those in positions of power, who quickly forget they even started at the bottom. And then there's the self-abuse. The drugs to push through a shift and stand the line through a bad back. The alcohol to ease the adrenaline at the end of a mad service of being screamed at by the drill sergeant, and this is just the tip. The final hit of this system, the result of this profession we call passion, is often depression, in the worst cases, suicide. And people ask why chefs are dying.[15]

Villarosa wrote these words at a time when the restaurant industry was making its way into our television screens, thanks to programmes such as *MasterChef* and *No Reservations*, *Kitchen Nightmares* and *Chef's Table*, up to the recent series *The Bear*. The fascination that has since surrounded the world of food often ends up contrasting with apparently inexplicable tragedies, such as the suicide of Anthony Bourdain, charismatic author of *Kitchen Confidential*; or that of Bernard Loiseau, who killed himself with a shotgun blast when the newspapers hypothesized the possible loss of a Michelin star; or the suicide of Luciano Zazzeri, who died as a result of long-term depression; or that of Benoit Violier, the multi-starred Franco-Swiss chef who took his own life in 2015 after being the victim of a fraud. These are just a few cases in a rather long sequence of tragedies. In fact, beneath the glamour of show business, we often find stories of depression, abuse and exhaustion.

Villarosa continues:

> They don't even see the scars the industry has left on all of us. Big-name chefs are chasing clout and money, so they've got to fake it, but the real know bro. Divorced, toiling away at a bullshit restaurant where the owners have you by the balls. It's real out here. Chefs are fucked up in the head, and physically fucked.

Understanding the hierarchical structure of the kitchen is fundamental to comprehending what goes on inside it, says Villarosa, who in his letter dwells on the migrants who populate the American kitchens, real cannon fodder.

> Exploited and underpaid, they've carried the restaurant industry on their backs, and when Covid-19 hit, we forgot about them like they shit. Why? Because they weren't high enough up Escoffier's chart? Or is it because of the color of their skin and the rampant racism we face in this industry also?

For Villarosa, the structure underpinning the restaurant industry uses racism to force migrants to do those essential jobs that nobody wants to do. Thus, while most chefs are white men, there are almost exclusively migrants in the galley. In Italian kitchens, the incidence of migrant workers is 15 per cent. Their conditions in the kitchens, in fact, are particularly harsh and subject not only to monstrous shifts and low wages, but also to explicit forms of racism.

Patrick, for example, recounts that he left the restaurant industry to work in a warehouse after spending five years in the same restaurant as a dishwasher, assistant cook and waiter. He never worked shifts of less than twelve hours: from 10.00 am to 4.00 pm and then from 6.00 pm to midnight. The problem was that he was treated badly.

> I used to argue a lot with the chef. He told me openly: 'I am a racist'. He didn't hide it from me, sometimes he would say 'n*ggh, come on, hurry up slave!', things like that. I worked there for five years.

Now I work in the warehouse, a demanding job, but better than the restaurant industry. They made me an offer: would you be OK with an apprenticeship? I was working in a restaurant, I was getting a salary. The internship, you know, is five hundred euro a month. I said OK, I just wanted to get out of that place. And then they gave me a permanent contract. Now I make one thousand five hundred euro a month. See the difference.[16]

Patrick started working in the restaurant industry as soon as he arrived in Italy. Often, working in the kitchen is the first job a migrant person takes when he or she arrives, because there is no need to know the language there. In those months, Patrick's pay was around eight hundred euro a month for doing up to sixty hours a week. It took four years to get a proper contract and receive a salary of about 1,200/1,300 euros per month. In the restaurant industry, shifts are long and wages are low. For Patrick, however, the main problem was racism.

The chef does not want us to come here. And if we come here, we have to do what the Italians say. Every day when he arrived in the kitchen he would start venting, saying that someone in my community had done something wrong. I was working, but he was not interested in that. He would spend the day complaining about migrants. That's why I quit my job.

Patrick took a long time before admitting that there was a problem of racism in the restaurant. Refugee Welcome volunteer Claudia recounts that the chef forced Patrick to listen to the fascist song 'Faccetta nera'[17] and that he only paid respect to whites. According to Claudia, he flaunted an almost caricatured racism. When Patrick threatened to leave, he offered him a pay rise to keep him there – he knew Patrick was a good worker. The latter, however, declined.

I stayed there because I'm an immigrant, I don't have my father here, I don't have family, I don't have anybody, I can't go sleep out, I had no other choice. So I stayed there and left as soon as I could.

The right time came when they offered him an internship for five hundred euros a month for six months in a warehouse. At first, Patrick hesitated: he needed a full salary and five hundred euro a month was too little to live on.

Claudia recounts to me that they discussed this situation at length, trying to contextualize it and process it because otherwise, 'you are in the dark and you don't *fully grasp* what is at stake'. People say you need a financial cushion to quit. Often, however, what it takes is to know that you are not alone.

> My instinct was to tell the chef to fuck off but then we had to mediate, because he had to have a job and so I advised him to visit the union to at least understand what his rights were. When they offered him an internship he took the risk. After all, he took the risk of jumping on a boat to cross the Mediterranean Sea, how can we expect him to be afraid to change jobs?

Claudia's words are important. Quitting a job is always frightening, but sometimes we underestimate the determination of the precarious class and its hunger for justice. Patrick is now a warehouse worker. It is hard work but the contract conditions, the shifts and the pay are better. He doesn't have to work on weekends and he doesn't have to put up with racism. The company has also hired him full-time after only two months of apprenticeship even though the latter was supposed to be six. 'I am better off', says Patrick. 'If I need one day off they give it to me. We work to also be happy. If I wake up in the morning and I'm already pissed off, what am I working for?'

That of Patrick is a story of redemption that has a positive outcome. It is not uncommon, however, that work in the restaurant industry, for migrants, consists of racism and exploitation. It is not uncommon to find wages of five hundred euros a month for sixty, seventy hours a week. Nor is it rare to find customers who do not like their dishes being prepared by 'foreign' hands, or managers who admit immigrant employees in the kitchen but not in the dining room, because they do not want them in contact with customers. And so in Italian kitchens there is often a *de facto* segregation, where racism and exploitation are swept under the rug.

Recently, studies focusing on abuses taking shape in the hospitality and restaurant industry have taken on alarming tones. Low wages, precariousness, staff shortages, inexperienced managers and gruelling shifts reveal a chaotic work culture often driven by harassment. What really describes these cases is mobbing—a brutal, primal logic that bases internal order on hierarchy and force. This is how, in times of tension, the kitchen uses fear and punishment to restore order, in line with what happens in a military context. It is not surprising that the restaurant industry has been at the centre of an intense international debate in recent years that attempts to understand the causes of mental health problems within it.

b. Working to exhaustion

Recently, the Order of Psychologists of the region of Lazio and the Italian Association of Taste Ambassadors have published the first research on mental health and work-related stress in the restaurant industry in Italy. The results of the survey, administered before and during the pandemic, highlighted several critical issues. Among these, staff turnover was considered problematic by 80 per cent of respondents, lack of work-life balance (55 per cent), working hours that were too long (55 per cent), workloads that were too high (54 per cent), sleep disorders (54 per cent), as well as anxiety (40 per cent), sadness (38 per cent) and social isolation (35 per cent).

In the UK, the United Union had released similarly disturbing figures[18] before the pandemic, claiming that the restaurant industry is endangering the mental and physical health of its employees. Seventy-nine per cent of chefs said that they work so hard that they have had an accident, or have risked one, due to fatigue, 51 per cent said that they suffer from depression due to overwork, 69 per cent reported that the hours negatively affect their health, and almost a third (27 per cent) confessed to drinking alcohol to get through their shifts. In these cases, the burnout culture the union explained, creates stress, depression, illness and deaths at work.

In this perspective, deteriorating mental health, depression, stress and burnout are not a personal problem but a managerial responsibility.

A dysfunctional governance creates mental health problems, burnout, emotional exhaustion, low satisfaction, low productivity and undermines the functioning of the organization. A report by the Order of Psychologists and the Italian Association on Taste Ambassadors:

> The 'burnout' so often reported by restaurant industry workers is to a large extent the effect of organisational rather than personal issues. According to psychology, personal issues never occur 'in isolation', but are always located within networks of interpersonal relationships and within the regulation processes that govern these networks, which escape the abstract rationality of the organisation and respond to the real, informal organisation, often driven by unspoken dynamics that override official rules.[19]

What is happening in the restaurant industry is also, and perhaps above all, a subject of discussion among workers, especially those who are trying to bring virtuous practices into the sector.

This anonymous letter sent to the Order of Waiters and Chefs à la Carte (Occca) founded in 2015 by Marco Natali – an exemplary attempt to create a community of professionals capable of giving voice to the reforms needed in the restaurant industry – is one of the many accounts of burnout that constellate the industry:

Hi Occca.

I am in the burnout phase, I have been working in the same restaurant for five years, my girlfriend and I run the restaurant as employees. We're completely burnt out — coming home utterly drained every night. We are both about to resign because we want to get our lives back. Back to playing sports, being with family, going out with friends, going to the cinema, watching a movie together without staying up till 4 am and then waking up dead tired to go to work. We love this job but unfortunately our life is *falling apart*. At this point I ask you: Am I right to change jobs?! Will I miss this job?! Do you think it is better to do a decent job that allows you to live or to continue living like this?[20]

A few months ago, journalist Lavinia Martini reported on similar stories.[21]

30 years spent in the restaurant industry, an inhuman life. Twelve years ago I managed to break out of that hell, I started living again. Just the idea of going back to the kitchen gives me the shivers, I still have nightmares about that job.

And this anonymous one:

After years in the industry I had started realising that the mental commitment, not so much the physical one, was unmanageable. Over the last few months my hands were shaking like the sheets of a newspaper, I had lost almost 10 kilos, my attention was waning more and more so I would cut myself, burn myself. I was crying every day until I realised I had to stop. I sat still and thought about it for at least six months, and then I looked for something else.

At present, the Italian restaurant industry seems to be experiencing a crisis of management and vision. For years, the lack of industrial policies has left the country in the grip of deindustrialization. In this context, the deterioration of mental health is frequently the sign of a world abandoned to itself, plagued by a very high risk of failure, and where the easiest solution, for too many restaurant owners, is to offload their costs and risks onto the workers.

c. Back to life

Andrea left the restaurant industry two years ago, after working for a long time as an executive chef in central Italy, with a salary that never earned him more than 5.60 euros per hour, often paid half on and half off the books. When he recounts that period, he speaks of a seven-day-a-week commitment, with shifts that could reach fifteen, sixteen hours a day, in often putrid board and lodging conditions, to the point that the cries of a colleague who found rats in the shower sounded like a colourful note. Andrea dwells on a hotel from which 'we all left', he says. In that hotel, he shared the kitchen with a man of Albanian origin, whom we shall call Lucio, who had been working twenty-four hours a day for 1100 euros a month for thirteen years.

Lucio, recounts Andrea:

did a tremendous job, and on his day off they would ask him to do work for free at the owners' place, as a favour. They tried to do this with me too. They asked me if I could go and do some work at the swimming pool, I told them I would bring my swimming costume. However, he felt already lucky enough to have a job. I told him, 'look, someone like you who knows how to do so many things will surely find something better'. I used to tell him that even though we are in Italy, where conditions are so bad, he shouldn't be afraid. But he was afraid of losing his job. He worked non-stop — and still, they kept piling on the pressure.

According to Andrea, the conditions were the same for everyone. The waitress in the dining room was constantly harassed by the boss, who put his hands all over her; Lucio was asked to pay for orders that came out wrong, to work harder to deserve the meagre pay they gave him. When I asked Andrea about the reasons for this sick taste for harassment, he replied:

It is counterproductive for the restaurant owner as well to do this, because everything works better if people can work properly. But instances like this happen systematically. The whole sector is badly organised. The employer will never admit it, but the moment you hire people off the books, you are aware that you are at fault, even if no one checks on it and so you are allowed to do it. But you are in the wrong, and you know it, and that, in my opinion, opens the door to a sequence of abuses. I remember, for example, that the owner of that hotel did not lift a finger, yet every morning she went round the rooms to collect the tips that people left. Tips should be given to the housekeeping staff. Instead she would steal the tips and confess it proudly, as if she had done something proper. Once you cross one threshold, then it's easy, you cross a second one, to reduce cognitive dissonance and see how far you can go.

In these cases, the workplace becomes a toxic environment.

The restaurant owner enjoyed putting everyone under pressure. He did it on purpose, somewhat sadistically. He would constantly put his hands on the waitress and when she came into the kitchen he would touch her butt. Until, at a certain point, I organised a silent revolution and after a year and a half we all left at once. Cora, the girl who worked as a waitress, remained in the restaurant business but changed place. Lucio got a job in a factory and now has a better salary than he did there.

Andrea himself left that hotel. During the pandemic, he managed to find a continuous collaboration in an NGO. With a contract of twenty hours per week he was paid 1100 euros per month. He said this with disbelief, as if having two days off a week had long been an inaccessible privilege for him. The fact that it was possible to work in a non-toxic and non-burdening way was something he no longer expected.

When the pandemic came, I found myself in absolute precariousness. As a seasonal worker, I managed to stay at most three years in the same place, but it was very difficult. The conditions were so harsh that at the end of each season, relationships soured. And between pots and slicers, my shoulders and back got wrecked.

When the pandemic arrived, I had to stop and ask myself what I had achieved over the years. I made a list. Disintegrated social life. After six or seven years as a seasonal worker, you don't even have a way to build a social life. At one point, I thought I'd be better off as a monk—because that's basically what my life looked like. So I asked myself: is it worth carrying on like this? No matter how tough things get, I'll never go back to that industry.

The pandemic was really hard on people in the restaurant industry. On the one hand, widespread labour informality made it difficult to access subsidies when hotels, bars and restaurants were closed. On the other hand, people used to working at a fast pace, can be destabilised when they stop. In these high-pressure jobs, you only notice the brutality once it stops—because the adrenaline keeps you going until then. In the restaurant industry, nicotine, coffee, alcohol, painkillers and narcotics are often used to relieve stress. The pandemic interrupted this.

> I needed to seek psychological support during those months and I still do. Maybe we were naive, fooled into thinking we'd all become MasterChef. There was a lot of media propaganda in this respect, and the result was disappointment. I invested in a sector where I hoped to find a decent situation but instead I never found it.

Some time ago, *the Economist* recounted the story of Steve, a young man who grew up as the only child of a wealthy family. High grades, a baseball team and an Ivy League scholarship had prepared him for the life he was destined for. 'It wasn't so much like I was doing all this great stuff, more like I was slotting into the role they'd already scripted for me'. Steve seems to live his entire existence in that character until, one fine morning, when his alarm clock goes off at 5.40 am, he turns it off, turns away and never shows up for work. We are not talking about the restaurant industry, in this case, but about a man who, at a certain point, breaks the mechanism of inertia that drove his life, and ceases to go back to work. 'His desire was a neglected muscle', writes psychoanalyst Josh Cohen[22] in recounting Steve's story. In his book entitled *Not Working: Why We Need to Stop*, Cohen reveals what happens in his practice when people like Steve seek his help: in many cases, his patients seem to delegate their life decisions to an autopilot until something forces them to take back control. There is no single reason why people quit, nor are these motives often comparable. The fundamental issue is that the body suddenly feels the urge to regain possession of its existence. Josh Cohen, not surprisingly, says that all these 'stories of confinement' are interrupted by a similar condition: *the urge to live.*

In Andrea's case, the decision stems from a simple cost-benefit analysis.

Benefits: a net of around one thousand five hundred euros per month, when it goes well.

Costs: no home, no family, a disintegrated social life, fifteen hours of work per day, crashed back and shoulders, zero prospects of future stability, no days off, permanent burnout and the obligation to start from scratch every year.

I challenge anyone, after years, to do otherwise.

In fact, in the cost-benefit calculation, every story is different.

d. Honey, where's the boss?

Susanna, a pastry chef, has a tiring career behind her, made of unpaid internships in starred restaurants and shifts of fourteen hours a day, of apprenticeships in world-famous pastry shops *filled with screaming and scoldings*, of endless shifts with catering companies that seem to be factories of undeclared work and illegality. Despite the environments in which she found herself – the latest being a catering company that demanded she worked strictly off the books with fifteen-hour shifts for €10 an hour — or €9, if you were a woman – Susanna says that the main problem was not wages, but the climate of toxicity and terror that pervades the industry. Susanna studied with prestigious chefs who were internationally admired, but so self-absorbed that would consistently exploit their apprentices. 'Everyone wants to be a chef, but at some point I realised that becoming a chef means that after being exploited all your life you start exploiting others', says Susanna. *Even people who love this job can't take it anymore.*

When I was beginning to write this book, I spoke at length with Giusi Palomba, author and translator,[23] who quit her job as a chef during the pandemic and decided to dedicate herself to writing.

For a long time she worked in the restaurant industry, first as a waitress and finally as a chef, with a career path that began in southern Italy, continued in Tuscany and ended in Barcelona. Giusi has a lucid, passionate and irreverent look at the problems that plague the restaurant industry. Being a woman in that environment, she says, is not easy. 'Cooking is considered to be a woman's business, but paradoxically chefs are almost all men'. One article summed up this issue in a few simple words: 'Honey, where's the boss?' Or: 'Do you know the chef? Is he in the kitchen?'[24]

For Giusi, the main problem in the restaurant industry is the 'logic of the transaction' that pervades the dining room, the idea that the customer pays for a service and that you are a complementary part of it.

> The logic is: I pay you for a service and I expect you to give something to me in return. This increases dramatically when it intersects with

the body of a racialised woman. The man goes into a complete frenzy over the possibility of exercising a minimal power over her body.

This is the case of Cora, which we mentioned earlier: the woman who, in Andrea's recounting, had to protect herself from her own boss. According to Giusi Palomba, it sometimes happens that the woman's body awakens a sense of nostalgia for an era where male dominance reigned supreme. 'It's like they're nostalgic for a time when they could harass women freely', writes an anonymous author in an article on 'Vice'.[25] Indeed, the few numbers we have on harassment in the restaurant industry are frightening.

According to a survey entitled *The Tipping Point,* 71 per cent of women working in the restaurant industry in the United States have experienced sexual harassment at least once.[26] The Equal Employment Opportunity Commission confirms that from the restaurant industry comes a higher rate of harassment complaints than from any other occupation.[27] A survey by the Hospitality management degree even reports that nine out of ten women have been subjected to sexual harassment at work.[28] In recent years, research has focused particularly on tip workers, the workers whose pay also depends, in part, on tips. Often, *tip* workers are the most exposed to harassment, to rude or sexist comments, to clients or employers who cannot resist the temptation to take advantage of the existing power imbalance.

Although it is largely normalized, the tipping system originated in the United States just after the Civil War, when slavery had been abolished but the supremacist culture then dominant refused to grant equal rights to minorities. Danny Meyer,[29] a well-known restaurant owner who advocated for the introduction of higher wages throughout the industry, recounts:

> The restaurant industry as well as the Pullman train car industry successfully petitioned the United States government to make a dispensation for our industries that we would not pay our servers, but it wasn't considered slavery because we would ask our customers to pay tips. And therefore no one could say they that were being enslaved.

In this context, it is not surprising.

The tip is the epitome of this logic of transaction and allows for the systematic abuse of devalued labour. For Giusi Palomba, these problems have long been underestimated.

In many TV shows, such as MasterChef, there is never any mention of the toxicity that exists in the restaurant industry. However, the sacrifice level is as high as the consumption of alcohol and painkillers. This means cocaine in clubs, *booze in bars* and paracetamol in kitchens. The problem is that with such strenuous shifts, you should take much better care of yourself. I was constantly switching jobs because of pain—exhaustion, sciatica, because they squeeze you to death if they can. It's much easier to leave than it is to get fired. Obviously, people with families have a harder time leaving, but even if you have a family, the hours you work prevent you from having a life. Where I worked, the afternoon shift ended at two in the morning and at three or four o'clock during weekends. In the morning you get up late, because you have so much adrenaline in your body, when you go to bed, that it takes some time before you go to sleep. So your life *ends up completely out of sync with the people you care about.* Meanwhile, you ignore the daily pain until it becomes normal. I remember a colleague who always had so much pain in her wrists, that she could no longer pick up frying pans, and she treated it all with paracetamol. *Painkillers numb it, but the pain doesn't leave just because you stop feeling it.*

As stated, Giusi Palomba left the restaurant industry during the pandemic.

Before the pandemic I was working as a full-time chef. Then I got sick and left. I took a part-time job in the mornings and I worked as a food and wine guide in the evenings. When the pandemic started, both jobs disappeared. Paradoxically, that dark moment was a breath of fresh air for me. I was able to stop for the first time in years. While people could not breathe because of the virus, I began to do so. *I still haven't wrapped my head around that paradox.* But it was then that I was able to find the strength to change my job. I realised that I could earn my living by writing and doing translations, and that it was the wildest dream I could have.

In recent years, various experiments have been launched to rethink the restaurant industry. For example, Fair Kitchens is working to make the sector fairer and more inclusive, focusing heavily on the training of restaurant owners and staff. The crisis in the restaurant industry is generating new visions of the profession, respectful of diversity, the environment and mental health, just as Harold Villarosa suggested. Perhaps the Great Resignation can become an opportunity to teach restaurant owners to find a more sustainable organizational model for their venues.

When I asked Susanna what she would do to improve working conditions in the industry, she listed three things.

1. More labour inspections to reduce undeclared work and create better working conditions.

2. Training courses for employers on how to treat employees, because you cannot have people shouting in your face and threatening your life, while you are making pastries.

3. Training staff: schools should dedicate a number of hours to teaching labour law, because those who work in the industry must be aware of their own rights.

Bringing staff up to standard, paying by the books for all the hours worked, ensuring that labour rights are respected: these small rules alone would improve working conditions in the restaurant industry and probably get to grips with the problem of staff shortages.

Instead of campaigning against those young people who allegedly don't want to work anymore, perhaps it is time to campaign against the pervasiveness of undeclared and unpaid work.

Chapter 6

HELL IS EMPTY AND ALL THE DEMONS ARE HERE. RESIGNATIONS IN RETAIL

1. A worthless piece of trash

I confirm these figures because I am one of them, I have just quit.
I have not worked in that retail store since November. A lot of
people have left alongside me and *in the last two years, turnover has
skyrocketed.*

This is Rose, a woman who worked for a long time as a sales agent
in the food department of a large grocery store, before resigning and
undertaking a training course to become a teacher. Now twenty-nine
years old, she started working in retail during her undergraduate
studies, and after graduation she continued. It is a common thing in
the business: students often start to work in the industry by chance,
because they need the money, and then continue due to lack of decent
alternatives.

In recent years, Rose has worked for three different department
stores with a permanent part-time contract of twenty hours per week.
For one reason or another, she has quit each of these times. In her
recount, large-scale retail is a tiring place to work, often with impossible
hours, no days off, weekends and holidays at work, which turn your life
into an eternal, interminable present.

Rose begins by describing her three years working for a multinational
company that has numerous outlets in Italy, each of which has a growing
turnover. In that company, she says:

all in all I wasn't too bad off because the shifts lasted half a day: the
morning shift started at six and ended at thirteen, the afternoon shift
went from thirteen until eight thirty.

Shakespeare, *The Tempest*.

While the shifts were manageable, the same could not be said of the work culture.

Rose usually worked in the food department, where she sold food products, took orders, made bread and used the slicer, a heavy monster that left bruises on her arms.

During the pandemic, on top of these rotas came the need to cover the shifts of sick colleagues.

> That week I had an argument with the manager because he said I was not fast enough. It was a very heated discussion. He argued that, in addition to being faster, I had to agree to work an extra ten minutes a day. I replied that it was OK for me to work an extra ten minutes a day, but he had to pay me, because nobody does anything for free. He is buying my work and I do not work for free.

After this quarrel, Rose was sent to a shop where there was a Covid outbreak. It was March 2020, the most difficult time of the pandemic.

> They sent me to work in an outlet where there was an outbreak of Covid, and didn't tell me anything. I was a worthless piece of trash. I get it - I said. You want to hurt me. I understand that you dislike me, but why send me to work in such a dangerous situation?

In those months, we operated in constant crisis mode. It was not uncommon for management to demand longer shifts, and in some cases to double them. Customers were nervous and aggressive, and there was a lack of masks, gloves, sanitizers and proper sanitization procedures; not to mention inadequate preparation to handle what was happening. And, on top of this, the company often asked to cover the absences of those on sick leave at other outlets, even though ministerial directives had prescribed the cancellation of business travel, in order to reduce the chances of contagion.

> There was general chaos, we had to work well over forty hours a week. We dealt with aggressive, panicked customers and we were all under great pressure. It was a really tiring situation.

Later on, the manager apologized for sending Rose to work in a grocery store where there was a surge of infections, adding that he had not been able to warn her of the risk 'because it was sensitive information'. The question, however, was not whether or not to inform Rose of the hazard she would be exposed to. It was not to expose her to it. By law, the employer has a statutory duty to protect the health, safety and welfare of employees, in line with the regulations for the prevention of accidents at work. But these proposals went unheeded.

According to a report published by the National Institute for Insurance against Accidents at Work (INAIL) in September 2022, essential workers faced higher risk of infection during those months. Between 2020 and 2022, there have been almost three hundred thousand reported infections, 2.6 per cent of which were in retail, while there have been almost one thousand reported fatal occupational accidents, 11.5 per cent of which were in retail.[1] Despite the risk of contagion, *cashiers* and *warehouse* workers made it possible for society as a whole to get by, while companies transferred the risks of the emergency onto them. 'It's not that we are afraid, we are terrified', stated one employee[2] in those days, 'when you are afraid it's because of something you know. But we don't know what we are up against, we are not used to working seven hours wearing a mask, we are not doctors, we don't know how to recognise the symptoms'. This sense of terror was exacerbated by the increasing number of workers on sick leave, while nobody explained why:

> The number of staff on sick leave has risen exponentially: in the supermarket where I work we are missing twenty people out of ninety. Are they sick? Are they afraid? Every day there is at least one colleague crying, or others who want to run away because they see endless queues, or who get palpitations from wearing face masks all those hours.

Rose recounts a similar story and recalls that nobody warned them when there was a new infection in the shop. Management's main concern was not to protect staff, but to prevent them from staying at home, leaving their shifts uncovered.

> The thing that made us most anxious was that when someone went on sick leave, no one warned you that a colleague had Covid, that maybe it would be better to get tested and stay under the radar. Nobody had to know anything. Infections had to be hidden, because employees would otherwise panic and stay at home. The principle was simple: they had to profit as much as possible. *Can we squeeze out more profit? Fine — let's do it.* You can't afford to stay at home, because otherwise I lose my profit. It's retail, there are no people, there is only profit.

In those days, fear that the pandemic would deprive people of the essential things they needed to survive, stormed the grocery stores, causing queues at the entrance, empty shelves, fights at the door.

They called it *apocalypse shopping*, the tendency to stock up on supplies in a panic, as if buying the last box of cereal on the market was the only way to survive. Psychologist Paul Marsden has spoken of *retail* therapy, to explain this phenomenon. According to Marsden, shopping therapy is an attempt to 'regain control' in a context of danger, even by doing unreasonable things such as buying toilet paper for a year. A study by sociologist Mayer[3] examined the consequences of this situation in grocery stores, showing how the obligation to face such risks on a daily basis without any adequate support contributed to the deterioration of the mental health of the employees. The testimonies speak of an insecure environment, which often became hostile, riddled with verbal and physical abuse, in which the only certainty was the need to work in order not to lose one's job, in a fear-driven coercion that almost always led to emotional or physical collapse.

> Verbal and sometimes physical abuse from customers, plus constant pressure and yelling from management, and the added stress of the last few weeks have brought me to a breaking point, causing me to lose my physical and mental balance.

A study by Roberta Valtorta, Cristina Baldisarri and Chiara Volpato, psychologists at Bicocca University,[4] emphasizes how working conditions in grocery stores led to a level of stress comparable to that in the healthcare sector. According to the authors, who surveyed a sample of 422 grocery store cashiers and warehouse workers during the pandemic, 'the outbreak of the coronavirus generated a mental health emergency in this group of workers'.

The survey highlights the link between burnout and dehumanization, and thus the impact on staff's mental health of feeling treated as a tool, which used to be the case at the time, when working hours doubled without warning and contagion became a risk to be taken in order to bring home the paycheck. In this context, dehumanization is the feeling of being at the mercy of corporate interests as mere pawns that can be moved as needed, with no possibility of keeping control.

'I feel treated as if I were a part of the till', said one worker. For Valtorta, Baldisarri and Volpato, the feeling of being dispossessed of one's existence and of the ability to refuse certain tasks and shifts has a negative impact on mental health. The results of the study confirm that 73 per cent of the staff experienced severe or major psychological distress: 32 per cent of the respondents showed symptoms of severe burnout, 41 per cent showed symptoms of exhaustion and cynicism.

It is interesting how Rose uses terms that are very similar to those used in this research. Rose said she felt like a worthless piece of trash as a result of the way she was moved from one shop to another, regardless of her will and of the hazard. Towards the end of the interview, she also made it clear that, for her, the worst thing about retail was the feeling of being annihilated as a person.

> In big retail we all quit for the same reasons. The worker practically does not exist.
>
> Employees are just working machines: they have to work and possibly stay put. The question also arises with regard to rotas, because rotas are the first form of respect for employees, because if you don't allow me to rest, I can't live. I cannot live if I finish work at 8 pm and have to go home and choose whether to eat, shower or sleep for eight hours because then at 5 am I have to wake up again to be in the shop at 6 am. The most unbearable thing was to be considered as an object, not as a person with needs. You have to be like a mere machine, stripped of any emotional drive.

After being transferred to the hazardous store, Rose asks to be sent to a different outlet. In the new place, however, conditions are no better.

> The store manager was the closest thing to a Nazi I have ever met. I had minor arguments with his partner, who worked in a different shop and insulted employees. In the mornings he would say to me 'you're ugly', 'the little communist has arrived', he would comment how I dressed, he would say I was arrogant. He didn't do this only with me: he used to psychologically bully the weaker girls and told them they couldn't do anything. Then said to a gay colleague: 'People like you are not to be trusted because you are all thieves'.

a. Little tyrants

'One day I was at work, I forgot to take out my earrings'. The manager started shouting 'The earrings, the earrings! Shame on you, the earrings'. For those working in the food department, food safety regulations require that no earrings, necklaces, rings, bracelets or watches should be worn, because they prevent thorough body and hand hygiene, as the HACCP (Hazard Analysis and Critical Control Points) control manual recites. It is true that Rose should not have worn earrings. However, the shouting and verbal aggression went well beyond the pretext and reflected a work culture that aims to control employees through harassment and threats. For Rose, the climate in that grocery store 'was one of pure terror'. The manager told her that she had to 'take a bath in humility'; that she and her colleagues should not make fools of him 'because you know what I'll do to you, I'll fire you in two days', and again: 'I am the law in here and you are nobody'.

In recent years, there has been much discussion of toxic culture in the workplace. In general, the term 'toxic culture' refers to a variety of causes, which include an environment where bullying, shouting and discrimination are the norm. Toxic culture, however, doesn't necessarily indicate a circumstantial or incidental condition resulting from problematic personalities. Often, toxic culture is a form of work organization whereby companies try to discipline employees. In some cases, one of the aims of toxic culture is to force employees to accept long hours and gruelling shifts, in order to squeeze the staff as much as possible and cut personnel costs.

Rose's recount recalls exactly this kind of purpose.

> The store manager used to keep an eye on me all the time. Every time I did a job, he would check if I had done it correctly. The supervisor would constantly put me under pressure and tell me: 'you have half an hour to do this', even if they took an hour and a half. It went on like this for months until, at a certain point, I was in despair.

According to Rose, the store manager exercised a form of control over all employees by shouting and threatening them in order to put them under pressure and increase revenues.

> For this reason he was very popular with the company because he had a very high revenue level. He squeezed people to the bone, until they were forced to resign or go to hospital because they couldn't take it anymore. That was the reason why that character was achieving very high results. However, recently he was forced to leave after 30 years of service. Maybe the company realised that he was the reason for the huge number of resignations.

Often, bullying has negative consequences on the mental health of the persecuted person, who is induced to feel inadequate, incapable and worthless. It is not uncommon for victims of psychological violence to end up suffering from post-traumatic stress disorder, a clinical condition characterized by psychological and emotional bruising, or to be deeply affected by the toxic environment in which they are immersed. In fact, it is very common for the retail sector to hit the headlines because of episodes aimed at mortifying workers, often forcing them to surrender to conditions far different from those stipulated by the law. For example, a scandal broke out at a grocery store in Pescara on 14 April 2022, when the store manager sent a voice message on WhatsApp to the employees, asking for the first and last name of the person who was on her menstrual cycle and threatening: *Or I'll drop her panties!*, in order to find out who had forgotten a tampon in the bathroom.

The affair was reported to the Filcams CGIL union, following the decision of the supervisors to draw up a list of the names of the women on duty that day, based on which they then carried out a body search in the toilets, forcing the employees to remove their trousers to prove that they were not menstruating. Immediately after the incident, the female employees who came forward and reported it to the union were afraid, because it was clear that the problem was not confined to the manager, but extended to the shop's supervisors, who were looking for both the woman who was guilty of *menstruating* and the one who had dared to report it. Interviewed by the national TV Channel RaiNews, one worker admitted that she was now afraid to use the bathroom.

> The employees were also looking for the offender in the following days, so much so that the bathrooms had to be permanently closed and we could only use another bathroom dedicated to customers or one where there is no *privacy* because it is a shared man/woman bathroom. [...] I am afraid because now there is a man-hunt for the person who dared to talk.[5]

Following the complaint, the retail chain Conad, which is the largest association of independent entrepreneurs in the Italian Food Retail sector, decided to discontinue its partnership with the store manager and to protect the employees. The incident, however, highlighted the wide range of vexations that pervaded the store. The store manager, in fact, was not new to this type of violence. In the past, her employees had documented how she controlled them, prevented them from using the bathroom and tried, in some cases, to push them to resign.

> I'll make your life in here hell if it's the last thing I do. You know me. I will not fire you, I will not pay your unemployment for two years. You will crawl out. You will crawl out, you 40-year-old little fool. If you have an ounce of dignity, go away first.[6]

It appears that cases such as this one do not refer to a simple 'moment of anger', as the store manager said in her own defence, but to real *government practices*, through which the management of a given business attempts to annihilate the resistance of the staff and to undermine a relationship of solidarity between the employees, so as to block workers from exercising their rights (such as sick leave, paid overtime and decent rotas, to name a few). The question to be answered is how deep and widespread these abuses run and how much they reflect the current way of organizing work in the retail sector.

b. Rituals of humiliation

One of the most interesting books on the subject is *Nickel and Dimed. On (Not) Getting By in America*, by Barbara Ehrenreich, published in the early 2000s.

In this text, the author documented, among other things, the working conditions in the world's largest retail store: Walmart. In the text, Ehrenreich spoke explicitly about *rituals of humiliation*: the practice that consists in humiliating employees and making them believe that they do not deserve anything good from life. 'My guess', says Ehrenreich in Nickel and Dimed:[7]

> is that the indignities imposed on so many low-wage workers – the drug tests, the constant surveillance, being 'reamed out' by managers – are part of what keeps wages low. If you're made to feel unworthy enough, you may come to think that what you're paid is what you're worth.

Barbara Ehrenreich's insight in this context is crucial. Not rarely, in fact, anyone studying retail is stunned by the disproportion that exists between the glossy image of the sector and the vastness of the malaise of those who work in it. Trade unionist Francesco Iacovone *describes various forms of workplace humiliation in this sector.*

When I talk to him, he tells me about a fellow cashier who was not informed about her mother's death until the end of her shift, for fear that she would leave it uncovered; about sick members of staff who are denied time off to attend a doctor's appointment; about shop assistants who are forced to pee in a bucket because management does not give them bathroom breaks during their shift. Ehrenreich, in turn, addressed similar issues in her book, highlighting the frequency of such incidents, starting with the denial of bathroom breaks. Bernard

Lown, a doctor at the Harvard School of Public Health, commented on this practice with 'disbelief and anger'[8] as the denial of bathroom breaks not only creates physical and psychological harm but leads to the degradation of human beings. In many ways, this is the secret of harassment. As difficult as it may seem to comprehend the logic of certain practices, the frequency of these rituals is such that we are forced to consider how, in some cases, the power to humiliate staff seduces employers. Humiliation rituals do not require a particular strategy. They leverage on the power imbalance that structures the workplace to annihilate staff.

In fact, having a boss is the most unnatural thing in the world, one worker told me.

> Anything that is normal outside the workplace is not normal inside of it, because you are in a condition of limited freedom: freedom of speech is limited, freedom of movement is limited. It is a violent matter, which you can tolerate only because of the paycheck and because there is some residual protection of the workers, but it is unnatural that there is a person who is equal to you before the law but is above you in reality. I think about this a lot: there is something inhumane at work that rarely gets acknowledged.

Harassment is an easy way to remind everyone of their place. Humiliation, in fact, undermines self-esteem. For a long time, these practices have been difficult to substantiate and effective in disciplining employees, leading them to accept low wages, long hours and gruelling shifts. It was a *win-win* solution that enabled the creation of workplaces in which staff was so scared and obedient, that fear could be used to increase profits. This continued until wages became so low that it was no longer worth it. And the workers started to quit.

2. An inhuman schedule

In Rose's interview, the theme of harassment kept returning. The problem was not just working seven days a week, Sundays and holidays included, without ever having a real break. It was being at the mercy of the store manager, as if the very possibility of increasing revenues depended on his ability to squeeze staff. Rose's case is interesting, because after quitting her job, she had no better luck in the next retail chain.

In this case, Rose had a permanent contract of twenty hours per week: a rather frequent condition in the retail business. Sociologist Ivana Fellini called it 'the poisoned product of the great recession',[9] pointing out that involuntary part-time contracts were the solution that many companies found to the drop in demand that followed the recession of the early 2000s. A report by the Ente bilaterale nazionale terziario,[10] which looks specifically at big retail, shows how in January 2015 there was a very strong growth in part-time contracts, which transformed precarious services into permanent contracts with a limited number of hours per week, thanks to the contribution waivers granted by the Financial Stability Act of 2014 and by the slight signs of growth that year.

Since then, the use of part-time work has been high. In most cases it has been involuntary part-time. According to the Italian Statistics Institute (ISTAT) annual report 2022,[11] 60.9 per cent of part-time contracts in 2021 were involuntary and involved primarily people who could not find full-time employment opportunities. The problem is that the widespread use of involuntary part-time, especially among young people and women, creates a condition of vulnerability, whereby in order to earn the right amount of money, one must be ready to be available *all the time*.

This is what Rose did, in a condition that translated into messy rotas and fluctuating shifts, made it impossible to plan her life. In addition, Rose could not escape working on Sundays or filling any uncovered shifts. As a result, during this period, she often worked for fifteen consecutive days without any time off. Her shifts started at 6.30 am and ended at 8.30 pm, with a long break in the middle, which forced her to choose, once she returned home in the evening, whether to sleep for eight hours, have dinner, or shower, as it was not possible for her to do all the three.

> It was inhuman. My working hours were 6.30–11.30 and 16.30–20.30, so I didn't even have an eleven-hour break between shifts, and many times I would miss my day off, so I worked fifteen days in a row. Overtime wasn't asked of you but simply assigned to you, you had to do forty-five hours a week, but you could even do fifty hours, while days off were constantly cut. At a certain point I could no longer manage these shifts, I no longer had a life.

It was also necessary to limit the days of sickness, so as not to become the target of criticism and suspicion.

I only happened to be on sick leave once, when I got Covid, but I tested positive in the promotional week offering 10% off groceries; so the workload had grown. Unfortunately I was positive on those very days. A colleague texted me, saying that I had done it on purpose because I didn't want to work. 'You see, she's home sick and you have to cover her shift: it's her fault!' they said in the grocery store. It was a war among the poor, their *goal was to pit workers against one another* because if we were busy waging war against each other, no one would look up to the crappy boss we had.

There is a logic to all this. As explained by the general secretary of the union Uiltucs, Paolo Andreani, in a recent interview with the newspaper 'la Repubblica',[12] over the years management decided that the work schedule had to be adapted to the flow of customers, so it required the presence of more workers at opening and closing times, and very long breaks throughout the day'.

In this context, time management fell totally in the hands of the company. As trade unionist Francesco di Martino stated, 'in the case of part-time hires, there are a thousand time slots that can be changed with as little as forty-eight hours' notice, which erodes the ability to have a second job, not to mention work-life balance'.[13] The inability to manage one's own time is one of the most criticized factors for those working in retail, who often find that they have no control over their shifts, or over their lives.

Annalisa Dordoni[14] has worked extensively on the consequences of the deregulation of working conditions approved by the Monti government, showing how the liberalization of Sunday openings introduced in 2011 forced staff to work on weekends and holidays and created great discontent.

Such was the case with Rose, who went on as long as she could and then, when they called her in on a Sunday morning, tired of being at the mercy of schedules that changed every day and relentlessly forced her into a life consumed by work, she decided to quit. On that occasion she realized that her presence was unnecessary. They did not need her to cover the shift. In fact, they asked her to scrub the fridge. For Rose, forcing her to work on her day off meant that they had no respect for her need, at least once a week, to do laundry and rest. It was at that point that she gave notice of her resignation, to regain a minimum amount of control over her life.

Rose was not the only one.

In early 2023, a long article in the newspaper *La Stampa*[15] dwelt on the deteriorating working conditions in retail.

The article was inspired by the experience of interns, who work for forty hours a week, seven days a week, for just over five hundred euros a month, earning barely two to three euros per hour. Between internships and apprenticeships, such remunerations are increasingly common. It is not uncommon to find people doing heavy work for five or six hundred euros a month. In fact, the combination of involuntary part-time and underpaid work has brought to the surface the pervasiveness of exploitation in retail.

In 2021, the conviction for manslaughter of the president of the Elpe[16] cooperative, a logistics giant responsible for recruiting employees to fill warehousing and shelving jobs for grocery stores and hypermarkets, sparked public outrage.

The investigation had been opened after a young woman, Chiara Riccomagno, lost her life during a car accident in 2015, at the end of a nineteen-hour shift. 'Chiara had been working at Elpe since April 2015 with a permanent part-time contract for eight-hour a day and a blue-collar status', wrote Christian Raimo in a 2016 investigation, which brought the facts to light.[17]

In that case, investigations revealed widespread exploitative practices based on very long shifts, marked by harassment and coercion, as well as starvation wages.

In recent months, resignations have alternated with strikes and labour disputes in the sector, showing cases of people forced to mop up outside and inside the store, including the parking lot and bathrooms, at the end of their shifts, often in conditions of insecurity;[18] of employees, as happened in Tropea, in the region of Sicily,[19] reduced to sleeping in their cars because they were transferred to a venue so far away that they did not have the time or money to go home; of hostile acts against union representatives or union members,[20] of migrants paid a few euros an hour to fill shelves in situations *often toeing — or crossing — the line of legality.*[21]

Online there are hundreds of stories of women and men who flee hypermarkets and grocery stores because of insecurity, low pay and abusive practices.

In the Italian region of Lazio:

Shifts from 6.30 a.m. until 9 p.m., with a two-hour lunch break in the middle. Unpaid overtime, inhuman shifts, toxic working environment, but it is understandable since everyone is locked in there without any normal life. Forget what they tell you at interviews and look elsewhere for a job, don't let yourself be exploited.[22]

In the region of Southern Italy, Calabria:

Low wages, exploitation guaranteed. You have no role, they put you where they need you. Good colleagues, but victims of this power, because either you do as they say or you're out. Beware of asking for raises. I chose to quit rather than be exploited. 7 hours of work for €480 is a disgrace. And split between the till and the department, there were days I couldn't even get up to drink water. I strongly advise against this company[23]

In the region of Southern Italy, Campania:

Hired as a cashier with a contract of 18 hours per week but actual work was 60 hours. In addition to the till you had to clean, wash the floor and restock the shelves. Positive aspects: none. Negative aspects: very bad management and work organisation.[24]

In Friuli, a region in the North-East of Italy:

Workers are subjected to continuous stress, the work-life balance announced during the interview was totally disregarded, the customer is your enemy is the motto, I was shocked at how it is organised. I quit after two months.

Again, in Friuli:

It is the worst place in which I have ever worked. Colleagues and lazy managers blaming others, constant gossip, tensions as if they were surgeons saving lives. Never again, I didn't even want to get up in the morning knowing I had to go there![25]

Reports such as these span from North to South, from big retail to small shopkeepers. In some cases, workers use terms such as 'pure slavery'[26] or 'get out while you can'.[27] Among the small shopkeepers, on the other hand, the case of Francesca,[28] a young woman from Secondigliano who turned down a job offer as a shop assistant, for two hundred and eighty euros per month, in a small shop where she was asked to work ten-hour shifts, Monday to Saturday, for a total of seventy hours per week with an hourly wage of around one euro per hour, has gone viral. There is no doubt that there are many decent working contexts in Italy where employees are well off. It is from the places described here, however, that we have to start in order to understand why people quit.

3. Something has broken

Today I summoned up the courage and at the end of my shift I went to the manager and handed in my resignation. I'm leaving a permanent job because I'm fed up with nagging, exhausting shifts, disrespectful customers, Sundays (three out of four a month) spent working there and away from my family. When I got home, I cried, out of fear, out of anger at how until the last moment they had acted like shit, making me feel that 'there are many out there ready to take your place'. But I also cried from a sense of liberation. I don't know what lies ahead of me, whether it will be for the better or for the worse, but I do know that if I had stayed, I would have gotten sick. I had stopped smiling; at home they couldn't stand seeing me like that. I still have sixteen days left after my notice. Perhaps they will be the longest. But I will live them with the spirit of a soldier waiting for his final discharge.

Anne quit her job in August 2022. She was a cashier with a permanent contract. She worked until 8.30 pm, including Sundays and holidays, and could not spend as much time as she wanted with her family.

I practically lived in there. Even the customers made fun of me, saying: 'But did you sleep here?' At home they never saw me, and when I came back, as soon as I sat down I couldn't get up because my swollen legs hurt, sometimes I felt like crying and felt that my body was leaving me, other times I wanted to get down on my knees to rest my legs a bit.

In the final months, Anne had been losing her hair, couldn't sleep at night, and had constant cystitis, sciatica and tendonitis. She had been intending to quit for a long time but was afraid of the consequences. As is often the case in these situations, certain decisions drag on for months, and for a long time they leave people trapped in an inner conflict in which there is, on the one hand, the fear that quitting would jeopardize the family's economic security and, on the other, the fear that staying would ruin one's own health. Workers feel cornered. One evening at the end of her shift Anne went to her boss and gave her notice. She had no other job in sight, nor had she planned to hand in her resignation. For some reason, the moment had come. In the days that followed, Anne confesses that she felt

> a myriad of conflicting states of mind, due to my fear of quitting a permanent contract, which makes you feel like you are in a forced and timeless prison, and which gradually wears down your soul and mind, and invariably affects your body. In addition to the scattered pain in my back, legs and shoulders, I had conspicuous hair loss, insomnia, constant cystitis, intestinal blockages, dull skin … wrinkles on my face that added at least eight years. And so you look in the mirror and no longer recognise yourself.

In August 2022, Anne's story had gone viral on social media, generating a long series of comments from people in similar situations.

> Exactly one year ago I quit. I was getting sick in the serious sense of the word. I am 55 years old, separated with a daughter at university. The spirit of survival took over and overcame fear and uncertainty. I scraped by with dozens of odd jobs that I managed with my schedule and am now paying for a course in cutting and sewing. I am going to learn a new job and *make it my own: I'll become a seamstress.* Finally, I am smiling again.

A man who is now a real estate consultant:

> I have taken the same decision a year ago and to this day the quality of my life has been priceless. […] I definitely work longer hours than before as a real estate consultant, but I work from home and manage my clients in peace. There is no more being humiliated and mortified, I had to undergo back surgery because of the amount of work I had before, between the warehouse, the sales area and the cashier. The warehouse slaughtered me with four hernias, today *I still regret not telling the area manager off.*

Another one who now works as an educational aide in schools:

> I did the same thing in July after four years in retail, I spent my notice days at home on sick leave. It's the best choice I've ever made. In

October I started a training program to become an educational aide in schools. I don't know where this will take me, but I know one thing for sure: I'm happy now and I hope I will NEVER have to work in the retail sector again.

One last person also observed that things are changing.

People are no longer lining up to take your place. It is becoming more and more difficult to find qualified workers. Be it for the gruelling shifts or for the mediocre salaries. Something has broken. And if we go on like this it will get to the point that nobody will want to work in retail anymore.

According to trade unionist Francesco Iacovone, resignations in retail have become common in recent years, due to the weakness of labour unions and to the solitude of workers. Today, the malaise in the sector has become so palpable that union organizers receive more phone calls from workers intending to quit than asking for advice on a case of redundancy. An article on these issues, published in 2018 on his blog, received around six hundred comments, twenty of which addressed cases of redundancy, while the others asked for advice on how or when to give a resignation notice. Among Italian retail and food store chains, Esselunga is one of the few to have commented on their voluntary resignation figures. For instance, the consolidated financial report for the year 2021[29] shows a growing trend, which leads the company to pay attention to 'the implementation of remuneration and *retention* policies, to the development of welfare policies in line with international standards, as well as through information, training and organisational development activities'. The company also notes that:

the upward trend in voluntary resignations of workers (in many cases without looking for another job, re-evaluating priorities related to well-being and work-life balance) has led to a significant drop in applications and a relative imbalance between supply and demand.

This transparency is not common. The impression is that companies do not like to share data on voluntary turnover. Perhaps this is because voluntary turnover is almost always a litmus test of organizational problems that manifest themselves in the inability to retain staff. Nevertheless, different analyses reflect similar concerns. In 2022, the seventeenth edition of the Marketing & Retail Summit brought to light that 73 per cent of companies report a skills shortage; that 90 per cent of employers admit that there is growing competition in attracting staff; and that 57 per cent of those working in retail say they are not adequately considered.[30]

For its part, research by the Fida Observatory[31] explains that in the last two years, one in three companies in the food distribution sector, particularly grocery stores and convenience stores, have had to look for new professional staff, especially sales counters (68.1 per cent), cashiers (58.5), butchers (42.2) and shelf stockers (39.3). About half of the companies (47 per cent) experienced difficulties in finding the personnel they needed, which had a negative impact on revenues. Among the main reasons for this shortage were a shortage of personnel with the required skills (64.1 per cent), long working hours (40.2) and unattractive tasks (31.3). Even the Eurospin Ceo[32] stated in October 2022 that: 'in the fifty years that I have been an entrepreneur, I have never encountered so many difficulties in finding staff for the shops and especially in logistics, which in our case is almost entirely outsourced'.

In general, the staff shortage in retail does not depend so much on a lack of expertise but on the inability to retain them. This is shown by the INPS Annual Report, from which we can see that, three months after the resignation date, excluding workers over sixty, the outplacement rate was 64.53 per cent, which means that only two-thirds of the resigning workers had another contract. If we look at the balance between incoming and outgoing redeployments, moreover, we see that it is negative, which means that those who quit to work in other areas outnumber those who redeploy in the same sector. In retail as in the restaurant industry, therefore, resignations often conceal a process of disaffection, which leads staff to quit even if they have no alternative. The problem is not the absence of expertise but the inability to offer conditions that prevent people from quitting.

Recently a study by Axonify and Nudge, a Toronto-based consultancy working with major North American retail brands, showed how this trend is in line with what is happening overseas. The report makes it explicit, moreover, that among the causes of this disaffection is what we might call the 'great misalignment'. In the *Deskless Report*,[33] Axonify and Nudge points out that, in North America, 42 per cent of employees in the industry wanted to quit their jobs in 2022 compared to 37 per cent in 2021: overseas, therefore, the so-called *quitting* intention increased in 2022. The study, based on a survey of managers and workers, pointed to an interesting reason for this crisis: the misalignment between what company leaders consider important and what is important to workers. Big retail is a stellar example of what we discussed at the beginning of this text, that is, the attempt to build the loyalty of workers and consumers by stimulating *brand love*, also thanks to uniforms, caps and T-shirts: a love for the company that can turn the brand into a big family. What workers need is something else, the report says: an adequate salary; the possibility to plan shifts and time off; decent and consistent hours and income. Instead, as one of the interviewees explains, companies 'try to get people excited about things they are not interested in.'[34] This misalignment is dragging the industry close to a breaking point. After all, why should employees care about the brand if they are denied bathroom breaks or can't afford to call in sick? When part of their salary is used to pay for a psychologist to cushion the traumatizing impact of bullying, or when the company's profits increase even though wages are stagnant? These sound like extreme situations, but unfortunately, they are the daily occurrence for too large a proportion of employees in the retail sector.

Chapter 7

THE 'SHE-SESSION'

1. It is not you, it is the organization

One of the most striking aspects of this research was the pervasiveness of discriminatory experiences. Rose, for example, recounted that it was normal for her to receive sexist jokes at work.

> Sometimes I thought: 'What did I do wrong to deserve this?' The answer was simple: I was a woman. They told me explicitly: you are good, but you will never have a career here. Not that it was my intention, but it was unbearable. I also had customers telling me: 'I don't want my ham sliced by a woman', so in addition to the discrimination from the management, there was also discrimination from the customers.

Sole quit her job at the grocery store because the store manager told her that, as a woman, she could not advance professionally, but had to stay at the till and could not even aspire to stock the shelves.

Unfortunately, cases of horizontal and vertical segregation are not isolated. As Mediobanca's Research Area[1] shows in detail, while women make up a similar proportion of the workforce in Italy and abroad (62.9 per cent and 58.3 per cent of the total, respectively), the share of women in managerial positions abroad is close to 40 per cent, in Italy it is 17 per cent. When WalMart's employees decided to sue the corporation in 2001 for its discriminatory practices, the numbers were not far off. On that occasion, Associate Justice Ruth Bader Ginsburg said that gender bias permeated its entire corporate structure. 'If you're not a man, you can't get on', said female employees, as they complained that they were excluded from promotions given to their male colleagues, many of whom had less experience.

Sole recounts very similar things:

> In a grocery store there is an internal hierarchy. The shelf-stockers

stand outside to load the products and when there is a queue at the checkout they are called to help the cashiers. This follows a hierarchy. For example, if you have been working there for ten years you are the last one to be called to the checkout, on the other hand if someone was hired yesterday, they will be called first, because they have to work their way up.

After three years working at the grocery store, Sole was convinced that she had moved up the hierarchy. Instead, the last newcomer was given more seniority than her. When she asked for explanations, the answer was always the same:

The manager will never let you overtake boys, because you are a woman, and they are men. He has an old mentality, they would tell me, and if they need help at the checkout, women go first, full stop. And I'm sorry if the new guy can do one fortieth of what you can do, you're a woman.

In an article in the *Washington Post*, economist Heidi Hartmann proposed analysing retail as a segregated industry. 'There's basically sex segregation within the retail industry', she wrote.[2] Women are working as cashiers in the food and clothing department and in discount stores, that is, in all low-paid positions. Men hold management position or work as salespeople in sectors with higher commissions, such as cars and electrical appliances. And then there are the racialized workers, who enter the shops at night only to leave at the crack of dawn, after stocking the shelves, thanks to the intermediation of shady cooperatives. Finally, are those who work along the entire supply chain, in conditions bordering on slavery, as Stefano Liberti and Fabio Ciconte showed.[3] White men at the top, women at the checkout and racialized workers in the supply chain: this set-up well describes big retail.

I was naive enough not to know that there was still this disparity between men and women, I really didn't expect it. I was convinced that, in 2022, when a woman doesn't make it, maybe it's because she doesn't try hard enough or doesn't deserve it. Instead, when I entered this company, I realised that patriarchy still exists. I had no idea it was so heavy and so pervasive, it had never happened to me. It traumatised me.

Because of that episode, Sole resigned.

I handed in my resignation. Then I called the store manager and said, 'look this is my last day'. It had been two weeks since the episode at the checkout. Twenty per cent of us have quit since the beginning of the year. So many leave due to the mismanagement of rotas and shifts. They may prefer to work at a factory, because they work Monday to Friday on single shifts and can spend the weekend at home. My main problem was misogyny. When I made up my mind, none of the hundred or so people working in that grocery store, not even one, told me 'are you sure?', 'think about it', 'look it's OK here.' Women and men, young or old, told me the same thing: go away, get out of here. I didn't know that patriarchy still existed. I learned it firsthand and I had the courage to quit, but many of my colleagues are still there because they have a child and they are afraid that they won't find anything else.

Sole is right: working women in Italy are still experienced as a nuisance, a problem, a cost, a risk in the workplace. It is common for them to be viewed with suspicion, treated as a threat, kept under surveillance and guarded as a danger.

The store manager once told me: if you ever want to have a career here, you must forget about having children. And you can never basically do anything wrong. He did not say this as a threat. He said so to help me, to warn me that the road was going to be uphill.

In her recent book, Alessandra Minello helps to frame the problem.[4]

According to data from the 2014–2017 Eurobarometer, a large segment of people in our country still thinks that the child suffers when the mother works, that if there are limited vacancies it is men who have to fill them so that women can stay at home to look after the children, that women are better suited to do care work than men. 51per cent of the sample believed that the most important job for a woman is to take care of the house and the family. This traditional view distances Italy from the rest of European countries. The idea that deeply permeates its imaginary is that women are genetically predisposed for the role of primary caregivers, which influences the division of domestic work. Empathy, emotions and caring are still considered to be feminine traits.

According to Minello, a working woman is still considered to be an anomaly. In Sole's case, such bias was explicit, and shared by the employer. Companies, observes a report by the Ente Bilaterale Nazionale Terziario, in many instances 'are not an engine for change', but 'reiterate behaviour and organisational models that penalise women', and reproduce 'prejudices that are still strong in the world of work'.[5]

'I have heard managers wonder why they should invest money on their female employees when all they think about is what to cook for dinner', says a remark reported in this study.[6] So it is that 'exhausted working mothers show up at the union to inquire about quitting, because the maternity allowance is too little to keep the family going, or because the employer is asking to go back to work full time', stated Elisa Berbieri, general secretary of the union Filcams CGIL in Piacenza.[7] There are also women like Sole, who have no intention of having children but wonder why this should be her boss's concern before it is hers.

Gillian Tett, a *Financial Times* columnist who has a background in anthropology, explains how such cases mark a misalignment between new and old generations.[8]

For the younger generations, she writes:

According to one survey, money is an issue, but it's definitely not the only issue. 'Meaningfulness of work' and 'adequacy of workforce flexibility' around issues such as working from home are also front of mind. The key, it seems, is a sense of personal control, both to define how and where work happens, as well as how it aligns with workers' personal values. Some readers will wince at this. Others will view it as a short-term phenomenon that emerged during the pandemic. [...] Corporate managers might fret about the great attrition. But they cannot tackle it unless they try to understand Gen P – and recognise that this mindset shift will not disappear soon. Even if there is a recession.

For Tett, behind the great attrition there is an underlying economic concern, but there is also a radical value misalignment. Technology, consumerism and user profiling over the years have accustomed the new generations to personalizing everything, 'from our travel plans to coffee choices and, of course, the music we listen to', spreading the habit of shaping things to our liking instead of making us fit into a preset package. Tett calls them the 'playlist generation', used to shaping the world according to their own needs, far more so than they are willing to adapt to those of others. 'Unsurprisingly, it's now seeping into our attitudes towards work', the journalist writes. Tett's discourse may seem lateral to what we are saying, but it is not. Disruptive timetables, the demands of devotion and the request to spend all one's life at the grocery store are, for Sole, inadmissible requests. Even worse is being expected to perform a version of femininity that waned several decades ago for the sake of her boss's appeasement.

> Their problem is that they do not keep up with the times. Priorities have changed. If you tell them that, they say that when they worked there thirty years ago, they started at six o'clock in the morning and finished at 11 p.m. But I frankly don't give a shit about what they did.

Quite rightly, Sole doesn't care how devotedly her bosses worked thirty years ago. She doesn't care what they think about women. She wants to do her job for a certain number of hours and she wants to be paid for it.

> I am telling you that I want to do something with my life that goes beyond the one thousand three hundred euro a month, and I don't give a damn if thirty years ago you were so devoted to the company that you worked like a slave.

The disconnect between her and the company's expectations could not be more obvious. Sole's identification with work is, understandably, limited. For Sole, who now works as an athlete and as a personal trainer, staying at the counter all day was torture. The company, on the other hand, took it for granted that she should do so with devotion, and that she should be the submissive and underpaid cashier that her boss wanted her to be. Not surprisingly, Sole experienced her occupation as an assault on her own existence. Society demanded of her not just to *do* her job, but to *be* what was asked of her. Clearly, this was alienating. It is naive to think that the new generations, who have grown up in an era marked by #MeToo and Black Lives Matter, where online platforms and social media have enabled the shaping of narratives and worldviews, as a recent report by Deloitte consultancy acknowledges,[9] would accept being catapulted into a culture that was already archaic in the 1950s, in order to keep an underpaid job that has never been able to engage them. For Sole, such an arrangement was simply too costly. If you consider the costs and benefits of that job, the outcome was clearly negative.

> *Benefits:*
> – One thousand three hundred euros per month

Costs:
- Remember that you are a woman, if you want to grow professionally
- Be grateful that you have a job, if you want more flexible hours
- Should you aspire to have nice colleagues, get used to a lump of macho men who attack your physical and mental health on a daily basis
- And remember: if all goes well, you will be doing a job you hate forever

Clearly, the numbers don't add up. As soon as she quits, in fact, Sole rejuvenates.

Since I quit, I've been able to digest my lunch. Previously I was a walking corpse. My partner couldn't stand to see me like that any more. I was mean, nervous, depressed. I was in a state of chronic sadness. Just endless sadness. Before going to work, I would get anxious and start feeling bad. *I couldn't bear the thought of going back in.* I would get anxious and I couldn't think about anything else. I would even ruin my day off because, even on those rare times that I was home on a Sunday, I would suddenly start thinking that I had to work the next day, and it was a crippling feeling. I couldn't simply enjoy myself and think that tomorrow was another day. On a Sunday afternoon I would start thinking, oh God, tomorrow is Monday and I have to get up and go to work. It was a paralyzing sense of dread.

The misalignment of values, the different expectations, starvation wages, uninspiring work and the attempt to segregate women who are eager to grow are some of the ways in which a company sets itself up to lose staff.

2. Make a sacrifice: We chose you!

One of the first people to share her story with me was Luna, a freelance worker in the cultural industry, for whom the pandemic was a *perfect storm*. I had recounted her story in the Italian magazine *Internazionale* in 2022,[10] when the Great Resignation was still unfolding. Luna is a woman in her forties, with extensive knowledge in the field of publishing, who until the summer of 2021 worked for a publishing company. In that company, Luna was an anomaly.

I was the only one with small children and the only freelance worker. The cultural industry is a vale of tears, full of short-term contracts and underpaid jobs. It was essential for me to have a little freedom. Self-employment obviously offers no career progression or salary increases, but you can cope with a situation like mine, where you have a job and small children. In addition, my job entailed working with newspapers and often this means not having a fixed schedule and working on weekends. From this point of view, self-employment can be helpful, but it has turned into an abusive tool that exploits people without giving them anything in return.

Luna has been self-employed since 2015. Hers, however, was a typical case of bogus self-employment.

Employers use bogus self-employment to dodge their fiscal and legal obligations. In the world of culture, and particularly in publishing, this practice is very common. Luna, for instance, had to abide by the employer's rules regarding working hours and presence on-site. 'I used to open the office every morning', she says. Yet, she did not have any of the social and legal protections that normally protect employees. When the pandemic hit, the limits of this situation came to the surface.

I immediately felt at fault, even though I had done nothing wrong, because I did not have access to certain forms of protection and could not claim them because in some cases they did not even exist. It was as if they had asked working women: make the human sacrifice, we have chosen you.

During the pandemic, Luna's condition as a freelance worker prevented her from taking time off work, while she also found herself at the centre of different caring responsibilities, many of which she could not meet.

Then the pandemic struck close to home—my father contracted the virus at the Day Hospital, and I suddenly found myself juggling quarantine with my family, a hospitalized parent, and growing turmoil at work. I remember waking up each day with a crushing sense of failure. Everything depended on me, and no matter how hard I tried—to be a good mother, a responsible citizen, a dedicated worker—it still felt impossible to hold it all together. By the end of each day, I was gripped by the fear that I'd come out of the pandemic with post-traumatic stress. It was burnout, plain and simple, and deciding to quit my job was my way of trying to survive it.

In Luna's case, the perfect storm stemmed from a series of structural deficiencies that manifested themselves simultaneously. It was not only an unprotected job, with a hostile and cynical boss, in a disorganized, chaotic office where the workload doubled from one day to the next without notice, in an arbitrary manner. It was also the lack of childcare services, the decision to shut down schools and an underfunded healthcare system that failed, despite the sacrifices of doctors and nurses, to protect the population. Under these circumstances, it was impossible for Luna to cope with the demands that were being placed on her.

You find yourself in this situation and say, I can't carry the burden of all this alone because the burden is just too heavy. I can't be the glue that holds this system together.

During those months, Luna expected someone to ask her if she needed a hand. Instead, her boss doubled her workload overnight.

I always thought that culture should be a laboratory for progressive ideas. But instead of receiving a phone call saying 'do you need help' my boss doubled my workload without warning. What's more, he took a support person away from me, without revising the economic agreement. 'That's the way it is', they said, 'take it or leave it'. Of course I am leaving, I replied.

In fact, he continues:

I am more and more convinced that it was the right decision, because if the cultural world doesn't uphold decent practices, our work is useless. Sometimes I feel dizzy about this choice, but it comforts me to know that I am not participating in a cannibal system. I think I am less toxic and more ecological if I earn a little less and do not accept certain conditions.

Luna's story is paradigmatic. In those months, too many women were forced to quit their jobs. With closed schools, for many of them, days became like this:

8 hours of childcare
8 hours of elder care
8 hours of domestic work
8 hours of remote work
8 hours of sleep

The catch? There were still only 24 hours in a day.

That is why so many quit their jobs. The debate spoke of a '*she-cession*': the exit of three hundred and thirty thousand women from the Italian labour market. The INAPP Report 2021[11] attributed the reasons for this haemorrhage to several factors, including the high incidence of non-renewal of fixed-term contracts, the drop in recruitment, and:

> The dynamics behind women's assessment of the opportunity cost of continuing employment, in a context that has intensified the traditional gender gap between paid market labor and unpaid work—particularly in the provision of care and assistance for children and the elderly.

According to Labour Inspectorate data concerning parents with children aged zero to three, in 2020 there were 42,377 voluntary resignations, 77.2 per cent of which came from women and 22.8 per cent from men. The most interesting information concerns the reasons. If in fact fathers quit mostly because they move to a different job, mothers quit primarily because they find it difficult to combine work and care duties, a trend that continued in 2021.

As Claudia Torrisi writes, 'what comes to the fore is the usual elephant in the room: the huge gender imbalance in care duties in Italy, the mirror of a stereotyped and deeply patriarchal society'[12] which is still based on the idea that the man is the breadwinner and the woman is the queen of the kitchen. In this context, women *collapse under the weight of it all*.

From this point of view, women's exit from the market is a symptom of the lack of material conditions able to guarantee employment and housing stability, welfare services, childcare and equal parental leave, as well as all those services that enable a work-life balance. Without these services, many of them will not be able to return to work.

In some instances, this dynamic forces women back into the caregiving roles historically assigned to them by society. It is a phenomenon that should not be underestimated, particularly in light of the long-standing pressure on women to quit their jobs so as to relieve employers of the responsibility to provide maternity leave coverage.

For many years, women have been required to sign an undated letter of resignation at the beginning of a new employment contract to allow employers to dismiss them for no apparent reason and without any compensation should they become pregnant.

In Italy this has been a widespread practice for a long time and has consolidated the tendency to consider women as mere accessories on the labour market, as well as inefficient, problematic and, ultimately, burdensome. This is why the question of women quitting their jobs has always been a sensitive one, because for too long the decision to quit has not been a personal choice, but a choice made for them by others.

In some instances, however, women actively choose to quit, refusing to endure the excessive workload and harassment imposed by the market. As Luna explains, her decision 'was a political one.

> In my opinion it is true that this large-scale resignation movement is partly rooted in depression. Surely, it stems from a journey through darkness. But sometimes, darkness brings clarity. Crises are opportunities, new worlds unfolding. They change the rules that are no longer sustainable.

For Luna, the Covid emergency was illuminating because it forced her to thoroughly reassess her priorities. Once it was established that she was not planning to carry on in a state of exhaustion, it was only a matter of quitting her job and bracing for a possible period of unemployment. Choosing to quit requires the contemplation of failure. Quitting a job can be a failure when it does not lead to an alternative. The decision to quit, however, exposes society's shortcomings. By ceasing to be the glue that holds the system together, Luna shed light on what was missing: childcare services, equal parental leave and employment protections. Often, it takes a sense of community to deal with this scenario. In the absence of universal social assistance, the ability to quit a toxic job depends on social and political forms of solidarity—something far from guaranteed in today's climate of social fragmentation. However, even in such a complex context, women's decision to quit brings us back to Alisa Del Re's analysis. Subtraction becomes a political gesture that challenges gendered norms. By withdrawing, women assert that they will not return to work unless the conditions are transformed. This act demands a rethinking of both productive and reproductive spheres— and a rejection of the expectation that women manage both.

For Luna, the decision to let go of these expectations was instructive.

> I took a leap of faith. I thought I would be out of work for three or four months. Instead, I was out of work for a fortnight. Now I work a fraction of what I used to and earn about the same, but, above all, I no longer have to do what for me was poison, i.e. flood the newspapers with news that were far from the truth.

When I spoke to Luna, a year after her decision to quit, she told me that she felt oddly grateful to her former bosses, because had it not been for their nastiness, she would not have had the courage to leave a comfort zone 'that was not comfortable at all'. Luna did not linger on the consequences of this wave of resignations, but only on their potential: 'Either you pay us fairly, or we stop working for you'.

3. The queer art of failure

Workplace prejudice doesn't stop at white, cisgender, heterosexual women—that's just the surface. Patrick's case made it clear: migrant workers are often subjected to far more brutal conditions, such as working for a boss who blared fascist music and acted with authoritarian cruelty. The same happens to LGBTQIA+ workers. Recently, the ISTAT-Unar[13] survey focused on discrimination against them. Based on a sample of around twenty thousand LGBTQIA+ individuals who were or had been in a civil union, the survey found that 26 percent of those identifying as homosexual or bisexual reported that their sexual orientation had negatively impacted their working life. Forty per cent report hiding their sexual orientation at work to avoid retaliation. Sixty per cent have experienced at least one microaggression, such as denigrating remarks and insults. About 30 per cent say they have suffered at least one incident of discrimination while looking for a job, and 68.2 per cent have avoided holding hands in public with their partner for fear of being attacked, threatened or harassed. In a deeply homophobic context, it is not unusual for people to feel pressured to quit their jobs. With respect to microaggressions, the report notes that 6.9 percent of those who experienced one seriously considered quitting their job but ultimately stayed, while 2.5 percent actually did resign.

This is what happened to Diamante, a lesbian woman who worked for a multinational cleaning company, part of a sector notorious for its high attrition rates. During that time, Diamante worked six hours a day for a net monthly salary of 500 euros. The company did not pay overtime, and the work culture was toxic, consisting of disciplinary measures and anti-union practices. Diamante, however, did not quit her job because of this. She did so because of repeated and ongoing discrimination by her co-workers. It all started when she was spotted holding hands with her girlfriend. Her coworkers cut her off and subjected her to a barrage of insults and verbal abuse. In line with the ISTAT-UNAR report, her colleagues were responsible for the micro-aggressions, as was the case in 57.2 per cent of the instances.

This specific cause of resignation is a cultural problem that starts in society and continues in the workplace, where it often goes unchecked. The absence of safeguards is what makes certain situations particularly insidious, because it undermines the mental health of the discriminated person in addition to creating isolation and exclusion.

'These things rot you from the inside,' said transfeminist activist Marte Manca in an interview with *Valigia Blu*. Italy still fails to confront the real toll of homophobia—something laid bare by the suicide of Cloe Bianco, a transgender woman who, in June 2022, could no longer bear the weight of 'continuous workplace discrimination, harassment, and bullying.' Manca adds: 'She stood her ground, she fought—but around her, there was only silence.

We are faced with a series of layered problems, the first of which is the poor culture concerning sexual orientation and gender identity, inside and outside the workplace.

This is confirmed by the spontaneity with which the first reports of Cloe Bianco's suicide used the woman's *deadname* to identify her – a practice that, by using her birth name to identify her as she was dying, disowned, instead of honouring, her courageous journey. Secondly, there is little acceptance of LGBTQIA+ people in the labour context, as there are insufficient forms of protection.

We often talk about the contrast between civil and social rights, as if attention to the former compromised the latter: but social rights have never really been universal.

Literature abounds with texts describing the monstrous deeds of marginalized communities. One need only think of Peter Linebaugh and Marcus Rediker's book, *The Many-Headed Hydra: Sailors, Slaves, Commoners, and the Hidden History of the Revolutionary Atlantic*, which described rebels and slaves as a seven-headed hydra, a terrible snake-like monster who had nine heads and was immortal, so as soon as one head was cut off, two more would be reborn from the wound.

We've heard this script before—again and again. In colonial times, it dehumanized Afro-descendants; in anti-migrant rhetoric, it portrayed newcomers as terrifying savages; during witch hunts, it cast women as malevolent figures wielding dark powers. Today, it resurfaces in the transphobic media hysteria that ricochets across the Atlantic. For social and civil rights to be extended to discriminated communities, first and foremost, they must be considered as human. In this respect, LGBTQIA+ activists and communities are doing invaluable work to bring to light existing forms of discrimination, in and outside the workplace. In this context, quitting is often not a choice, but rather a way of protecting oneself from a persecutory and hostile culture.

On the other hand, it must be said that some of the most insightful interpretations of quitting have come precisely from the queer world. It is the radical dis-identification with a context of production that has long marginalized the LGBTQIA+ community that has enabled many to reject an idea of self-fulfilment inscribed within a framework of economic success. 'When we first heard of failure as an art, we were already bankrupt', writes the *Craaazi collective* in the afterword to the Italian translation of Jack Halberstam's text, *The Queer Art of Failure*. 'Indebted, without family, asocial, indecent', they continue:

> We were already embodying the ongoing unraveling of binary gender and sexual norms—living through both its fertile possibilities and its inherent tensions. That's why it was almost intuitive to transpose the queer art of failure onto the terrain of economic and existential precarity, and to glimpse in the crisis an opening for change in our sideways ways of existing and imagining.

The ability to trace the causes of failure back into the very structure of our society is the foundation of a radical process of dis-identification capable of subverting expectations and 'reconstructing an imaginary of liberation at the time of crisis'.

'There is something powerful about making mistakes, losing and failing', they go on to write. All our failures, if experienced beyond the individual dimension, 'could be enough, if we practice them well and together, to bring down the winners'.[14]

4. The art of subtraction

There is one last story I would like to tell before we close: Viola's.

Viola quit her job at the beginning of 2023, she had a permanent position in a company working in the cultural industry: the field that takes us from media to publishing, from art to communication, from teaching to cultural heritage, and that is increasingly inhabited by the new *cognitive working poor* – that part of the precarious class that often works in poverty, despite its very high professional profiles.

Viola worked at the same company for almost eight years: a small company of about twenty people, each of whom had a different contract: part-time, permanent, freelance and bogus freelance, casual, temporary, fixed term contract or internship. Viola was cut out for the job: she was passionate and talented. However, she wanted her work situation to be regulated by clear rules. To this end, she embarked on a political journey within the company in an attempt to place limits on the constant encroachment on her free time and the relentless increase in her workload. Slowly, the attitude of the people around her changed. Viola was no longer seen as a talented and brilliant woman, but as an element out-of-tune, a disturbing note, an inconvenient person. In time, she began to feel isolated. When she went to work, she felt ill: she felt out of space, started to question herself and to feel trapped. Her story, at that point, became the story of a *quiet quitter*: the experience of a woman who gradually distanced herself from work until she abandoned it.

Viola's story lays bare the reality of labour in Italy. It shows how the 'passion trap'—selling work as a calling or a devotion—often masks a brutal demand for constant availability, seven days a week, with no real break and no room to even want one. Passion becomes the bait to justify exploitation and unpaid presence. Her choice to walk away invites us to rethink the act of stepping back—not as failure, but as a political stance against a system that demands our total identification with work.

To reconstruct Viola's story, we have to start with the company: a fragmented place, with a predominantly female staff, where each person had a different labour contract. The logic was to make sure that bogus freelancers would show the same devotion to work as the employee and that employees would have the same self-entrepreneurial spirit as the self-employed.

On one hand, self-employed workers were pressured to maintain office-hour presence, displaying a commitment indistinguishable from that of salaried staff—without, however, receiving any of the protections such as social security or paid sick leave. On the other hand, employees were recast as self-entrepreneurs, tasked with constantly enhancing their own productivity to benefit the company. This tendency is paradigmatic: Sergio Bologna and Anna Soru, in their valuable report on working conditions in publishing and the audiovisual market,[15] dwell at length on the ways in which the cultural industry, and more specifically the Italian one, is teeming with hybrid figures, in which the distinction between self-employed and subordinate work is blurred. Outsourcing has become the cultural industry's preferred method for slashing labour costs—especially in publishing—producing what amounts to 'job disinsertion' for many professionals: a systematic detachment from stable, protected employment. To make up for this, outsourced workers were pressured to show loyalty to the company just to hold on, while regular employees were driven to overperform in order to justify their continued presence.

Viola did not like this kind of constraint: she did not want to be forced into something she was not: an entrepreneur of herself, always available, including weekends and holidays, to 'bring the loot to the office'.

Her conflicts start here. For the company, Viola kept placing boundaries on the management's demands and in doing so, she did not give everything she could.

> To them I was outdated. On the one hand they told me that my pursuits brought lifeblood to the company, on the other they considered me to be unaligned with their goals.

Viola felt robbed of her time. Phrases such as 'we don't spare ourselves', 'it's not a job, it's a privilege' well describe the range of strategies deployed by management to seize ever larger portions of her life.

> For them, the work we do is not work, it is a privilege, and the moment I started to track my hours, I became almost insulting to them. 'You are here in a prestigious reality, and you come to me nitpick about every cent?' They would always tell me, 'you are very good. The problem is your attitude'. It's not enough to work with passion, rigour, method, working as a team, achieving the goals you are given: you have to be dedicated. You have to think, when you are there, 'I like being at work more than anything else'. You don't grow by showing that you do things well or that you are autonomous, you grow by doing more and more, and by showing that you are willing to do more and to work on weekends and evenings. They were irritated that I, despite being so attuned to the things we do in our work, refused to accept this. They were never lacking in appreciation, but I did not correspond to the image they had of an employee, to the image that many of my colleagues embodied of a person who does not spare him or herself. 'We don't spare ourselves', they kept telling me, whereas you, they said, set boundaries. And it was true.

Viola wanted her work to be regulated by clear rules: how does overtime work? How do make-up hours work? Is there any form of economic compensation in spite of overtime pay? For the company, these were inappropriate questions.

> There was this unspoken idea that working there was already a privilege. We weren't waiting tables or stacking boxes in a warehouse—so raising certain issues was seen as inappropriate. That's how I earned the label of 'the unionist'. But all I was doing was asking basic questions: How do make-up hours work? What about overtime? How is it paid? Just asking these questions was enough to disturb the balance, to brand me as some kind of ideological, leftist, nineteenth-century nuisance. It made me feel not only isolated, but fundamentally out of place. How could this be? I was working in an organisation that prided itself on being left-wing and feminist—and yet, as soon as I asked perfectly ordinary questions, the responses I got were grimaces, dismissals, discomfort. People would tell me: *You're the off-key note, because here, we don't hold back.* And that 'we' wasn't just management—it was collective. '*We* don't spare ourselves. But you—what are you trying to do? set boundaries? Say no?' I could feel their irritation.

Over time, anything turned into an opportunity for conflict, even leaving on time was a form of non-compliance.

> I was trying to leave on time and this was frowned upon. Can we come to terms with the fact that we are not perpetually living in an emergency, that work can be organised? That it's not normal if we all work past scheduled time, every day, to the point where even those who overstay are just pretending to work. Why? Because they know that staying beyond regular hours gives them the image of the devoted person. […] I always went out on time, where it was not necessary to stay.

Simply asking to recover hours worked over the weekend was seen as a transgression.

> I once told my boss that if I was away all weekend I needed make-up time, just to do something as basic as my laundry. 'Get your partner to help you', he replied.

For the company, ours was basically not a job: it was a kind of hobby that can be carried out in one's spare time, like it's just another night out at the cinema. The company was so insistent on the equivalence between work and leisure that Viola had to explain that there is a big difference between the two.

They would say to me: why ask for time off, when what you do in your free time is basically the same as what we ask you to do? And I'd reply: because going to the movies to watch a film I choose is not the same as meeting the people *you* tell me to meet. They couldn't grasp the idea that if there's a task, that's work. If there's a report to be written, that's work. Sure, it might be enjoyable and I might even be good at it—but it's still work. When I go to a business meeting, I dress a certain way, I adopt a certain attitude. That's not the same as just doing my own thing. If I'm off the clock and a performance bores me, I can just leave. I don't have to take notes. I don't have to write a report. My whole perspective is different. Is it really that hard to understand that there's a difference between leisure and labour?

It may seem paradoxical, but Viola was forced to specify the difference. The 'passion trap', as Annalisa Murgia and Barbara Poggio[16] have called it, blurs the boundaries between life and work: what need is there for leisure if work is a passion? If you love your work, what more can you dream of doing on weekends? The encroachment of work into leisure time finds, in passion, a persuasive Trojan horse, subtle, but all-encompassing in its effects. Transforming work into passion, in fact, changes the very concept of it. 'When I go to a business meeting, I dress a certain way, I adopt a certain attitude', says Viola. But her explanations fall on deaf ears. After all, describing work as a passion allows one to break through all the boundaries that regulate it.

I once remarked, 'but I answer emails when I'm on holiday, on sick leave, out of office, I'm here! I'm always here'. And they replied, 'but that is a given for us'. They took it for granted. But if you don't appreciate that *extra* there, then I have to stop. I don't have to do more: I necessarily have to stop. It's heartbreaking to think that I had to give up a job that I liked because I ended up going to the office and feeling sick. From a certain point on I started to feel physically ill: I would go to the office and ask myself, why am I here?

In recent years, the least explored aspect of passion has been complicity, the way in which a part of the precarious class accepts to have a passion for work that slips into a regime of exploitation, in the hope that their sacrifice will somehow be rewarded. This kind of unwritten agreement continually shifts the bar, normalizing the supply of an ever-larger slice of unpaid labour.

In Viola's case, however, there was no complicity. Viola felt the corporate encroachments and the attempt to claim ownership over her time. She sought the support of her colleagues, but did not find it: no one wanted to be exposed.

Gradually it became clear to her that those were not just petty arguments. Those who obeyed, in fact, received financial or professional recognition. When Viola asked for a raise, however, she did not get it. The concept was: how can we give it to you if you do not give us that kind of availability? At that point, says Viola, 'I had a breakdown. I was physically sick': she felt punished because of her own persona, not because of her work, and felt anger at a situation that made her feel problematic and wrong.

a. Quiet quitting or quiet grabbing?

There is a pervasive, preventive, undeclared form of psychological warfare in today's workplace. A war that says, simply put, that in order to grow professionally or to gain recognition, one must demonstrate complete commitment. We have said it before: the love of work is not innocent. It implies the demand to consider the company as a family and put it above everything else.

Viola made it very clear. We are not a family. We are at best a condominium.

> We are not a family. At best, we're a condo. I've always preferred the condo metaphor: you're the administrators, the tenants have rights and duties, and once the doors close, everyone minds their own damn business. A family is about unconditional love—and I don't offer you that, because you don't offer it to me. You never will. The moment I leave this job, you'll forget I ever existed. And I want to remain something else. I want to be able to say: no, I'm not doing that thing tonight because it's my friend's birthday. Because that friend— if I get sick—will bring me my meds. You won't.

Viola has a visceral repulsion for that continuous attempt to capture her life within an exploitative regime, using love as a pretext. For her, this repulsion is a kind of *ick* moment, a confirmation of manipulation.

Viola's story allows us to say is what work *is not*: it is not a hobby, it is not passion, it is not self-fulfilment, it is not a privilege, it is not a favour. 'Society has convinced us that work is a favour',[17] said Ornela Casassa, a construction engineer, in a viral video explaining why she had decided to turn down a 900 euros gross job as a freelancer, about 750 euros net per month: 'We have to stop setting the bar low'. For Angela McRobbie, author of a text titled: *From Holloway to Hollywood: Happiness at Work in the Cultural Economy*,[18] the idea of work as passion is pernicious: 'No initiative has been more successful than this in trying to undermine organised labour and trade unionism'.[19] These conceptions of work are primarily forms of deregulation, through which a gradual dismantling of labour law is legitimized, clearing the way for individual bargaining that leaves people at the mercy of employer discretion.

From here on, Viola's is a story of *quiet quitting*, an attempt to escape from corporate interference and stick strictly to her contractual obligations. Viewed closely, though, Viola's case begs the question of whether the real problem in her experience is quiet *grabbing*, rather than quiet *quitting*: the silent hoarding of her work skills, emotions, time and livelihood. Sarah O'Connor, a brilliant journalist for the *Financial Times*, put it this way: behind the issue of quiet *quitting* is 'an unhealthy conception'[20] of work, cleverly created to make people not just do what they have to do but go above and beyond. The whole debate on the engagement of staff at work is an emblematic example of this culture of encroachment, which instead of regulating work continuously attempts to eliminate all norms.

This also applies to self-employment. Taking publishing as an example, Sergio Bologna and Anna Soru recount how this sector outsources a whole range of skills, from communication to marketing, from translation to graphics. The 'passion trap' is particularly heavy on the new *cognitive working poor*, highly skilled individuals who do piecework for starvation wages. Unfortunately, while resignations from employed positions leave a trace, it is very difficult to reconstruct the stories of the self-employed who decide to change sectors. Precisely because of the conditions they are subjected to, however, we know that these stories exist. It is thanks to independent unions like Acta and Redacta, which aim to unite Italian freelancers, that it is possible to break the physical and emotional isolation of those who work in the publishing industry.

b. Make hoarding impossible

It is no coincidence that, in order to escape from all this, Viola turns to a world of culture that focuses on dis-identification from work.

> At home, on the fridge, I hung pictures of plays and quotes from books that, in moments of greatest frustration, helped me imagine different scenarios. I wrote this phrase on the fridge: 'act by subtraction, make hoarding impossible'. It is a phrase that Blu used when he cancelled all his artworks in Bologna. I had to do that. So much so that when someone translates quitting as 'renunciation' I think it is not so. I did not renounce. I withdrew from a system in which I could not recognise myself. I tried to ensure that it could not get the best of me.

'Make hoarding impossible' is the phrase used by the writing collective Wu Ming and the graffiti writer Blu, a globally recognized street artist, in a script dated 12 March 2016. In those days, the city of Bologna had announced the exhibition *Street Art. Banksy & Co. Art in the Urban State,* which took the graffiti that Blu had gifted to the streets for twenty years and confined them to a museum. It was a real process of capture, which allowed private individuals to move the artist's work to a museum, in order to make it available on payment of a ticket. In an article in Giap,[21] Blu and Wu Ming lay bare the contradictions of a city council that on the one hand prosecuted '16-year-old writers' and on the other privatised Blu's works. 'The exhibition *Street Art. Banksy & Co.* is the symbol of a concept of the city that must be fought, based on private hoarding and on the appropriation of everyone's life and creativity to the advantage of a few', they wrote. In support of this position, Blu deleted the paintings and subtracted them from private capture.

> Faced with the arrogance of those who feel they are entitled to take drawings from the walls like *landlords,* or colonial rulers, there is nothing left to do but make the artwork disappear. Act by subtraction, make hoarding impossible.

Viola uses the same phrase: 'act by subtraction. Make hoarding impossible'. In fact, the point does not change: her intention was to prevent work from taking the best part of her creative capacity, of her time, of herself.

Viola, here, begins to ask herself: what does it mean to withdraw, to stop doing what you love and start doing any job that pays the bills, to withdraw from the manipulative exploitation of passion? What kind of subjective repercussions does it have, to quit a job? Does a person's value change if they stop working? 'Let us get used to the fact that a job is just a job, it is not a passion, it is not a status, it is not a lifestyle or an identity', she says. Work does not qualify a person: it has nothing to do with their value.

Viola places a space between herself and her work. In these statements, her life and her work do not coincide. 'I am not my work and my work does not qualify me', she repeats. Listening to her, I am reminded of the work of Diane Arbus, the fascinating American photographer who committed suicide in 1971. In her work Arbus immortalized masks, disguises, postures of discomfort, eyes looking at the camera almost begging not to be seen, a bit like the wallpaper with the sea and tall palm trees pasted on the walls of a grey waiting room, or like a dilapidated house in Hollywood of which only the façade remained. 'It's all', she said, 'in the gap, or rather the space between what a person is and what a person thinks they are'.[22] That crack, that space between what we are and what society wants us to be, is the crack that allows us to be free. In order to enact a process of liberation, we need to see a crack through which we can escape from the roles that society forces upon us. In a context of psychological warfare that tends to render pathological anything that does not meekly accept subordination, Viola seeks a crack, between herself and her social role, and embraces it to flee.

> Had there not been Mark Fisher's books, had I not read Byung-chul Han's *The Burnout Society*, had I not read Sarah Jaffe, had there not been Blu, had there not been Zerocalcare, had there not been Daria Deflorian and Antonio Tagliarini staging *Quasi niente*, had there not been Cecilia Vicuna at the Biennale with her painting la Comegente, which depicts a woman who eats villains to nurture the planet, if I had not had this imagery around me that suggested that I was not alone in what I was experiencing, *I could have thought they might be right—maybe I really was the problem.* 'You're the one who doesn't get it, the one always pushing back— while others sing along in harmony.

Viola drew on these artworks to redefine herself and her way of inhabiting the world. And then she left—liberated.

> I started to breathe again. I started to feel good again. I could see the end. I was counting the weeks, how many weeks to go, how many days to go, how many hours to go. It is over.

CONCLUSION

1. *The failure of a production model*

Every unhappy workplace is unhappy in its own way, we could say paraphrasing Tolstoy. Despite this, there are similar underlying patterns in the stories we have read. One of these is that quitting is often described as a liberating, though not decisive, gesture. A gesture that affirms the primacy of life over exploitation, as if moving away from the source of one's own suffering allowed a neglected part of oneself to speak out. As if affirming the primacy of life over harassment evoked disbelief, even awe. As if listening to one's deepest truths, even though it involves great risks and costs, allowed individuals to trust themselves again and reclaim an idea of the future that has been too long neglected. Often, the thrill of quitting stems here, from the resolve workers show show, which indicates that it's no longer time to keep their heads down.

It is certain: subtraction is an individual act and, often, it is not decisive. Occasionally, moreover, it can lead from one hellscape to another. But that affirmative gesture is, for once, a rare moment of real liberation.

Over the last few months, I have listened to hundreds of resignation stories. For each published interview, approximately twenty more did not make it to the final draft of the text. These are stories of people working in the hospitality and restaurant industry, museums or business services, logistics or cleaning, social services or cooperatives, real estate agencies or consulting companies, marketing or communication, food delivery couriers and factory workers, art directors and social media managers, architects and archaeologists, who have tried to redefine their relationship with their own work and lives. In addition to these, hundreds of testimonies reached me by e-mail and through social media. None of the people I spoke to said they had left their job thanks to the Citizenship income, although the dominant vulgate says so. Instead, each spoke of an untenable situation that forced them to re-examine their relationship with work. What does it mean to work? What does work give and what does it subtract? How do you limit its negative impact on your life?

If I had to summarize what has emerged, I would say that some of the reasons that drive people to quit have distinct similarities.

- Cuts in workforce, idle time, costs
- The extensive use of precarious, part-time or shady contracts, the widespread tendency to outsource parts of the production process, the reliance on cooperatives for the supply of labour with near-zero wages and rights
- A constant surveillance, consisting of authoritarian forms of control or digital feedback mechanisms, used to track performance and quietly ramp up workloads
- An anti-union culture, which cuts across the world of work

In a sense, the Great Resignation sanctions the crisis of a production model. It can be understood 'in light of the lean production model focused on the reduction of wastes and on the continuous improvement of performances'. What is at stake is 'the survival of a business model based on lean production, *just-in-time*, flexible labour and outsourcing'.[1]

Marco Revelli foresaw this back in the early 2000s, when he wrote that lean production is 'a system that tries to wring water out of dry towels'.[2]

In many ways, the deterioration of working conditions starts here, from those transformations that, in the beginning, the business world hailed as a win-win strategy, which would benefit the company and also its workforce, whereas, after about four decades, they appear as lose-lose models, in which both sides lost.

In this context, we've likely underestimated a few things.

First of all, an economic scenario in which micro and small enterprises account for 95 per cent of all businesses whose internal organization is almost always centred on the figure of the boss, who tries to make up for the lack of technological investment by squeezing labour costs. 'They act like gods', said a worker as he was telling me about his boss in a small company in Central Italy, 'in the sense that you are their own property'. 'At best they are paternalistic, at worst they are despots', he continued. Under these conditions, harassment proliferates, leading, in too many cases, to only one law: *here you do as I say*. This is also where some of the most glaring deficiencies and serious accidents occur, particularly in the world of subcontracting.

The second problem is a widespread union-busting culture, enforced through reward mechanisms as well as sanctions, as Bruno Trentin predicted years ago.[3] In logistics, for instance, union organizers are being repressed and criminalized. The Parliamentary Commission of Inquiry into working conditions in Italy offers a merciless picture of work in the country, showing how it is characterized by the imposition of 'unsustainable working rhythms and conditions, harassment, episodes of violence, intimidation and threats. Exploitation and illegal forms of labour intermediation are present everywhere and this is not worthy of a civilized country', the survey concludes.[4]

The Grafica Veneta scandal is an illustration of this. In 2021, investigations on the leading book printing company in Italy brought to light conditions of exploitation close to slavery. Police found migrant workers employed for up to twenty-four hours a day with no breaks, holidays or other labour protections and starvation wages. It is impressive, in retrospect, that this very company, a few years earlier, had complained that it could not find workers, despite the attractive job opportunities.[5]

The third thing we have underestimated is the malaise that this generates.

Isolation and union-busting have created a situation of blackmail and loneliness, in which all too often the only option other than obedience is to quit. From this point of view, the Great Resignation describes a *double failure*: the failure of the union in its mandate to create an organized workforce able to collectively resist repeated and continuous intimidation and harassment. And the failure of the company, in its quest to tame employees, because in the absence of an organized workforce, when working conditions deteriorate, they quit.

A disincentive to work

There is one last aspect to consider: wages.

In Italy, there has been a (rather long) phase during which wage compression has become a reason for national pride. Think of the complacency surrounding the then Prime Minister Matteo Renzi's suggestion that foreign firms should invest in the country because 'we have the lowest wages in Europe'.[6] From 1990 to 2020, wages in the Baltic states more than tripled. In Central European countries they doubled. In Germany they increased by 33 per cent and in France by 31 per cent. In Italy, over the same years, wages decreased by 2.9 per cent.[7]

'Citizenship income should be abolished because it is a disincentive to work', we have been told for years. Yet, the first, real disincentive to work is underpaid work.

'First they cut wages', says Lorenzo, who himself left a job in the cultural industry.

> They convinced you the job would give you status. Meanwhile, you gave everything you had—and now you're stuck trying to make ends meet. By then, you're older, and you think: you know what? Screw them. They told you anyone could become whatever they wanted, as long as they tried hard enough. But here you are, burnt out while they celebrate with the money they never paid you. In the end, you can't help but wonder: was this all just a joke?

In many ways, the Great Resignation started here, when burnout, exhaustion and dissatisfaction appeared behind the promises of a successful future that never came. Eventually, people began to question whether it was worth it.

Is it worth ruining your health for a pittance?

Is it worth suffering the abuse of a boss that pays you seven hundred euros a month?

Is it worth going to work for a few hundred euros a month and spending the same on childcare?

These matters cannot be reduced to low pay. But low pay does not offer a sufficient counterpart to those seeking the motivation to endure them. The purchase and sale of labour-power is not eternal.

As Karl Marx notably observed:

> Nature does not produce on the one side owners of money or commodities, and on the other men possessing nothing but their own labour-power. This relation has no natural basis, neither is its social basis one that is common to all historical periods. It is clearly the result of a past historical development, the product of many economic revolutions, of the extinction of a whole series of older forms of social production.[8]

The purchase and sale of labour-power only exists within specific socio-economic conditions as an exchange that bears, as its minimum limit, the value of the 'physiologically indispensable' means of subsistence. What happens when the value of such an exchange falls below this threshold?

This question frightens the business world.

Across the West, rising interest rates mark the attempt to counter the scandalous disorganized revolt of the Great Resignation. The Italian government's choice to eliminate the Citizenship Income, in order to recall workers to 'their responsibilities', goes in the same direction.

The government's response, in many ways, is punitive: its hope is that the war on benefits will force the unemployed to sell themselves on the market, once deprived of other means of livelihood. Although the logic of the scheme is clear, it is not necessarily resolutive. We have seen this in the early twentieth century, when the low wages and high workloads of the early Fordist factories generated high rates of absenteeism and voluntary turnover. There is only one effective way to retain staff: to introduce direct, indirect and deferred forms of compensation that can reward people for their efforts. We have said it before: for a labour relationship to exist, it is necessary to listen to the needs of the workers: raise wages, hire more staff, increase inspections and safety at work, discourage the use of undeclared work, introduce a legal minimum wage, fight contractual dumping and involuntary part-time work, introduce equal parental leave, new childcare services, abolish free internships and all those forms of unpaid work that accustom students to exploitation. It is also imperative to extend and strengthen welfare measures such as a Universal Basic Income, to enable people to refuse work when it poses inadequate conditions.

This is partly what has happened in Spain, where Minister Yolanda Díaz has pushed through a comprehensive labour market reform that goes in the opposite direction to what has happened in the last forty years. It is not science fiction: it is possible.

2. Life is not a commodity

For years, national and international policies have ignored the most pressing issues of our time. For a long time, the sole objective of our economic system has been to reduce labour costs and increase profits.

In this context, important issues have received little attention, namely the need to defend and extend labour rights and to rethink the purpose of production in an era marked by climate change, automation and artificial intelligence, as well as by the growing need for care of the population. Almost a century ago, the British economist John Maynard Keynes gave a major speech in Madrid, entitled *Economic Possibilities for Our Grandchildren* whereby he predicted that, in our time, the growth of productive capacity would solve the problem of scarcity and marginalize the role of work in our lives. One hundred years later, productive capacity has increased to such an extent that humanity must reduce its pressure on the environment, in order not to find itself in a situation of extreme drought, water scarcity and food shortages. In this context, the great potentials of our time have become problems. The challenges of the present have become so abysmal that politics, unable to respond, looks the other way. Today, there is no single solution to the multiple crises in which we live. Most viable answers come from the labour movement and from the movement for climate justice.

For three years, the GKN Factory Collective, a group of workers from the automotive factory in Campi Bisenzio, near Florence, has been able to transform a collective dismissal procedure carried out by the British investment fund Melrose into a laboratory of theoretical and political transformation on the need to reconvert production and to imagine a worker-managed socially integrated factory with low environmental impact, capable of protecting jobs and the labour rights acquired over time. Despite many adversities and the neglect of institutions, the GKN Factory Collective has been able to open a breach in the collective imaginary, showing how the future can go in the direction of a sustainable production that respects the environment and the population.

In the face of so many discussions about climate change, the GKN Factory Collective has been the only political actor in Italy to carry this conversation forward. In the absence of such a conversation, it is not surprising that people feel disengaged with work. A system that responds only to the demands of profit cannot arouse enthusiasm. In this context, the Great Resignation is a showcase of the misalignment between the purpose of production and the needs of society. In the absence of a transformative perspective, this disaffection promises to continue, as an expression of the unwillingness to accept a production system that is incapable of offering a future other than war and climate collapse.

In recent years, the Great Resignation has been an unexpected and disorganized response to this situation. Alongside a growing number of protests and strikes, demonstrations and assemblies, it has caused enterpreneurs to fear that they will no longer be able to carry on production due to the unavailability of workers. From the United States to France, the streets have said it loud and clear: 'Life is not just work'; we want to 'work less and live more'. In the 1970s, the refusal of work was a theoretical construct, the idea was that automation would slowly create the conditions for a society free from work. Today, to liberate life from work is a matter of survival. Jean-Luc Mélenchon put it beautifully on 21 January 2023, during a large demonstration against the pension reform in France.

> We are not simply defending the right to a pause in life, we are saying that the time that counts, in life, is not only the time that is considered useful because it produces. Living, loving, caring for your family, reading poetry, painting, singing or doing nothing: unproductive time is the only time in which we have the opportunity to be fully human. This is what we are talking about.[9]

The problem is not the labour shortage. It is that life is not a commodity. Wealth is not money. That is why people refuse to work: to live. 'The rich steal our time', one could hear in the streets of France. In a widespread and pervasive way, these words crossed nations and boundaries to appear in our daily conversations, giving voice to the urgency of reclaiming time to live, rest, and help the planet heal. We find traces of this in books, films, songs and poetry. Historically, such cultural transformations have punctuated the emergence of struggles that are able to disrupt work until new rights are won. The world is ready for a system of production not built on the exhaustion of our physical and mental energy and of the planet's resources. As GKN Factory Collective repeats, the sky is the only limit. Everything else is possible. Together.

NOTES

Introduction

1   Petersen, H., 'How Millennials Became the Burnout Generation', *BuzzFeed.news*, 5 January 2019, https://www.buzzfeednews.com/article/annehelenpetersen/millennials-burnout-generation-debt-work.

2   Ibid.

3   McClure, T., 'Jacinda Ardern: Political Figures Believe Abuse and Threats Contributed to PM's Resignation', *The Guardian*, 20 January 2023, https://www.theguardian.com/world/2023/jan/20/jacinda-ardern-speculation-that-abuse-and-threats-contributed-to-resignation.

4   'Nicola Sturgeon Resigns: "I Don't Expect Violins, but I Am a Human Being"', *Sky News*, 15 February 2023, https://www.youtube.com/watch?v=VtRTplMuus0.

5   Kang, C. and Griffith, E., 'What Sheryl Sandberg's Exit Reveals about Women's Progress in Tech', *The New York Times*, 3 June 2022, https://www.nytimes.com/2022/06/03/technology/sheryl-sandberg-women-in-tech.html.

6   Harris, M., *Kids These Days: The Making of Millennials*, Back Bay Books, New York, 2018, pp. 132–43, quoted in: Jaffe, S., *Work Won't Love You Back: How Devotion to Our Jobs Keeps Us Exploited, Exhausted, and Alone*, Bold Type Books, New York, 2021, p. 250.

7   Petersen, H., *Can't Even: How Millennials Became the Burnout Generation*, Mariner Books, Boston, 2020, p. 13.

8   Page, Michael, *The Great X*, https://www.michaelpage.co.in/sites/michaelpage.co.in/files/2022-04/Talent_Trends_2022_GreatX_report_MPIN.pdf.

9   'Self-Help Singh – Do Nothing (Full Speech)', https://www.youtube.com/watch?v=3rerBnAKPn0.

10   Clifton, J., 'The World's Broken Workplace', *Gallup*, https://news.gallup.com/opinion/chairman/212045/world-broken-workplace.aspx.

11   Graeber, D., *Bullshit Jobs: A Theory*, Simon & Schuster, New York, 2018.

12   Gini, Al and Sullivan, T., 'Work: The Process and the Person', *Journal of Business Ethics*, 6 (1987), pp. 649–55, pp. 649, 651, 654. Quoted in Graeber, *Bullshit Jobs*, p. 183.

13   Godwin, R., 'Work Less, Live More. Is It Time to End the Five-Day Week?' *The Guardian*, 22 January 2023, https://www.theguardian.com/society/2023/jan/22/work-less-live-more-is-it-time-to-end-the-five-day-week.

14   Kiderlin, S., '4-Day Work Week Firms Are Seeing a Surge in Job Applications', *Cnbc.com*, 18 October 2022, https://www.cnbc.

com/2022/10/18/is-the-four-day-work-week-the-key-to-recruiting-and-retaining-workers.html?&qsearchterm=4-Day%20Work%20Week%20 Firms%20Are%20Seeing%20a%20Surge%20in%20Job%20 Applications.

15   Schor, J. B., Fan, W., Kelly, O., Gu, G., Bezdenezhnykh, T. and Bridson-Hubbard, N., 'The Four Day Week. Assessing Global Trials of Reduced Work Time with No Re-duction in Pay', *Four Day Week Global*, 2022, https://autonomy.work/wp-content/uploads/2023/02/The-results-are-in-The-UKs-four-day-week-pilot.pdf.

16   Godwin, R., 'Work Less, Live More. Is It Time to End the Five-Day Week?; Working Less Could Solve 21st-Century Problems', *The Guardian*, 20 February, available at: www.theguardian.com (Accessed: 15 March 2024).

17   Taylor, M., 'Four-Day Working Week Would Slash UK Carbon Footprint, Report Says', *The Guardian*, 27 May 2021, https://www.theguardian.com/environment/2021/may/27/four-day-working-week-would-slash-uk-carbon-footprint-report.

18   Schulz T., Beyer S. and Book S., 'Hatte Marx doch recht?', *Der Spiegel*, (2023), n. 1.

Chapter 1

1   'Richmond enquirer', 17 January 1860, Semi-weekly edition, Image 1, (Image provided by) Library of Virginia; Richmond, VA, https://chroniclinga-merica.loc.gov/lccn/sn84024735/1860-01-17/ed-1/seq-1/.

2   'The Stockton Review and Rooks County Record', *Newspapers.com*, 27 April 1984, https://www.newspapers.com/newspage/379643726/.

3   Blasi, W., 'Nobody Wants to Work Anymore Has Been Said for 100 Years. It Wasn't True Then and It Isn't True Now', *Market Watch*, 28 July 2022, https://www.marketwatch.com/story/nobody-wants-to-work-anymore-has-been-said-for-100-years-it-wasnt-true-then-and-it-isnt-true-now-11659019444.

4   White, M., 'Blair Hails Middle Class Revolution', *The Guardian*, 15 January 1999, https://www.theguardian.com/politics/1999/jan/15/uk.politicalnews1.

5   Douglas, Paul H., 'The Problem of Labor Turnover', *American Economic Review*, 8 (1918), n. 2, pp. 306–16, https://www.jstor.org/stable/1811123#metadata_info_tab_contents.

6   Owen, L., 'History of Labor Turnover in the U.S.', *EH. Net Encyclopedia*, 29 April 2004, https://eh.net/encyclopedia/history-of-labor-turnover-in-the-u-s/.

7   Owen, L., 'Worker Turnover in the 1920s. What Labor-Supply Arguments Don't Tell Us', *The Journal of Economic History*, 55 (1995), n. 4, pp. 822–41, doi:10.1017/S0022050700042170.

8   Raff, D. and Summers, L., 'Did Henry Ford Pay Efficiency Wages?' *Nber Working Paper Series*, December 1986, p. 9, https://www.nber.org/system/files/working_.

9   Ibid.

10   Webster, F. M., 'Loyalty. An Outmoded Concept?' *PM Network*, June 1993, 7, n. 6, pp. 30, 32 and 35, https://www.pmi.org/learning/library/employers-employe-es-no-longer-demonstrate-loyalty-5032.

11   Lancaster, H., 'A New Social Contract to Benefit Employer and Employee', *The Wall Street Journal*, 29 November 1994.

12   Webster, 'Loyalty. An Outmoded Concept?' pp. 30–2, 35, https://www.pmi.org/learning/library/employers-employees-no-longer-demonstrate-loyalty-5032.

13   Coin, F., *Il produttore consumato. Saggio sul malessere dei lavoratori contemporanei*, Il Poligrafo, Padua, 2006.

14   Mitchell, W. and Muysken, J., *Full Employment Abandoned. Shifting Sands and Policy Failures*, Edward Elgar, Cheltenham (UK) – Northampton (MA), 2008, http://pombo.free.fr/mitchellmuysken.pdf.

15   Webster, 'Loyalty. An Outmoded Concept?' pp. 30–2, 35, https://www.pmi.org/learning/library/employers-employees-no-longer-demonstrate-loyalty-5032.

16   Royce, J., *The Philosophy of Loyalty*, editado por John J. McDermott, Vanderbilt University Press, Nashville, 1995, https://www.vanderbiltuniversitypress.com/9780826512673/the-philosophy-of-loyalty/.

17   'The Importance of Loyalty in the Workplace', https://www.youtube.com/watch?v=bfhKC4MZy7k.

18   Kahn, W. A., 'Psychological Conditions of Personal Engagement and Disengagement at Work', *Academy of Management Journal*, 33 (1990), n. 4, pp. 692–724, https://journals.aom.org/doi/abs/10.5465/256287.

19   Bersin, J., 'It's Time to Rethink the Employee Engagement Issue', *Forbes*, 10 April 2014, https://www.forbes.com/sites/joshbersin/2014/04/10/its-time-to-rethink-the-employee-engagement-issue/.

20   Harris, J., *Getting Employees to Fall In Love with Your Company*, Amacom, New York, 1996.

21   Ibid.

22   Ibid.

23   'How Employee Engagement Is Like a Marriage', *Schoop.co.uk*, https://www.schoop.co.uk/2019/05/02/how-employee-engagement-is-like-a-marriage/.

24   Grey, K., 'Can't Pay Your Employees What You'd Like? Praise Them Instead', *CBS News*, 19 January 2010, https://www.cbsnews.com/news/cant-pay-your-employees-what-youd-like-praise-them-instead/.

25   Herbert, G., 'A Successful Marriage Starts at the Engagement', https://www.grantherbert.com/blog/a-successful-marriage-starts-at-the-engagement

26   Mandell, N., *The Corporation as Family: The Gendering of Corporate Welfare (1890–1930)*, University of North Carolina Press, Chapel Hill, 2022.

27   Herrera, T., 'Your Workplace Isn't Your Family (and That's O.K.!)', *The New York Times*, 13 August 2018, https://www.nytimes.com/2018/08/13/smarter-living/your-workplace-isnt-your-family-and-thats-ok.html.

28   Goffee, R. y Jones, G., *The Character of a Corporation: How Your Company's Culture Can Make or Break Your Business*, Profile Books, London, 2003.

29   Luna, J. A., 'The Toxic Effects of Branding Your Workplace a "Family"', *Harvard Business Review*, 27 October 2021, https://hbr.org/2021/10/the-toxic-effects-of-branding-your-workplace-a-family?registration=success.

30   Cortez, J., 'Airline Organization Blames Great Resignation for Operational Difficulties', *FlyerTalk.com*, 7 December 2021, https://www.flyertalk.com/articles/airline-organization-blames-great-resignation-for-operational-difficulties.html.

31   Jaffe, S., *Work Won't Love You Back: How Devotion to Our Jobs Keeps Us Exploited, Exhausted and Alone*, Bold Type, New York, 2022, p. 33.

32   Austin, A., Capper, B. y Deutsch, T., 'Wages for Housework and Social Reproduction. A Microsyllabus', *Radical History Review*, 27 April 2020, https://www.radicalhistoryreview.org/abusablepast/wages-for-housework-and-social-reproduction-a-microsyllabus/.

33   O'Reilly, J., 'The Housewife's Moment of Truth', *New York Magazine*, 14 April 2018, https://nymag.com/news/features/46167/.

34   *Our Time Is Coming Now* (BBC, Selma James & Michael Rabiger, 1970), https://www.youtube.com/watch?v=jHkRWteXNTc.

35   Ratti, Fondazione Antonio, 'La dimensione dell'esodo. Etica della diserzione', 9 March 2023, https://vimeo.com/807476618.

36   George, '"Anti-work": The Movement That Gained Strength in the Pandemic and Spreads through Online Communities', *News Bulletin*, 7 February 2022, https://newsbulletin247.com/economy/44218.html.

37   Miller, B., 'Dear White Staffers is Lifting the Lid on the Reality of Life as a Congressional Staffer Working on Capitol Hill', *Abc.net.au*, 15 February 2021, https://www.abc.net.au/news/2022-02-16/dear-white-staffers-instagram-reveals-congress-work-conditions/100824260.

38   French, L., Hanna, P. e Huckle, C., 'If I Die, They Do Not Care: UK National Health Service Staff Experiences of Betrayal-based Moral Injury During Covid-19', *Psychological Trauma: Theory, Research, Practice, and Policy*, 14 (2022), n. 3, pp. 516–21, https://doi.org/10.1037/tra0001134.

39   'Mom Died… Employer Didn't Care', https://www.reddit.com/r/relationship_advice/ comments/mwzcr4/mom_diedemployer_didnt_care/.

40   French, Hanna, and Huckle, 'If I Die, They Do Not Care', pp. 516–21, https://doi.org/10.1037/tra0001134.

41   Ibid.

42   Ibid.

43 Rosenblum, C., 'Work Is a False Idol', *The New York Times*, 22 August 2021, https://www.nytimes.com/2021/08/22/opinion/lying-flat-work-rest.html.

44 Three weeks ago, my sister died, and my boss told me to try to attend an online funeral for her so I wouldn't have to miss work for travel. https://www.reddit.com/r/antiwork/comments/sncbhw/three_weeks_ago_my_sister_died_and_my_boss_told/.

Chapter 2

1   Cohen, A., 'How to Quit Your Job in the Great Post-Pandemic Resignation Boom', 10 May 2021, https://www.bloomberg.com/news/articles/2021-05-10/quit-your-job-how-to-resign-after-covid-pandemic?embedded-checkout=true.

2   Malesic, J., 'The Future of Work Should MeanWorking Less', *The New York Times*, 23 September 2021, https://www.nytimes.com/interactive/2021/09/23/opinion/covid-return-to-work-rto.html?searchResultPosition=9.

3   BlackRock, 'After the Great Resignation. Shifting Expectations for Employers', October 2022, https://www.blackrock.com/corporate/literature/whitepaper/after-the-great-resignation-shifting-expectations-for-employers.pdf.

4   Ferguson, S., 'Understanding America's Labor Shortage', *U.S. Chamber of Commerce*, 22 February 2023, https://www.uschamber.com/workforce/understanding-americas-labor-shortage.

5   Gillispie, C., Codella, C., Merchen, A., Davis, J. y Cappo, A., 'Equity in Child Care Is Everyone's Business', *U.S. Chamber of Commerce Foundation*, https://www.uschamberfoundation.org/sites/default/files/Equity_ChildCare_Final_web.pdf.

6   Richter, F., 'The Great Resignation', *www.statista.com*, 9 January 2023, https://www.statista.com/chart/29071/number-of-resignations-in-the-us-since-january-2021-by-industry/#:~:text=U.S.

7   Restaurant Opportunities Centers United, 'The Impact of Covid-19 on Restaurant Workers across America', January 2022, https://rocunited.org/wp-content/uploads/sites/7/2022/06/ROC_COVID_Impact_2.pdf.

8   Ibid.

9   Coin, F. and Jaffe, S., 'Il lavoro non ti ama (e nemmeno noi lo amiamo)', *Jacobin Italia*, 24 October 2022, https://jacobinitalia.it/il-lavoro-non-ti-ama-e-nemmeno-noi-lo-amiamo/.

10 Worktango, 'How the Great Resignation Has Impacted 10 Industries', https://www.kazoohr.com/blog/10-industries-great-resignation.

11 Popa, I., Lee, L., Yu, H. and Madera, J. M., 'Losing Talent Due to Covid-19. The Roles of Anger and Fear on Industry Turnover Intentions',

Journal of Hospitality and Tourism Management, 54 (March 2023), pp. 119–27, https://www.sciencedirect.com/science/article/pii/S14476770 22001978?via%3Dihub.

12   Bui, Q. and Wolfers, J., 'The Staggering Rise in Jobless Claims This Week', *The New York Times*, 19 March 2020, https://www.nytimes.com/interactive/2020/03/19/upshot/coronavirus-jobless-claims-states.html.

13   Rushe, D. and Holpuch, A., 'Record 3.3m Americans File for Unemployment as the US Tries to Contain Covid-19', *The Guardian*, 26 March 2020, https://www.the-guardian.com/business/2020/mar/26/us-unemployment-rate-coronavirus-business.

14   Hussain, S., 'Just Wear a Mask and Don't Tell Anyone. Workplaces Are Filling Up with Sick Employees', *Los Angeles Times*, 26 January 2022, https://www.latimes.com/business/story/2022-01-26/covid-testing-rapid-tests-access-sick-leave-cdc-quarantine-workplace-risks.

15   Desilver, D., 'As Coronavirus Spreads, Which U.S. Workers Have Paid Sick Leave – and Which Don't?' *Pew Research Center*, 12 March 2020, https://www.pewresearch.org/fact-tank/2020/03/12/as-coronavirus-spreads-which-u-s-workers-have-paid-sick-leave-and-which-dont/.

16   Fuller, D., Logan, B. and Valkova, A., 'The Great Attrition in Frontline Retail – and What Retailers Can Do about It', *McKinsey & Company*, 22 July 2022, https://www.mckinsey.com/industries/retail/our-insights/the-great-attrition-in-frontline-retail-and-what-retailers-can-do-about-it.

17   Parker, K. and Menasce, J., 'Majority of Workers Who Quit a Job in 2021 Cite Low Pay, No Opportunities for Advancement, Feeling Disrespected', *Pew Research Center*, 9 March 2022, https://www.pewresearch.org/fact-tank/2022/03/09/majority-of-workers-who-quit-a-job-in-2021-cite-low-pay-no-opportunities-for-advancement-feeling-disrespected/.

18   Ibid.

19   Ferguson, 'Understanding America's Labor Shortage: The Most Impacted Industries', *U.S. Chamber of Commerce*, 22 February 2023, https://www.uschamber.com/workforce/understanding-americas-labor-shortage.

20   Walker, T., 'Survey: Alarming Number of Educators May Soon Leave the Profession', *Nea News*, 21 January 2022, https://www.nea.org/advocating-for-change/new-from-nea/survey-alarming-number-educators-may-soon-leave-profession.

21   Lampert, J., 'Why That One Tweet Went Viral (and What We Must Do Now to Fix Teacher Shortages)', *EduResearch Matters*, https://www.aare.edu.au/blog/?p=14048.

22   https://www.reddit.com/r/antiwork/comments/11bdwsy/this_is_just_real_sad/.

23   Kush, J. M., Badillo Goicoechea, E., Musci, R. J. and Stuart, E. A., 'Teacher Mental Health during the Covid-19 Pandemic', *Educational*

Researcher, 14 November 2022, 51, n. 9, https://www.doi.org/10.3102/001 3189X221134281.

24	Coin, F., 'On quitting', *Ephemera*, 17, n. 3, https://epheme-rajournal.org/ contribution/quitting/.

25	Gewin, V., 'Has the "Great Resignation" Hit Academia?' *Nature*, 31 May 2022, https://www.nature.com/articles/d41586-022-01512-6.

26	'UK Higher Education. A Workforce in Crisis', *University and College Union*, March 2022, https://www.ucu.org.uk/media/12532/ HEReport24March22/pdf/HEReport24March22.pdf.

27	Ibid.

28	Threlkeld, K., 'Employee Burnout Report: Covid-19's Impact and 3 Strategies to Curb It', *Indeed*, https://www.indeed.com/lead/preventing-employee-burnout-report.

29	Burchi, S., 'Lavorare da casa durante la pandemia. Donne e smart working', https://www.ingenere.it/sites/default/files/ricerche/ workingpaper-smartworking_burchi.pdf.

30	BlackRock, 'After the Great Resignation, Shifting Expectations for Employers', October 2022, https://www.blackrock.com/corporate/ literature/whitepaper/after-the-great-resignation-shifting-expectations-for-employers.pdf

31	De Smet, A., Dowling, B., Mugayar-Baldocchi, M. and Schaninger, B., 'Gone for Now, or Gone for Good? How to Play the New Talent Game and Win Back Workers', *McKinsey & Company*, 9 March 2022, https://www.mckinsey.com/capabilities/people-and-organizational-performance/our-insights/gone-for-now-or-gone-for-good-how-to-play-the-new-talent-game-and-win-back-workers.

32	Fleming, S., 'This Is the World's Biggest Mental Health Problem – and You Might Not Have Heard of It', *World Economic Forum*, https://www. weforum.org/agenda/2019/01/this-is-the-worlds-biggest-mental-health-problem/.

33	Part of this chapter was previously published on the website of the Italian magazine Valigia Blu, for which I am grateful.

34	Briggs, J., 'US Daily: Why Isn't Labor Force Participation Recovering? (Briggs)', *Goldman Sachs*, 1 November 2021, https://www.gspublishing. com/content/research/en/reports/2021/11/12/4f72d573-c573-4c4b-8812-1d32ce3b973e.html.

35	Herrman, J., 'Quitting Your Job Never Looked So Fun', *The New York Times*, 29 October 2021, https://www.nytimes.com/2021/10/29/style/ quit-your-job.html.

36	Ibid.

37	Ibid.

38	https://twitter.com/dixie3flatline/status/1426937846678446084.

39	'The Amount of Companies That Do This', https://www.reddit.com/r/ antiwork/comments/ls8cdp/the_amount_of_companies_that_do_this/.

40   'They Ask for so Much and in Return You Can Get 11-13 Dollars an
     Hour', https:// www.reddit.com/r/antiwork/comments/olr5st/they_ask_
     for_so_much_and_in_return_you_can_get/.

41   '37 cents', https://www.reddit.com/r/antiwork/comments/woxjr5/37_cents/.

42   '2020 Edelman Trust Barometer', https://www.edelman.com/node/7936.

43   Malone, N., 'The Age of Anti-ambition', *The New York Times*,
     15 February 2022, https://www.nytimes.com/2022/02/15/magazine/anti-
     ambition-age.html.

44   Ibid.

45   Ibid.

46   Ibid.

47   Tiwari, A., '12 Honest but Savage Resignation Letters Where People Quit
     Their Jobs in Style', *Indian Times*, 18 June 2022, https://www.indiatimes.
     com/trending/wtf/creative-funny-resignation-letters-572555.html.

48   Malone, N., 'The Age of Anti-ambition', *New York Times*, 15 February
     2022, https://www.nytimes.com/2022/02/15/magazine/anti-ambition-age.
     html

49   Reich, R., 'Is America Experiencing an Unofficial General Strike?'
     The Guardian, 13 October 2021, https://www.theguardian.com/
     commentisfree/2021/oct/13/american-workers-general-strike-robert-
     reich.

50   https://www.bls.gov/opub/ted/2022/number-of-unemployed-people-per-
     job-opening-unchanged-at-0-6-in-december-2021.htm#:~:text=Onper
     cento20thepercento20lastpercento20businesspercento20day,downperc
     ento200.1percento20frompercento20Octoberpercento202021.&text=L
     inepercento20chartpercento20withpercento20181percento20data
     percento20points.

51   https://www.nber.org/papers/w29739.

52   Greenhouse, S., '"Striketober" Is Showing Workers' Rising Power – but
     Will It Lead to Lasting Change?' *The Guardian*, 23 October 2021, https://
     www.theguardian.com/us-news/2021/oct/23/striketober-unions-strikes-
     workers-lasting-change.

53   Deaux, J., 'Deere Climbs as End of Monthlong Strike Eases Sales
     Concern', *Bloomerg*, 18 November 2021, https://www.bloomberg.com/
     news/articles/2021-11-18/deere-union-workers-accept-latest-deal-
     ending-monthlong-strike?sref=CIpmV6x8.

54   Thorbecke, C., 'Kellogg Restarts Talks with Workers as Strike Enters
     Seventh Week', *abcnews.com*, 22 November 2021, https://abcnews.
     go.com/Business/kellogg-restarts-talks-workers-strike-enters-seventh-
     week/story?id=81327465.

55   Yrkevich, V. and Isidore, C., 'Striking Alabama Mine Workers Bring
     Protest to New York City', *Cnn*, 4 November 2021, https://edition.cnn.
     com/2021/11/04/business/mine-workers-protest-nyc/index.html.

56   Greenhouse, S., 'A Slap in the Face. Nurses' Strike Signals Kaiser's
     End as Union Haven', *The Guardian*, 13 November 2021, https://www.

theguardian.com/us-news/2021/nov/13/kaiser-permanente-nurses-unions-strike.

57	Aiken, A., 'Workers Pin Brutal Resignation Letter to Storefront after Quitting Jobs over Low Pay', *Dailystar*, 8 November 2021, https://www.dailystar.co.uk/news/weird-news/workers-pin-brutal-resignation-letter-25405712.

58	Handbury, M. and Reuter, D., 'We All Quit. A Photo of a Burger King Sign Went Viral after Workers Protested Long Hours, Low Pay, and Kitchen Temperatures That Reached 97 Degrees', *Insider*, 13 July 2021, https://www.businessinsider.com/burger-king-we-all-quit-sign-viral-workers-labor-shortage-2021-7?r=US&IR=T.

59	Elk, M., '1,650th Strike Recorded by Payday in Richmond – NoLa Garbage Workers Strike – Rural NC Bojangle Workers Strike', *Paydayreport*, 8 November 2021, https://paydayreport.com/1650th-strike-recorded-by-payday-in-richmond-nola-garbage-workers-strike-rural-nc-bojangle-workers-strike/.

60	Molla, R., 'How a Bunch of Starbucks Baristas Built a Labor Movement', *Vox*, 8 April 2022, https://www.vox.com/recode/22993509/starbucks-successful-union-drive.

61	Lucas, A., 'Here's a Map of Starbucks Stores That Voted to Unionize', *CNBC*, 9 December 2022, https://www.cnbc.com/2022/12/09/map-of-starbucks-stores-that-voted-tounionize.html?__source=sharebar|twitter&par=sharebar.

62	'Labor Action Tracker', *ILR Workers Institute*, 21 February 2022, https://www.ilr. cornell.edu/worker-institute/blog/reports-and-publications/labor-action-tracker-annual-report-2021.

63	Ibid.

64	Ho, J., 'U.S. Labor Strikes Went Up Almost 50% Between 2021 and 2022', *Marketplace.org*, 16 January 2023, https://www.marketplace.org/2023/01/16/labor-strikes-went-up-almost-50-percent-between-2021-and-2022/.

65	Brusie, C., 'NYC Nurse Strike Ends – Nurses Win Historic Victory', *Nurse*, 12 January 2023, https://nurse.org/articles/new-york-nurse-strike/.

66	Gurley, L. K., 'Apple Illegally Fired Five Labor Activists, Union Says', *The Washington Post*, 28 March 2023, https://www.washingtonpost.com/technology/2023/03/28/apple-union-firings/.

67	Del Rey, J., 'Leaked Amazon Memo Warns the Company Is Running Out of People to Hire', *Vox*, 17 June 2022, https://www.vox.com/recode/23170900/leaked-amazon-memo-warehouses-hiring-shortage.

68	Streitfeld, D., 'How Amazon Crushes Unions', *The New York Times*, 16 March 2021, https://www.nytimes.com/2021/03/16/technology/amazon-unions-virginia.html.

69   Dimitrov, N., 'Why Amazon's Attrition Is Higher than Attrition at Other Tech Companies', *Amazonbound.medium.com*, 26 October 2018, https://amazonbound.medium.com/why-amazons-attrition-is-higher-than-attrition-at-other-tech-companies-b0de9cb2c4fe.

70   Brancaccio, D., Morbey M. G., Conlon, R. Shin, D., 'Is Amazon's High Turnover a Huge Red Flag or the Secret to Its Dominance?' *Marketplace.org*, 18 June 2021, https://www.marketplace.org/2021/06/18/amazon-workforce-turnover-dominance-investigation/.

71   Ibid.

72   Kantor, J., Weise, K. and Ashford, G., 'The Amazon That Customers Don't See', *The New York Times*, 15 June 2021, https://www.nytimes.com/interactive/2021/06/15/us/amazon-workers.html.

73   Del Rey, J., 'Leaked Amazon Memo Warns the Company Is Running Out of People to Hire', Vox, 17 June 2022, https://www.vox.com/recode/23170900/leaked-amazon-memo-warehouses-hiring-shortage.

74   Menegus, A., 'Exclusive: Amazon's Attrition Costs $8 Billion Annually according to Leaked Documents. And It Gets Worse', *Engadget*, 17 October 2022, https://www.engadget.com/amazon-attrition-leadership-ctsmd-201800110.html.

75   Anderson, G., 'Can Amazon Afford to Keep Churning through Its Frontline Workers?' *RetailWire*, 19 October 2022, https://retailwire.com/discussion/can-amazon-afford-to-keep-churning-through-its-frontline-workers/.

76   Kantor, Weise and Ashford, 'The Amazon That Customers Don't See'.

77   Menegus, 'Exclusive: Amazon's Attrition Costs $8 Billion Annually according to Leaked Documents. And It Gets Worse'.

78   Boyd, J. H., 'Still Booming', *Supply Chain [quarterly]*, 25 August 2022, https://www.supplychainquarterly.com/articles/7000-still-booming.

79   Ibid.

80   Allyn, B., 'Amazon Ceo Says Company Will Lay off More *than* 18,000 Workers', *NPR*, 4 January 2023, https://www.npr.org/2023/01/04/1147034858/amazon-ceo-says-company-will-layoff-more-than-18-000-workers#:~:text=In%20a%20blog%20post%2C%20Amazon,not%20affect%20hourly%20warehouse%20workers.

81   Coin, F. and Jaffe, S., 'Il lavoro non ti ama (e nemmeno noi lo amiamo)', *Jacobin Italia*, 24 October 2022, https://jacobinitalia.it/il-lavoro-non-ti-ama-e-nemmeno-noi-lo-amiamo/.

82   Aldrick, P., 'Larry Summers Says US Needs 5% Jobless Rate for Five Years to Ease Inflation', *Bloomberg*, 20 June 2022, https://www.bloomberg.com/news/articles/2022-06-20/summers-says-us-needs-5-jobless-rate-for-five-years-to-ease-cpi#xj4y7vzkg.

83   International Labour Organization, 'Global Wage Report 2022-23', https://www.ilo.org/digitalguides/en-gb/story/globalwagereport2022-23#intro.

84   https://x.com/RBReich/status/1539362473517559808.

85   Weber, I. M. and Wasner E., 'Sellers' Inflation, Profits and Conflict. Why
      Can Large Firms Hike Prices in an Emergency?' 27 February 2023,
      https://scholarworks.umass.edu/econ_workingpaper/343/; '*Central
      Bankers Warn Companies on Fatter Profit Margins*', *Financial Times*,
      https://www.ft.com/content/a35d1da4-60f6-4b34-9c04-a5c4f3b4d2cc.

86   'Transcript of Chair Powell's Press Conference', 15 June 2022, https://
      www.federalreserve.gov/mediacenter/files/FOMCpresconf20220615.pdf.

87   Blanchard, O., Domash, A. and Summers, L., '22-7 Bad News for the Fed
      from the Beveridge Space', *Peterson Institute for International Economics*,
      July 2022, https://www.piie.com/sites/default/files/documents/pb22-7.pdf.

88   Reich, R., 'Corporate Greed, Not Wages, Is behind Inflation. It's Time
      for Price Controls'. *The Guardian*, 25 September 2022, https://www.
      theguardian.com/commentisfree/2022/sep/25/inflation-price-controls-
      robert-reich.

89   Kalecki, M., 'Political Aspects of Full Employment', The *Political
      Quarterly*, 14 (1943), n. 4, pp. 322–30.

90   'Best Books of 2022: Economics', *Financial Times*, https://www.ft.com/
      content/634c1974-bc76-4f56-9548-274816dcc638.

91   Mattei, C., 'Don't Be Fooled: Policymakers Are Quietly Invoking
      Austerity by Other Names', *The Guardian*, 8 October 2022, https://www.
      theguardian.com/commentisfree/2022/oct/08/us-policymakers-austerity-
      by-other-names.

92   Ibid.

93   Ibid.

94   Covert, B., 'The Fed's War on Inflation Is a Class War', *The New York
      Times*, 31 March 2023, https://www.nytimes.com/2023/03/31/opinion/
      federal-reserve-inflation-jerome-powell.html.

95   Wang, V., '12-Hour Days, Six Days a Week', *The New York Times*, 2 August
      2021, https://www.nytimes.com/2021/08/02/briefing/china-economy-
      gig-workers.html.

96   Huang, Z., 'China Spells Out How Excessive "996" Work Culture Is
      Illegal', *Bloomberg*, 27 August 2021, https://www.bloomberg.com/news/
      articles/2021-08-27/china-s-top-court-says-excessive-996-work-culture-
      is-illegal?leadSource=uverify%20wall.

97   https://996.icu/#/zh_CN.

98   'The Extreme 996 Work Culture in China', https://www.youtube.com/
      watch?v=l8wWoQ3_F00.

99   Dou, E., 'Death of Chinese Tech Worker Fuels Anger over Brutal Hours',
      The Washington Post, January 2021, https://www.washingtonpost.com/
      world/asia_pacific/china-tech-death-pinduoduo/2021/01/05/c68bdd76-
      4eff-11eb-a1f5-fdaf28cfca90_story.html.

100   Jiayun, F., 'Pinduoduo Worker Dies by Suicide While on Leave, Ex-
      Employee's Video on Disturbing Work Culture Goes Viral', *The China
      Project*, 11 January 2021, https://thechinaproject.com/2021/01/11/

pinduoduo-worker-dies-by-suicide-while-on-leave-prompting-ex-employee-to-reveal-disturbing-work-culture/.

101 Flannery, R., 'Pinduoduo Founder Passes Alibaba's Jack Ma as China's Second-Richest Man', *Forbes*, 22 June 2020, https://www.forbesmiddleeast.com/billionaires/world-billionaires/pinduoduo-founder-passes-alibabas-jack-ma-as-chinas-second-richest-man.

102 '"Gwarosa": Why Koreans Are Working Themselves to Death', *The Week*, 6 November 2018, https://www.theweek.co.uk/97569/gwarosa-why-koreans-are-working-themselves-to-death.

103 'Why China's Workers Die so Young', https://www.youtube.com/watch?v=WKLUvEx1-gE.

104 Li, J., 'Death of Bilibili Staff Member Renews Discussion about Overwork in Chinese Tech Companies', *KrASIA*, 8 February 2022, https://kr-asia.com/death-of-bilibili-staff-member-renews-discussion-about-overwork-in-chinese-tech-companies.

105 'Authorities Investigate Sudden Death of 22-Years-Old Woman after Days of Overworking', *Global Times*, 28 July 2022, https://www.globaltimes.cn/page/202207/1271648.shtml.

106 'Long Working Hours Can Increase Deaths from Heart Disease and Stroke, Say Ilo and Who', *International Labour Organization*, 17 May 2021, https://www.ilo.org/global/about-the-ilo/newsroom/news/WCMS_792131/langen/index.htm.

107 Chen, E., 'These Chinese Millennials Are "Chilling", and Beijing Isn't Happy', *The New York Times*, 3 July 2021, https://www.nytimes.com/2021/07/03/world/asia/china-slackers-tangping.html.

108 Deepak, B. R., 'Chinese Millennials Take to Lying Flat', *The Sunday Guardian*, 3 July 2021, https://sundayguardianlive.com/opinion/chinese-millennials-take-lying-flat.

109 Ferri, G., 'Cosa c'è dietro il tangping, la protesta dei giovani lavoratori tech in Cina', *Wired*, 4 August 2021, https://www.wired.it/economia/lavoro/2021/08/04/cina-tangping-protesta-giovani-lavoratori-tech/.

110 Angran, L., 'What Happened When China Expanded Its Higher Education System?' *Sixth Tone*, 11 January 2023, https://www.sixthtone.com/news/1012037/.

111 'Let It Rot: China's Tech Workers Struggle to Find Jobs', *Financial Times*, https://www.ft.com/content/cc3e25c3-a8a4-4b4c-9f0c-77cf0777fd4b.

112 'Property Prices Index by City 2023', *Numbeo*, https://www.numbeo.com/property-investment/rankings.jsp.

113 《躺平是王道》躺平即正义, Zhang Busan, 'Lying Flat is King', https://www.youtube.com/watch?v=corZx0a1yRU.

114 Zhou, V., '"iPhones Are Made in Hell". 3 Months Inside China's iPhone City', *Rest of World*, 3 January 2023, https://restofworld.org/2023/foxconn-iphone-factory-china/.

115 Ibid.

116 Anonymous, 'Tangpingist Manifesto. Tangpingists of the World, Unite!',
     The *Anarchist Library.com* (2021), https://www.theanarchistlibrary.org/
     library/anonymous-tangpingist-manifesto.

117 长平观察:中国'屌丝'的'内卷'与"躺平", Dw.com, https://www.
     dw.com/zh/%E9%95%BF%E5%B9%B3%E8%A7%82%E5%AF%9F%
     E4%B8%AD %E5%9B%BD%E5%B1%8C%E4%B8%9D%E7%9A%84
     %E5%86%85%E 5%8D%B7%E4%B8%8E%E8%BA%BA%E5%B9%B3
     /a-57594567.

118 Yu, S., 'In Charts. Why Women in China Are Climbing High – or
     Quitting Work', *Financial Times*, 8 March 2023, https://www.ft.com/
     content/4c47ddba-0e1a-467e-9f7c-33d71b0e843a. It is interesting to add
     a gender perspective to this picture. Over the past decade, the number
     of women in leadership positions in Chinese companies has tripled.
     This growth has gone hand in hand with the number of women leaving
     the workforce. An article in the *Financial Times* shows how the labour
     force participation rate of women has dropped to an all-time low to 61.6
     per cent from 63.8 per cent. The lack of support networks and childcare
     services has forced many female professionals to reduce, if not abandon,
     the world of work.

119 Xiao, H. Y., 'I've Had Enough of My Parents' "No Pain, No Gain"', 26
     December 2022, https://www.nytimes.com/2022/12/26/opinion/china-
     society-culture-youth-covid-protests.html.

120 Qianni, W. y Shifan, G., 'How One Obscure Word Captures Urban China's
     Unhappiness', *Sixth Tone*, November 2020, https://www.sixthtone.com/
     news/1006391/how-one-obscure-word-captures-urban-chinas-unhappiness.

121 https://www.newyorker.com/culture/cultural-comment/chinas-
     involuted-generation.

122 Liu, Y-L., 'China's "Involuted" Generation', *The New Yorker*, 14 May
     2021, https://www.newyorker.com/culture/cultural-comment/chinas-
     involuted-generation.

Chapter 3

1   Ambrosio, L., 'What's Going On? 07/06/2022', *Radio Popolare*,
     7 June 2022, https://www.radiopopolare.it/podcast/gli-speciali-di-
     martedi-07-06-2022/.

2   Girardi, A., 'Se ci fosse un referendum sul reddito di cittadinanza la
     metà degli italiani voterebbe per abolirlo', *FanPage*, 6 June 2022, https://
     www.fanpage.it/politica/se-ci-fosse-un-referendum-sul-reddito-di-
     cittadinanza-la-meta-degli-italiani-voterebbe-per-abolirlo/.

3   INPS, 'Conoscere il Paese per costruire il futuro', *XXI Rapporto Annuale*,
     June 2022, https://servizi2.inps.it/docallegati/Mig/Dati_analisi_bilanci/
     Rapporti_annuali/XXI_Rapporto_Annuale/XXI_Rapporto_Annuale.pdf.

4   'ISTAT', *Rapporto Annuale 2022*, 8 June 2022, https://www.istat.it/it/
     files//2022/07/Rapporto-Annuale-2022_estratto-sintesi-5.pdf.

5   Rocco, S., 'Flavio Briatore: Mai visto un povero creare posti di lavoro,
     rompono invece di ringraziare', *FanPage*, 7 September 2022, https://www.
     fanpage.it/spettacolo/personaggi/flavio-briatore-mai-visto-un-povero-
     creare-posti-di-lavoro-rompono-invece-di-ringraziare/.

6   'Spot Volontari Expo Milano 2015', https://www.youtube.com/
     watch?v=6pRUMN5cV7k.

7   Brancaccio, E., *Democrazia sotto assedio*, Piemme, Milan, 2022.

8   Zaccardi, M., 'Viaggio nel fenomeno delle grandi dimissioni: le aziende
     ancora non capiscono perché le persone si licenziano', *Forbes*, 7 February
     2022, https://forbes.it/2022/02/07/grandi-dimissioni-causa-cosa-le-
     azienda-non-capiscono/.

9   Fubini, F., 'Lavoro, giovani in fuga: Non cerco piú un'azienda, mi vogliono
     a X Factor', *Corriere della Sera*, 10 August 2022, https://www.corriere.it/
     cronache/il-racconto/22_agosto_10/lavoro-giovani-in-fuga-654cede2-
     181c-11ed-9a9b-5d6d627908eb.shtml.

10   Boralevi, A., 'Da commercialista a rider felice', *La Stampa*, 15 January
     2021, https://www.lastampa.it/rubriche/lato-boralevi/2021/01/15/news/
     da-commercialista-a-rider-felice-1.39776762/.

11   'Giuseppina', *bidella*, January 2023, https://gazzettadelsud.it/articoli/
     cronaca/2023/01/18/giuseppina-bidella-pendolare-tutti-i-giorni-tra-
     napoli-e-milano-treno-costa-meno-dellaffitto-d37b9096-ec8a-4a77-
     b908-826e02706363/.

12   'La storia, smentita, del 35enne che chiude il suo studio di commercialista
     per diventare un rider felice', *Open*, 18 January 2021, https://www.open.
     online/2021/01/18/la-storia-smentita-del-35enne-che-chiude-il-suo-
     studio-di-commercialista-per-diventare-un-rider-felice/.

13   'State of the Global Workplace: 2022 Report', *Gallup*, https://www.gallup.
     com/workplace/349484/state-of-the-global-workplace-2022-report.aspx.

14   Marazzi, C., *E il denaro va. Esodo e rivoluzione dei mercati finanziari*,
     Bollati Boringhieri, Turín, 1998, p. 37.

15   Kent, G., 'The Benefits of World Hunger', *Un Chronicle*, 45 (2008), n. 2/3,
     p. 81, https://www2.hawaii.edu/~kent/BenefitsofWorldHunger.pdf.

16   Istat, 'Posti vacanti nelle imprese dell'industria e dei servizi – stime
     preliminari', https://www.istat.it/it/files//2022/11/Posti_vacanti_nelle_
     imprese_novembre_2022.pdf.

17   Garnero, A. and Taddei, M., 'Domanda e offerta di lavoro: un incontro
     difficile', *LaVoce.info*, 26 November 2021, https://www.lavoce.info/
     archives/91171/domanda-e-offerta-di-lavoro-un-incontro-difficile/.

18   'Banca d'Italia. Il mercato del lavoro. Dati e analisi', *marzo de 2023*,
     https:// www.lavoro.gov.it/documenti-e-norme/studi-e-statistiche/
     Documents/Il%20mercato%20del%20lavoro%20dati%20e%20analisi%20
     -%20marzo%202023/MLPS-Bankitalia-Anpal-marzo-2023.pdf.

19   Armilleri, F. 'Le grandi dimissioni hanno precedenti', *La voce info*,
      https://www.lavoce.info/archives/99876/le-grandi-dimissioni-hanno-
      precedenti/.

20   CENSIS, 'V Rapporto Censis-Eudaimon sul welfare aziendale', https://
      www.censis.it/sites/default/files/downloads/5°%20Rapporto%20Censis-
      Eudaimon%20sul%20welfare%20aziendale_SINTESI.pdf.

21   'Banca d'Italia. Il mercato del lavoro. Dati e analisi', March 2023, https://
      www.lavoro.gov.it/documenti-e-norme/studi-e-statistiche/Documents/
      Il%20mercato%20del%20lavoro%20dati%20e%20analisi%20-%20
      marzo%202023/MLPS- Bankitalia-Anpal-marzo-2023.pdf.

22   Censis, 'Il valore delle nuove forme del lavoro nelle aziende', *VI Rapporto
      Censis-Eudaimon sobre el bienestar empresarial*, 1 March 2023, https://
      www.censis.it/sites/default/files/downloads/6_Rapporto%20Censis-
      Eudaimon%20sul%20welfare%20azien-dale_sintesi.pdf.

23   Coin, F., 'I lavoratori si sentono in gabbia', *L'Essenziale*, 19 March 2022, n.
      19, p. 27.

24   https://www.inps.it/it/it/dati-e-bilanci/rapporti-annuali/xxi-rapporto-
      annuale.html.

25   Randstad, 'Il rapporto tra posti vacanti e disoccupazione', https://research.
      randstad.it/rapporti/il-rapporto-tra-posti-vacanti-e-disoccupazione.pdf.

26   Alloway, T., 'A New Type of Beveridge May Explain a Stubborn Labor-
      Market Mystery', *Bloomberg*, 27 September 2022, https://www.bloomberg.
      com/news/articles/2022-09-27/a-new-type-of-beveridge-may-explain-a-
      stubborn-labor-market-mystery#xj4y7vzkg.

27   Randstad, 'Il rapporto tra posti vacanti e disoccupazione'.

Chapter 4

1   'C'era una volta la sanità pubblica, Presa diretta, 2020–2021', *RaiPlay.
     it*, https://www.raiplay.it/video/2021/02/Presa-diretta—Cera-una-volta-
     la-sanita-pubblica-0b7d6ab0-bb1e-4abf-a1a9-ced2de43d5d2.html?wt_
     mc=2.google.yt.rai_ presadiretta.&wt.

2   Folino, F., *Legge 161/2014: direttiva europea sull'orario di lavoro
     e turni massacranti*, en NuoveFrontiereDiritto.it, https://www.
     nuovefrontierediritto.it/legge-1612014-direttiva-europea-sullorario-di-
     lavoro-e-turni-massacranti/.

3   Maslach, C., *Burnout: The Cost of Caring*, Malor Books, San José (CA),
     2011.

4   Maslach, C. and Leiter, M. P., *The Truth about Burnout: How
     Organizations Cause Personal Stress and What to Do about It*, Jossey-Bass,
     San Francisco, 1997.

5   Young, E., 'What Happens When Americans Can Finally Exhale',
     The Atlantic, 20 May 2021, https://www.theatlantic.com/health/
     archive/2021/05/pandemic-trauma-summer/618934/.

6   'Rinnovo contratto. Nursing Up "gravi carenze di personale,
     infermieri con piú di 100 giorni di ferie arretrate"', *Nurse Time*, 7 May
     2022, https://nursetimes.org/rinnovo-contratto-nursing-up-gravi-
     carenze-di-personale-infermieri-con-piú-di-100-giorni-di-ferie-
     arretrate/140680.

7   Nacoti, M., Ciocca, A. et al., 'At the Epicenter of the Covid-19 Pandemic
     and Humanitarian Crises in Italy: Changing Perspectives on Preparation
     and Mitigation', *Nejm Catalyst*, 21 March 2020, https://catalyst.nejm.org/
     doi/pdf/10.1056/CAT.20.0080.

8   SIAARTI, 'Raccomandazioni di etica clinica per l'ammissione a
     trattamenti intensivi e per la loro sospensione, in condizioni eccezionali
     di squilibrio tra necessità e risorse disponibili', 6 March 2020, https://
     www.sicp.it/wp-content/uploads/2020/03/SIAARTI-Covid19-
     Raccomandazioni-di-etica-clinica.pdf.

9   Revelli, M., 'Siamo arrivati a una sorta di ground zero', *il manifesto*, 11 March
     2020, https://ilmanifesto.it/siamo-arrivati-a-una-sorta-di-ground-zero.

10   Lydersen, K., 'Nurses in the U.S. Are Suffering "Moral Injury"',
     Inthesetimes.com, 18 July 2022, https://inthesetimes.com/article/nurses-
     moral-injury-pandemic-staffing-crisis-work-conditions.

11   Litz, B. T., Stein, N., Delaney, E. et al., 'Moral Injury and Moral Repair in
     War Veterans: A Preliminary Model and Intervention Strategy', *Clinical
     Psychology Review*, XXIX (2009), pp. 695–706, https://icds.uoregon.edu/
     wp-content/uploads/2015/03/Litz-et-al-2009-Moral-Injury-and-Moral-
     Repair-in-War-Veterans.pdf.

12   Molendijk, T., Kramer, E.-H. and Verweij, D., 'Moral Aspects of "Moral
     Injury": Analyzing Conceptualizations on the Role of Morality in
     Military Trauma', *Journal of Military Ethics*, 17 (2018), n. 1, pp. 36–53,
     14 giugno 2018, https://www.tandfonline.com/doi/full/10.1080/15027570
     .2018.1483173?cookieSet=1.

13   Coin, F., 'L'abisso della guerra raccontato dai veterani', *Jacobin*, 20
     March 2022, https://jacobinitalia.it/labisso-della-guerra-raccontato-dai-
     veterani/.

14   Nakashima Brock, R., What Is Moral Injury? It Can Teach Us About Our
     Own Humanity, Voa.org, 21 March 2018, https://www.voa.org/blog/
     what-moralinjury.-teaches-us-about-our-own-humanity

15   Ibid.

16   Ibid.

17   Roy, A., *The God of Small Things*, Flamingo, London, 1997.

18   Bulli, F., 'Coronavirus: la ferita morale degli operatori sanitari', *Ipsco.it*, 8
     July 2020, https://www.ipsico.it/news/coronavirus-la-ferita-morale-degli-
     operatori-sanitari/.

19   DeMarco, M., 'Moral Injury and the Agony and Power of Love',
     Psychology Today, 3 September 2022, https://www.psychologytoday.com/
     us/blog/soul-console/202209/moral-injury-and-the-agony-and-power-
     love.

20   Talbot, S. G. and Dean, W., 'Physicians Aren't "Burning Out". They're
     Suffering from Moral Injury', *Stat*, 26 July 2018, https://www.statnews.
     com/2018/07/26/physicians-not-burning-out-they-are-suffering-moral-
     injury/.

21   Talbot, S. G. and Dean, W., 'Physicians Aren't "Burning Out". They're
     Suffering from Moral Injury', *Stat*, 26 July 2018, https://www.statnews.
     com/2018/07/26/physicians-not-burning-out-they-are-suffering-moral-
     injury/.

22   DeMarco, M., 'Moral Injury and the Agony and Power of Love',
     Psychology Today, 3 settembre 2022, https://www.psychologytoday.com/
     us/blog/soul-console/202209/moral-injury-and-the-agony-and-power-
     love.

23   Carucci, R. and Praslova, L. N., 'Employees Are Sick of Being Asked to
     Make Moral Compromises', *Harvard Business Review*, 21 February 2022,
     https://hbr.org/2022/02/employees-are-sick-of-being-asked-to-make-
     moral-compromises.

24   Schneider, F. H., Brun, F. and Weber, R. A., 'Sorting and Wage Premiums
     in Immoral Work', June 2020, https://www.econ.uzh.ch/static/wp/
     econwp353.pdf.

25   Palermo, C., Rivetti, C., Di Silverio, P. et al., 'La grande fuga dagli ospedali
     del Ssn. Negli ultimi tre anni 21mila medici li hanno abbandonati. Lo
     studio Anaao Assomed', *Quotidiano Sanità*, 21 April 2022, https://www.
     quotidianosanita.it/studi-e-analisi/articolo.php?articolo_id=104156.

26   Anaao Assomed, 'Via dal Ssn 8mila medici l'anno tra pensione e
     dimissioni. È emergenza', 23 September 2021, https://www.anaao.it/
     content.php?cont=32793.

27   Anaao Assomed, 'Covid-19: la grande fuga dagli ospedali. Il sondaggio
     dell'Anaao Assomed', 7 January 2021, https://www.anaao.it/content.
     php?cont=30576.

28   'Nursing Up: "Fuga di infermieri e Oss, oltre 2mila dimissioni in sei
     mesi"', *Affari Italiani*, 12 January 2022, https://www.affaritaliani.it/
     medicina/nursing-up-fuga-di-infermieri-oss-oltre-2mila-dimissioni-in-
     sei-mesi-774387.html.

29   July 2022, https://www.adnkronos.com/sanita-ogni-giorno-7-medici-
     danno-le-dimissioni_3lw1yy3PFMpKZrkREg262e.

30   Agenas, 'Il personale del Servizio Sanitario Nazionale', 23 December
     2022, https://www.agenas.gov.it/comunicazione/primo-piano/2147-il-
     personale-del-servizio-sanitario-nazionale.

31   Palermo, C. and Liuzzi, G., 'Quanta confusione sulla carenza dei medici',
     Quotidiano Sanità, 26 October 2022, https://www.quotidianosanita.it/
     lettere-al-direttore/articolo.php?articolo_id=108389.

32 Spandonaro, F., D'Angela, D. and Polistena, B., 'Senza riforme e crescita, Ssn sull'orlo della crisi', *XVIII Rapporto sanità, Creasanita.it*, https://www. quotidiano-sanita.it/allegati/allegato1674639068.pdf.

33 Mastrillo, A., 'Professioni sanitarie. Ecco il Report annuale con tutti i dati tra carenze ed esuberi. Appello alle Università: rivedano i criteri nella determinazione dei posti da mettere a bando, serve piú equilibrio', *Il Sole 24 Ore*, 15 November 2022, https://www.sanita24.ilsole24ore. com/art/lavoro-e-professione/2022-11-10/professioni-sanitarie-ecco-report-annuale-tutti-dati-carenze-ed-esuberi-appello-universita-rivedano-criteri-determinazione-posti-mettere-bando-serve-piu-equilibrio-104653. php?uuid=AEcKFpFC.

34 Studio Multicentrico Nazionale, 'Gli episodi di violenza rivolti agli infermieri italiani sul posto di lavoro', https://www.fnopi.it/wp-content/ uploads/2022/06/UNIGE-studio-multicentrico-Universita-Genova-1.pdf.

35 Anaao Giovani, 'Ospedali. L'inesorabile declino del pubblico. Confronto 2010/2017', *Quotidiano Sanità*, 4 February 2020, https://www. quotidianosanita.it/studi-e-analisi/articolo.php?articolo_id=80953.

36 Beneventi, N., 'Stress, ansia, disturbi del sonno: i sanitari a rischio burn-out durante il Covid', *TrendSanità*, 9 December 2021, https://www.pphc. it/stress-ansia-burn-out/.

37 Tavolaro, A., 'Sempre piú infermieri vogliono abbandonare la professione', *Nurse24.it*, 18 May 2022, https://www.nurse24.it/infermiere/professione/ sempre-piu-infermieri-vogliono-abbandonare-professione.html.

38 Giorgi, C. e Taroni, F., *Il Servizio sanitario nazionale di fronte alla pandemia. Passato e futuro delle politiche per la salute*, https://www. futura-editrice.it/wp-content/uploads/2020/04/Il-Servizio-sanitario-nazionale-di-fronte-alla-pandemia_Giorgie-Taroni.pdf.

39 Ibid.

40 Taroni, F., 'Prima e dopo quel difficile dicembre 1978', http://www. cortisupremeesalute.it/wp-content/uploads/2019/06/7_Prima-e-dopo-quel-difficile-dicembre-1978-1.pdf.

41 Ibid.

42 Ibid.

43 Gimbe, Report 7/2019. 'Il definanziamento 2010–2019 del SSN', https://www.gimbe.org/pagine/1229/it/report-72019-il-definanziamento-20102019-del-ssn#:~:text=Il per cento20finanziamento per cento20pubblico per cento20 per centoC3 per centoA8 per cento20stato,per per cento20esigenze per cento20di per cento20finanza per cento20pubblica.

44 'Dossier Sanità Allarme Rosso', *Federazionecimofesmed.it*, https://www. federazionecimofesmed.it/2022/09/08/dossier-sanita-allarme-rosso/.

45 Ibid.

46 Palermo, C. and Rivetti, C., 'Covid. Meno posti letto, piú morti. Indagine Anaao', *Quotidiano Sanità*, 1 March 2021, https://www.quotidianosanita. it/studi-e-analisi/articolo.php?articolo_id=93013.

47   Anaao Piemonte, *#iomenevado*, 22 April 2022, https://www. anaaopiemonte.info/anaaopiemonte/iomenevado/.

48   'Congresso nazionale Anaao. La tempesta è servita. Servono investimenti per uscire dalla crisi', *Quotidiano Sanità*, 24 June 2022, https://www. quotidianosanita.it/lavoro-e-professioni/articolo.php?articolo_id=105810.

49   Huebner, L. C., *Catheters, Slurs, and Pickup Lines: Professional Intimacy in Hospital Nursing*, West Chester University of Pennsylvania, Philadelphia (PA), 2021, https://digitalcommons.wcupa.edu/casfaculty_books/16/.

50   Ravizza, S. and Viafora, G., 'I medici a gettone arruolati in chat senza controlli: Guadagnano 3.600 euro in 48 ore', en *Corriere della Sera*, 1 October 2022, https://www.corriere.it/cronache/22_ottobre_01/medici-gettone-3600-euro-48-ore-8e419eca-40fb-11ed-8b65-55aa2f703574.shtml?refresh_ce.

51   Anaao Assomed, 'Via dal Ssn 8mila medici l'anno tra pensione e dimissioni. È emergenza', 23 September 2021, https://www.anaao.it/ content.php?cont=32793.

52   'Il mercato dei gettonisti', *Vvox.it*, https://vvox.it/video/il-mercato-dei-gettonisti/.

53   Strippoli, S., 'Lascio il posto fisso in pronto soccorso, da medico mi conviene lavorare a gettone', *la Repubblica*, 31 agosto 2022, https://torino. repubblica.it/cronaca/2022/08/31/news/dottoressa_pronto_soccorso_ meglio_lavoro_a_gettone-363609140/.

54   'Ilaria, Infermiera: Mi dimetto dal Ssn perché non mi fa crescere come professionista', *Assocarenews.it*, 1 November 2021, https://www. assocarenews.it/primo-piano/ultim-ora/nurse24/ilaria-infermiera-mi-dimetto-dal-ssn-perche-non-mi-fa-crescere-come-professionista#.

55   Bocci, M., 'L'addio dei medici di famiglia lascia quasi 3 milioni di italiani senza il dottore. Lombardia e Veneto le regioni più in difficoltà', *la Repubblica*, 15 November 2022, https://www.repubblica. it/cronaca/2022/11/15/news/carenza_medici_di_famiglia_ regioni-374586896/.

56   'Bisogni di salute nelle aree interne, fra desertificazione sanitaria e PNRR', *Aiponet.it*, http://www.aiponet.it/news/104-ufficio-stampa/3129-bisogni-di-salute-nelle-aree-interne-fra-desertificazione-sanitaria-e-pnrr.html.

57   Antonino, C., 'Simeu, De Iaco: Da novembre altri 600 medici si sono dimessi dai pronto soccorso: fughe in accelerazione', *Emergency-live.com*, 13 May 2022, https://www.emergency-live.com/it/news/simeu-de-iaco-da-novembre-altri-600-medici-si-sono-dimessi-dai-pronto-soccorso-fughe-in-accelerazione/.

58   'Pronto soccorso a rischio estinzione: mancano quasi 5mila medici e 100 al mese lasciano', *Il Sole 24 Ore*, 9 May 2022, https://www. sanita24.ilsole24ore.com/art/lavoro-e-professione/2022-05-09/pronto-soccorso-rischio-estinzione-mancano-quasi-5mila-medici-e-100-mese-lasciano-130050.php?uuid=AE5UVPXB.

59   Antonino, C., 'Simeu, De Iaco: Da novembre altri 600 medici si sono dimessi dai pronto soccorso: fughe in accelerazione', *Emergency-live.com*, 13 May 2022, https://www.emergency-live.com/it/news/simeu-de-iaco-

da-novembre-altri-600-medici-si-sono-dimessi-dai-pronto-soccorso-
fughe-in-accelerazione/.

60   'Mezzogiorno per l'unità e la crescita del Paese – Intervento di Giuseppe
      Visone', https:// www.youtube.com/watch?v=KtRIzNFzNAw.

61   ES. M., 'Al Cardarelli di Napoli il PS "esplode" e i medici si dimettono',
      Quotidiano Sanità, 4 May 2022, https://www.quotidianosanita.it/regioni-
      e-asl/articolo.php?articolo_id=104491#:~:text=di%20Es.,adeguata%20
      e%20dignitosa%20ai%20pazienti%E2%80%9D.

62   'Mezzogiorno per l'unità e la crescita del Paese – Intervento di Giuseppe
      Visone', https:// www.youtube.com/watch?v=KtRIzNFzNAw.

63   ISTAT, 'Il benessere equo e sostenibile in Italia', *Quotidianosanita.it*,
      https:// www.quotidianosanita.it/allegati/allegato1650530891.pdf.

64   Ibid.

65   'La famiglia di Sara Pedri: "L'hanno annientata". Tateo a Chi l'ha
      visto: "Non parlo, momento particolare"', *l'Adige*, 21 October 2021,
      https://www.ladige.it/cronaca/2021/10/21/la-famiglia-di-sara-pedri-
      l-hanno-annientata-tateo-a-chi-l-ha-visto-non-parlo-momento-
      particolare-1.3031696.

66   'Worldwide Shortage of Health Workers Threatens Effective Health
      Coverage', *en Healthdata.org*, 23 May 2022, https://www.healthdata.org/
      news-release/worldwide-shortage- -workers-threatens-effective-health-
      coverage.

67   Brophy, S. A., Sriram, V., Zong, H., Andres, C., Mawyin, M. P. and
      Narayanan G., 'Heroes on Strike. Trends in Global Health Worker Protests
      during Covid-19', https://accounta-bilityresearch.org/wp-content/
      uploads/2022/04/ARC-Accountability-Note_Health-Worker-Protests_
      WEB.pdf.

Chapter 5

1   Bascetta, M., *Economia politica della promessa*, Il Manifesto Libri, Roma,
     2015.

2   Oxfam, 'Disuguitalia. Ridare valore, potere e dignità al lavoro', May
     2022, https://www.oxfamitalia.org/wp-content/uploads/2022/05/WEB_
     Disuguitalia_2022_CLEAN.pdf.

3   FIPE, 'Dumping contrattuale nel settore dei pubblici esercizi', March
     2022, https://www.fipe.it/wp-content/uploads/2022/05/Guida_dumping_
     PE-web.pdf.

4   Lazzeroni, L., 'Il parossistico "mercato" dei contratti collettivi', *Labour*,
     5 (2021), n. 2, pp. 135–53.

5   Garnero, A. e Lucifora, C., 'Sui contratti "pirata" chiudere un occhio non
     paga', *Lavoce.info*, 8 aprile2022, https://www.lavoce.info/archives/94305/
     contratti-pirata-chiudere-un-occhio-non-paga/.

6   For the sake of completeness, it should be said that these 393 thousand beneficiaries with an active employment position make up about 40 per cent of the households benefiting from the RdC (326,000 out of 855,000) and about 20 per cent of the beneficiary persons (393,000 out of 2 million).

7   Polanyi, K., *The Great Transformation*, Beacon Press, Boston, 1944, https://inctpped.ie.ufrj.br/spiderweb/pdf_4/Great_Transformation.pdf.

8   Gainsforth, S., *Cameriera*, Einaudi, Torino, 2022.

9   Aimone Gigio, L. and Camussi, S. A. M., 'Questioni di economia e finanza. Cambiamenti nella struttura qualitativa dell'occupazione', July 2022, https://www.bancaditalia.it/pubblicazioni/qef/2022-0705/QEF_705_22.pdf.

10   Cavalcoli, D., 'Ristoranti e alberghi, 2 addetti su 3 sono lavorativamente poveri', *Corriere della Sera*, 12 July 2022, https://www.corriere.it/economia/lavoro/cards/ristoranti-alberghi-2-addetti-3-sono-lavorativamente-poveri/lavoro-povero-italia_principale.shtmll.

11   'Fipe: in 14 mesi di pandemia persi 514mila posti di lavoro', *Il Sole 24 Ore*, 18 May 2021, https://www.ilsole24ore.com/art/fipe-14-mesi-pandemia-persi-514mila-posti-lavoro-AEi0xBK.

12   Natali, M., 'Quello che il ristoratore non vuole capire', http://www.occca.it/quello-ristoratore-non-vuole-capire/.

13   Matteini, C., 'Lavoro sottopagato – Turni "spezzati", niente riposi, 17 ore dietro il bancone per 800 euro al mese: per i lavoratori la ristorazione è una giungla. Vessazioni e minacce sono la regola', *il Fatto Quotidiano*, 11 November 2021, https://www.ilfattoquotidiano.it/2021/11/11/lavoro-sottopagato-turni-spezzati-niente-riposi-17-ore-dietro-il-bancone-per-800-euro-al-mese-per-i-lavoratori-la-ristorazione-e-una-giungla-vessazioni-e-minacce-sono-la-regola/6384416/.

14   Nguyen, T., 'Amanda Cohen's Sage Advice on Becoming a Professional Chef: "Don't"', *Mediaite.com*, 13 December 2021, https://www.mediaite.com/food/amanda-cohens-sage-advice-on-becoming-a-professional-chef-dont/.

15   Villarosa, H., 'Why Escoffier's Brigade System Has to Go', *FinediningLovers.com*, 13 August 2020, https://www.finedininglovers.com/article/escoffiers-brigade-system.

16   Radio Popolare, 'Mancano lavoratori stagionali, i ristoratori: "È colpa del reddito di cittadinanza"', https://www.radiopopolare.it/mancano-lavoratori-stagionali-i-ristoratori-e-colpa-del-reddito-di-cittadinanza/.

17   Fascist song written by Renato Michele in 1935 during Italy's invasion of Ethiopia.

18   'Two-Thirds of London Chefs Believe Long Hours' Culture Is Harming Their Health, Unite Survey Reveals', *UniteLegalService.org*, 27 April 2017, https://www.unitelegalservices.org/news-stories/two-thirds-of-london-chefs-believe-long-hours-culture-is-harming-their-health-unite-survey-reveals.

19   Pelusi, D., Corradini, I. and Amore, F., 'La psicologia al servizio
      della ristorazione', https://www.ambasciatoridelgusto.it/wp-content/
      uploads/2022/02/2022.02.25-Ricerca-conoscitiva-e-best-practice_3rid.pdf.

20   https://www.facebook.com/OCCCAofficial/posts/faccio-bene-a-
      cambiare-lavoro-di-un-cameriere-anonimociao-occcaio-sono-nella-
      fas/3171073246257626/.

21   Martini, L., 'Nel 2022 i cuochi non vogliono piú rischiare il burnout
      in cucina', *Vice*, https://www.vice.com/it/article/wxdanb/burnout-
      ristorazione.

22   Cohen, J., 'Minds Turned to Ash', *The Economist*, 29 June 2016, https://
      www.economist.com/1843/2016/06/29/minds-turned-to-ash.

23   Palomba, G., *La trama alternativa. Sogni e pratiche di giustizia
      trasformativa*, Minimum Fax, Roma, 2023.

24   Keohane, J., 'The Horrors, Degradations & Ass-Kicking Triumphs of
      NYC's Female Chefs', *Thrillist.com*, 17 April 2015, https://www.thrillist.
      com/eat/nation/horrors-of-being-a-female-chef-nyc-female-chef-stories.

25   Anonymous, 'How I Feel as a Bar Waitress When You Sexually Harass
      Me', *Vice*, 30 August 2016, https://www.vice.com/en/article/9agnxa/how-
      i-feel-when-you-sexually-harass-me-as-your-bar-waitress.

26   'One Fair Wage. The Tipping Point', March 2021, https://onefairwage.site/
      wp-content/uploads/2021/03/OFW_TheTippingPoint_3-1.pdf.

27   Thuy Vo, L., 'We Got Government Data on 20 Years of Workplace Sexual
      Harassment Claims. These Charts Break It Down', 5 dicembre 2017,
      https://www.buzzfeednews.com/article/lamvo/eeoc-sexual-harassment-
      data.

28   'Sexual Harassment in the Hospitality Industry', https://
      hospitalitymanagementdegre-es.net/features/sexual-harassment-in-
      hospitality-infographic/.

29   Cohn, E., 'Shake Shack Founder Danny Meyer Calls Tipping a Massive
      Hoax That Was Born out of Slavery', *Business Insider*, 11 January 2017,
      https://www.businessinsider.com/tipping-is-a-hoax-born-out-of-slavery-
      danny-meyer-says-2017-1?r=US&IR=T.

Chapter 6

1   INAIL, 'Scheda nazionale infortuni sul lavoro da Covid-19', https://
      www.inail.it/cs/inter-net/docs/alg-scheda-tecnica-contagi-covid-31-
      agosto-2022.pdf.

2   Liberatore, R., 'Coronavirus, il fronte dei supermercati a Milano:
      Paura? Siamo terrorizzati. Vedo colleghi piangere tutti i giorni – Le
      testimonianze dei commessi', *Open*, 22 March 2020, https://www.open.
      online/2020/03/22/coronavirus-fronte-supermercati-milano-siamo-
      terrorizzati-vedo-colleghi-piangere-testimonianze/.

3   Mayer, B., Helm, S., Barnett, M. and Arora, M., 'The Impact of Workplace
     Safety and Customer Misbehavior on Supermarket Workers' Stress and
     Psychological Distress during the Covid-19 Pandemic', https://www.
     emerald.com/insight/content/doi/10.1108/IJWHM-03-2021-0074/full/
     pdf?title=the-impact-of-workplace-safety-and-customer-misbehavior-
     on-supermarket-workers-stress-and-psychological-distress-during-the-
     covid-19-pandemic.

4   Valtorta, R., Baldissarri, C. and Volpato, C., 'Burnout and Workplace
     Dehumanization at the Supermarket. A Field Study during the Covid-19
     Outbreak in Italy', *Journal of Community & Applied Social Psychology*,
     32 (July 2022), n. 4, pp. 587–795, https://onlinelibrary.wiley.com/
     doi/10.1002/casp.2588.

5   'Pescara, caccia alla lavoratrice con il ciclo: la testimonianza di
     una dipendente', *RaiNews*, 29 April 2022, https://www.rainews.
     it/video/2022/04/pescara-la-caccia-alla-lavoratrice-con-il-ciclo-
     la-testimonianza-di-una-dipendente-878f3128-0e6c-452d-9a15-
     5d0ff407c6f6.html.

6   '"Chi ha il ciclo?": il messaggio e le parole della direttrice del
     supermercato, Le Iene', 4 May 2022, https://www.iene.mediaset.it/video/
     messaggio-e-parole-direttrice-supermercato_1144869.shtml.

7   'Ehrenreich on Walmart part 1', https://www.youtube.com/
     watch?v=FNfjeEz113w.

8   Ibid.

9   Riva, P., 'Donne e giovani, quelli costretti a fare il part time', *Corriere
     della Sera*, 9 October 2022, https://www.corriere.it/buone-notizie/22_
     ottobre_09/donne-giovani-quelli-costretti-fare-part-time-efda59d6-41f2-
     11ed-b75b-b72dca12f1fd.shtml.

10   Ente Bilaterale Nazionale Terziario, 'L'organizzazione del lavoro nelle
     imprese della Gdo negli anni della crisi', https://www.ebinter.it/ebinter-
     site/wp-content/uploads/2016/12/LOrganizzazione-del-lavoro-nelle-
     imprese-della-GDO-negli-anni-della-crisi.pdf.

11   ISTAT, 'Le diverse forme della disuguaglianza', Rapporto annuale
     2022, chapter 4, https://www.istat.it/storage/rapporto-annuale/2022/
     Capitolo_4.pdf.

12   Amato, R., 'Contratti pirata e part-time imposto: tra gli scaffali sempre
     meno diritti', *la Repubblica*, 29 April 2022, https://www.repubblica.it/
     cronaca/2022/04/29/news/contratti_pirata_e_parttime_imposto_tra_gli_
     scaffali_sempre_meno_diritti-347326265/.

13   Viarengo, P., 'Nella grande distribuzione al lavoro per 3 euro l'ora', *La
     Stampa*, 13 January 2023, https://www.lastampa.it/asti/2023/01/13/news/
     grande_distribuzione_lavoro_per_3_euro_lora-12533227/.

14   Dordoni, A., *Sempre aperto*, Mimesis, Milan, 2019.

15   Viarengo, P., 'Nella grande distribuzione al lavoro per 3 euro l'ora', *La
     Stampa*, 13 January 2023, https://www.lastampa.it/asti/2023/01/13/ news/
     grande_distribuzione_lavoro_per_3_euro_lora-12533227/.

16 Martinenghi, S., 'Si schianta in autostrada dopo turno di 19 ore, la collega muore: datori di lavoro condannati per omicidio colposo', *la Repubblica*, 27 July 2021, https://torino.repubblica.it/cronaca/2021/07/27/news/l_autista_alla_guida_era_troppo_stanco_dopo_un_turno_massacrante_condannati_i_datori_di_lavoro_per_l_incidente_in_cui_era_m-311981473/.

17 Ibid.

18 Franchi, M., 'Nuove frontiere del lavoro senza diritti: Pam-Panorama vuol imporre le pulizie ai cassieri', *il manifesto*, https://ilmanifesto.it/nuove-frontiere-del-lavoro-senza-diritti-pam-panorama-vuol-imporre-le-pulizie-ai-cassieri.

19 'Protesta dipendenti Eurospin a Lamezia Terme', https://www.youtube.com/watch?v=LwFteAzdlHU.

20 'Sciopero in tutti i supermercati Eurospin dell'Umbria, la denuncia dei sindacati', *Perugia Today*, 16 August 2022, https://www.perugiatoday.it/economia/sciopero-eurospin-supermercati-16-agosto-2022.html.

21 Staglianò, R., 'Gli schiavi che lavorano da mezzanotte all'alba', *la Repubblica*, 9 October 2017, https://www.repubblica.it/venerdi/articoli/2017/10/09/news/supermercati_notte-177802768/.

22 Indeed.com: https://it.indeed.com/cmp/Conad/reviews/ambiente-tossico-sfruttamento?id=837394a5f8507dd9.

23 Indeed.com: https://it.indeed.com/cmp/Conad/reviews/non- percentoC3 per centoA8-tutto-oro-quello-che-luccica?id=6d9b9c1c91dc3370.

24 Indeed.com: https://it.indeed.com/cmp/Conad/reviews/ambiente-pessimo-e-poco-organizzato?id=abe1f82da6b3643d.

25 Indeed.com: https://it.indeed.com/cmp/Eurospin/reviews/terrificante?id=2d54b2615d0e3058.

26 Indeed.com: https://it.indeed.com/cmp/Aldi/reviews/schiavismo-puro?id=532c6dedb98904b4.

27 Ibid., 4.

28 '"Daresti 280 euro al mese ai tuoi figli?": la storia di Francesca che rifiuta il lavoro', *Ansa*, 23 June 2022, https://www.ansa.it/sito/videogallery/economia/2022/06/23/daresti-280-euro-al-mese-ai-tuoi-figli-la-storia-di-francesca-che-rifiuta-il-lavoro_f34a8549-.

29 Gruppo Esselunga, 'Bilancio consolidato al 31 dicembre 2021', https://www.esselunga.it/content/dam/istituzionale20/azienda/investor-relations/new/Esselunga%20-%20Bilancio%20Consolidato%202021_IT.pdf.

30 'L'importanza del fattore umano nel retail', *Dealer*, 7 October 2022, https://dea-lermagazine.it/limportanza-del-fattore-umano-nel-retail/.

31 FIDA, Osservatorio FIDA 2022, Informe de investigación, https://www.fidaonline.it/wp-content/uploads/2022/05/Osservatorio-Fida-2022-Format-Research.pdf.

32 https://twitter.com/RobertoPacific3/status/1577616167279202304?cxt=H HwWgMC4qfXi6OQrAAAA.

33 Axonify & Nudge, 'The Deskless Report', http://deskless.nudge.co/ report/#Download-Report.

34 Ibid.

Chapter 7

1 *GDO*, 'l'analisi di Mediobanca 2022. Eurospin ed Esselunga campioni di utili', *Fruitbook Magazine*, 17 March 2022, https://www. fruitbookmagazine.it/gdo-lanalisi-di-mediobanca-2022-eurospin-ed-esselunga-campioni-di-utili/.

2 Paquette, D., 'Why Are Women Losing Retail Jobs while Men Are Gaining Them?' *The Washington Post*, 19 December 2017, https://www. washingtonpost.com/news/wonk/wp/2017/12/19/why-are-women-losing-retail-jobs-while-men-are-gaining-them/.

3 Ciconte, F. and Liberti, S., *Il grande carrello. Chi decide cosa mangiamo*, Laterza, Bari, 2019.

4 Minello, A., *Non è un paese per madri*, Laterza, Roma-Bari, 2022.

5 Ente Nazionale Bilaterale Terziario, 'Ricerca sull'evoluzione del mercato del lavoro nel terziario', p. 160, https://www.ebinter.it/ebinter-site/ wp-content/uploads/2022/09/RICERCA-SULLEVOLUZIONE-DEL-MERCATO-DEL-LAVORO-NEL-TERZIARIO.pdf.

6 Ibid.

7 'Barbieri al vertice di Filcams Cgil. Mamme lavoratrici: troppe dimissioni', *Libertà*, 7 December 2022, https://www.liberta.it/news/ cronaca/2022/12/07/barbieri-al-vertice-di-filcams-cgil-mamme-lavoratrici-troppe-dimissioni/.

8 Tett, G., 'What Musk Misses about How This Generation Works', *Financial Times*, https://www.ft.com/content/2ecc2819-d54c-4539-9c9d-e849cfe618ba.

9 Deloitte, 'A Call for Accountability and Action', https://www2.deloitte. com/con- tent/dam/Deloitte/mk/Documents/about-deloitte/2021-deloitte-global-millennial-survey-report.pdf.

10 Parts of Luna's story have been published originally in this article: Coin, F., 'Il nuovo rifiuto del lavoro', en *Internazionale*, 25 July 2022, https:// www.internazionale.it/essenziale/notizie/francesca-coin/2022/07/25/il-nuovo-rifiuto-del-lavoro.

11 INAPP, 'Lavoro, formazione e società in Italia nel passaggio all'era post Covid-19', https://www.aranagenzia.it/attachments/article/11990/Inapp_ Rapporto_2021.pdf.

12 Torrisi, C., 'Le Grandi Dimissioni delle donne con figli espulse dal mondo del lavoro', *Valigiablu.it*, 16 December 2021, https://www.valigiablu.it/grandi-dimissioni-donne-figli/.

13 Istat 'L'indagine Istat-Unar sulle discriminazioni lavorative nei confronti delle persone lgbt+ (in unione civile o già in unione)', https://www.istat.it/it/files//2022/03/RE- PORTDISCRIMINAZIONILGBT_2022_rev.pdf.

14 Halberstam, J., L'arte Queer del Fallimento, Minimum Fax, Roma, 2021. Postazione e cura del Collettivo Craaazi.

15 Bologna, S. and Soru, A. (eds.), 'Dietro le quinte. Indagine sul lavoro autonomo nell'audiovisivo e nell'editoria libraria', https://www.fondazionebrodolini.it/sites/default/files/pubblicazioni/file/Q62.pdf.

16 Murgia, A. and Poggio, B., *La trappola della passione. Esperienze di precarietà dei giovani highly skilled in Italia, Spagna e Regno Unito*, Cordella, G. and Masi, S. (eds.), *Condizione giovanile e nuovi rischi sociali. Quali politiche?* Carocci, Roma, 2013.

17 'Lo sfogo fa il giro del web: Ecco cosa dovrebbe fare la sinistra', *La7*, https:// www.la7.it/intanto/video/lo-sfogo-fa-il-giro-del-web-ecco-cosa-dovrebbe-fare-la-sinistra-04-02-2023-470839.

18 McRobbie, A., *From Holloway to Hollywood: Happiness at Work in the Cultural Economy*, Du Gay, P. and Pryke, M., *Cultural Economy: Cultural Analysis and Commercial Life*, SAGE, London, 2002, pp. 97–114.

19 McRobbie, A., 'The Smile Economy in the Teaching Machine: Undoing Neoliberalism in the Academy Today?' *Versobooks.com*, 24 August 2018, https://www.versobooks.com/blogs/3989-the-smile-economy-in-the-teaching-machine-undoing-neoliberalism-in-the-academy-today.

20 'The Term Quiet Quitting Is Worse than Nonsense', *Financial Times*, https:// www.ft.com/content/a09a2ade-4d14-47c2-9cca-599b3c25a33f.

21 'Wu, Ming, Street Artist #Blu Is Erasing All the Murals He Painted in #Bologna', *Wumingfoundation.com*, 12 March 2016, https://www.wumingfoundation.com/giap/2016/03/street-artist-blu-is-erasing-all-the-murals-he-painted-in-bologna/.

22 DeCarlo, T., 'A Fresh Look at Diane Arbus', *Smithsonian Magazine*, May 2004, https://www.smithsonianmag.com/arts-culture/a-fresh-look-at-diane-arbus-99861134/.

Conclusion

1 Marazzi, C., 'Diario della crisi – II', *Euronomade.info*, http://www.euronomade.info/?p=15437.

2 Taiichi Ohno, Lo spirito Toyota, Einaudi, Torino, 2001.

3   Trentin, B., 'Sulla questione del merito', *Sinistra in Europa*, 24 October
     2022, https://www.sinistraineuropa.it/approfondimenti/sulla-questione-
     del-merito-un-articolo-di-bruno-trentin/ /.

4   'Commissione parlamentare di inchiesta. Sulle condizioni di lavoro in
     Italia, sullo sfruttamento e sulla sicurezza nei luoghi di lavoro pubblici
     e privati', https://www.senato. it/documenti/repository/commissioni/
     condizioni_lavoro_18/documenti_approvati/Doc_XXII-bis_n9.pdf.

5   D. F., 'Azienda che stampa Harry Potter cerca 25 operai. Il titolare:
     "Si sono presentati solo in 4"', en *FanPage*, 17 April 2018, https://www.
     fanpage.it/attualita/azienda-che-stampa-harry-potter-cerca-25-operai-il-
     titolare-si-sono-presentati-solo-in-4/.

6   Mackinson, T., 'Lavoro, la gaffe del governo sugli stipendi Investite qui,
     gli italiani costano meno', *Il Fatto Quotidiano*, 2 October 2016, https://
     www.ilfattoquotidiano.it/2016/10/02/lavoro-la-gaffe-del-governo-sugli-
     stipendi-investite-qui-gli-italiani-costano-meno/3070627/.

7   'L'Italia è l'unico paese europeo in cui i salari sono diminuiti rispetto al
     1990', *Openpolis.it*, 15 June 2022, https://www.openpolis.it/numeri/litalia-
     e-lunico-paese-europeo-in-cui-i-salari-sono-diminuiti-rispetto-al-1990/.

8   Marx K., *Capital: A Critique of Political Economy*, vol. 1, Book 1, p. 118,
     First published: in German in 1867, English edition first published in
     1887; Source: First English edition of 1887, https://www.marxists.org/
     archive/marx/works/download/pdf/Capital-Volume-I.pdf.

9   'Francia, oltre un milione di persone in piazza contro la riforma delle
     pensioni. La premier Borne: Nessun passo indietro – Foto e video',
     Open, 31 January 2023, https:// www.open.online/2023/01/31/francia-
     manifestazione-vs-riforma-pensioni-31-gennaio-foto-video/.

BIBLIOGRAPHY

Autonomy Collective (2020) *The future of work: Autonomy, technology, and sustainability*. London: Autonomy Press.

Fisher, M. (2009) *Capitalist realism: Is there no alternative?* Winchester: Zero Books.

Frayne, D. (2015) *The refusal of work: The theory and practice of resistance to work*. London: Zed Books.

Frayne, D. (2019) *The work cure: Critical essays on work and wellness*. London: PCCS Books.

Godwin, R. (2023) 'Working less could solve 21st-century problems', *The Guardian*, 20 February. Available at: www.theguardian.com (Accessed: 15 March 2024).

Halberstam, J. (2011) *The queer art of failure*. Durham, NC: Duke University Press.

Han, Byung Chul (2015) *The burnout society*. Stanford, CA: Stanford University Press.

Hester, H. & Srnicek, N. (2023) *After work: The politics of free time*. London: Verso Books.

Hirschman, A.O. (1970) *Exit, voice, and loyalty: Responses to decline in firms, organizations, and states*. Cambridge, MA: Harvard University Press.

Jaffe, S. (2021) *Work won't love you back: How devotion to our jobs keeps us exploited, exhausted, and alone*. London: Hurst.

Lazzarato, M. (2014) *Marcel Duchamp and the refusal of work*. Los Angeles, CA: Semiotext(e).

Linebaugh, P. & Rediker, M. (2000) *The many-headed hydra: Sailors, slaves, commoners, and the hidden history of the revolutionary Atlantic*. Boston, MA: Beacon Press.

Malesic, J. (2022) *The end of burnout: Why work drains us and how to build better lives*. Berkeley: University of California Press.

Maslach, C. (1982) *Burnout: The cost of caring*. Englewood Cliffs, NJ: Prentice-Hall.

Mattei, C. (2022) *The capital order: How economists invented austerity and paved the way to fascism*. Chicago and London: University of Chicago Press.

Mélenchon, J-L (2025) *Now, the people! Revolution in the 21 century*. London: Verso Books.

Saitō, K. (2024) *Slow down: The degrowth manifesto*. New York: Astra House, 2024.

Srnicek, N. & Williams, A. (2015) *Inventing the future: Postcapitalism and a world without work*. London: Verso Books.

Weeks, K. (2011) *The problem with work: Feminism, marxism, antiwork politics, and postwork imaginaries*. Durham, NC: Duke University Press.